RICH DAD POOR DAD

Robert T. Kiyosaki

RICH DAD POOR DAD

WITH **UPDATES** FOR TODAY'S WORLD – AND 9 **Study Session Sections**

ROBERT T. KIYOSAKI

PLATA® PUBLISHING

Published by Plata Publishing, LLC

Plata Publishing, LLC
4330 N. Civic Center Plaza
Suite 100
Scottsdale, AZ 85251
(480) 998-6971
Visit our websites: PlataPublishing.com and RichDad.com
Printed in the United States of America

First Edition: 1997
First Plata Publishing Edition: March 2011
20th Anniversary Edition: April 2017
25th Anniversary Edition: April 2022

042022

ISBN: 978-1-61268-112-2

Cover photo credit: Seymour & Brody Studio

"*Rich Dad Poor Dad* is a starting point for anyone looking to gain control of their financial future."

– *USA TODAY*

Why Milestones Are Important

People of all cultures and countries celebrate milestones. We use them to measure time, mark progress, reflect on the lessons we've learned, and celebrate accomplishments. They are a way that we integrate past, present, and future… looking back at where we started, where we are today… and the promise of all that the future can hold.

Milestones give meaning to a journey and help us to not only savor each small step but celebrate the leaps and bounds that catapult us forward. Whether it's a birthday or anniversary, the number of years a business has outlasted the competition, the death of an icon, or an innovation that will change our lives, milestones are a part of all that we are… and all that we will become.

A quarter century has passed since *Rich Dad Poor Dad* was first published — 25 years since April 8, 1997 — and so many things in our world have changed. One thing that has not changed is the pressing need for and the power of financial education.

Money is still a mainstay of our lives, like it or not, and technology has brought both speed and innovations to the world of money. All the more reason, it seems, to do all that we can to get smarter with our money, learn as much as we can, and take control of our financial futures.

As The Rich Dad Company celebrates this milestone, I am humbled by the stories from around the world of people who have put the Rich Dad principles to work in their lives and who are sharing what they've learned and achieved with their family and friends… their children and grandchildren.

Twenty-five years have flown by in the blink of an eye. And in so many ways we've traveled this road, this *road less traveled*, together. I have learned that there are still so many things I don't know… and I continue to be a student. One thing I do know: My life is richer today thanks to the millions of people around the world who have embraced financial education as an essential and powerful tool in creating the future they deserve.

Robert Kiyosaki

The Lessons of *Rich Dad Poor Dad* Have Stood the Test of Time

Although 25 years have passed since *Rich Dad Poor Dad* was first published, you'll find that very little in the book itself has changed.

We've done a few updates to the cover over the years and added some sidebars and 20/20 Hindsight notes at the 20th Anniversary milestone… but that's about it. Because the lessons about money and the principles of *Rich Dad Poor Dad* haven't changed.

That's important to point that out because it speaks to the fact that this book — often referred to as a "classic" in personal finance — has truly stood the test of time.

New generations have found that its timeless wisdom and no-nonsense lessons can be applied to anyone's life and I am grateful to all the parents and grandparents, aunts and uncles, mentors and teachers and thought leaders around the world who have shared copies of *Rich Dad Poor Dad* with those they love.

As this 25th Anniversary edition goes to print, *Rich Dad Poor Dad* still ranks as the #1 Personal Finance book of all time, hits bestseller lists around the world, and consistently tops Amazon's best seller lists at #1 in the categories of Personal Finance, Parenting, and Investing. It has been translated into 38 languages and has sold more than 40 million copies around the world.

—RTK

Best-selling Books
by Robert T. Kiyosaki

Rich Dad Poor Dad
What the Rich Teach Their Kids About Money –
That the Poor and Middle Class Do Not

Rich Dad's CASHFLOW Quadrant
Guide to Financial Freedom

Rich Dad's Guide to Investing
What the Rich Invest in That the Poor and Middle Class Do Not

Rich Dad's Rich Kid Smart Kid
Give Your Child a Financial Head Start

Rich Dad's Retire Young Retire Rich
How to Get Rich and Stay Rich

Rich Dad's Prophecy
Why the Biggest Stock Market Crash in History Is Still Coming...
And How You Can Prepare Yourself and Profit from It!

Rich Dad's Guide to Becoming Rich
Without Cutting Up Your Credit Cards
Turn Bad Debt into Good Debt

Rich Dad's Who Took My Money?
Why Slow Investors Lose and Fast Money Wins!

Rich Dad Poor Dad for Teens
The Secrets About Money – That You Don't Learn In School!

Escape the Rat Race
Learn How Money Works and Become a Rich Kid

Rich Dad's Before You Quit Your Job
Ten Real-Life Lessons Every Entrepreneur Should Know
About Building a Multimillion-Dollar Business

Rich Dad's Increase Your Financial IQ
Get Smarter with Your Money

Robert Kiyosaki's Conspiracy of the Rich
The 8 New Rules of Money

Unfair Advantage
The Power of Financial Education

Why "A" Students Work for "C" Students
Rich Dad's Guide to Financial Education for Parents

Second Chance
For Your Money, Your Life and Our World

8 Lessons in Military Leadership
For Entrepreneurs

Why the Rich Are Getting Richer
What Is Financial Education ...Really?

FAKE
Fake Money • Fake Teachers • Fake Assets

BOOKS CO-AUTHORED WITH DONALD TRUMP

Why We Want You To Be Rich
Two Men | One Message

Midas Touch
Why Some Entrepreneurs Get Rich—and
Why Most Don't

BOOKS CO-AUTHORED WITH EDWARD SIEDLE

Who Stole My Pension?
How You Can Stop the Looting

Dedication

To parents everywhere,
a child's first and most important teachers,
and to all those who educate, influence,
and lead by example

Contents

---

25 YEARS... MILESTONES AND HINDSIGHTS

Five years ago, when we reached our first major milestone — marking 20 years since *Rich Dad Poor Dad* was first published — I wrote these words:

The Beatles released the *Sgt. Pepper's Lonely Hearts Club Band* album on June 1, 1967. It was an immediate commercial and critical success, spending 27 weeks at the top of the albums chart in the UK and 15 weeks at number one in the United States. *Time* magazine declared *Sgt. Pepper's* "a historic departure in the progress of music." It won four Grammy Awards in 1968 as well as Album of the Year—the first rock album ever to receive that honor.

Rich Dad Poor Dad was released 20 years ago, on my 50th birthday, on April 8, 1997. Unlike The Beatles' story, the book was not an immediate commercial success. It was not a critical success. In fact, the book's release and the firestorm of criticism that followed was quite the opposite.

Rich Dad Poor Dad was originally self-published because every book publisher we approached turned my book down. A few rejection slips offered comments like "You do not know what you are talking about." I learned that most publishers are more like my highly-educated poor dad, than my rich dad. Most publishers disagreed with my rich dad's lessons on money… as did my poor dad.

Twenty Years Today

In 1997, *Rich Dad Poor Dad* was a warning, a book of lessons about the future.

Twenty years later, millions of people around the world are more aware of my rich dad's warnings and his lessons about the future. With 20/20 hindsight, many have said that his lessons were prophetic… predictions come true. A few of those lessons are:

Rich Dad's Lesson #1: "The rich don't work for money."

Twenty years ago, a few publishers turned my book down because they did not agree with rich dad's number one lesson.

Today, people are more aware of the growing divide between the rich and everyone else. Between 1993 and 2010, over 50 percent of the increase in the national income in the United States went to the wealthiest one percent. Since then, things have only gotten worse. Economists at the University of California found that 95 percent of the income gains between the years 2009 and 2012 also went to that wealthiest one percent.

The lesson: The increases in income are going to entrepreneurs and investors, not to employees—not to the people who work for money.

Rich Dad Lesson: "Savers are losers."

Twenty years ago, most publishers vehemently disagreed with this lesson from rich dad. For the poor and middle class, "saving money" is a religion, financial salvation from poverty and protection from the cruel world. For many people, calling savers "losers" is like taking god's name in vain.

The lesson: A picture is worth a 1,000 words. Take a look at the chart of 120 years of the Dow Jones Industrial Average and you will see why and how savers became losers.

The chart shows there are have been three massive stock market crashes in the first 10 years of this new century. The chart on the next page illustrates these three crashes.

120 Years of the Dow

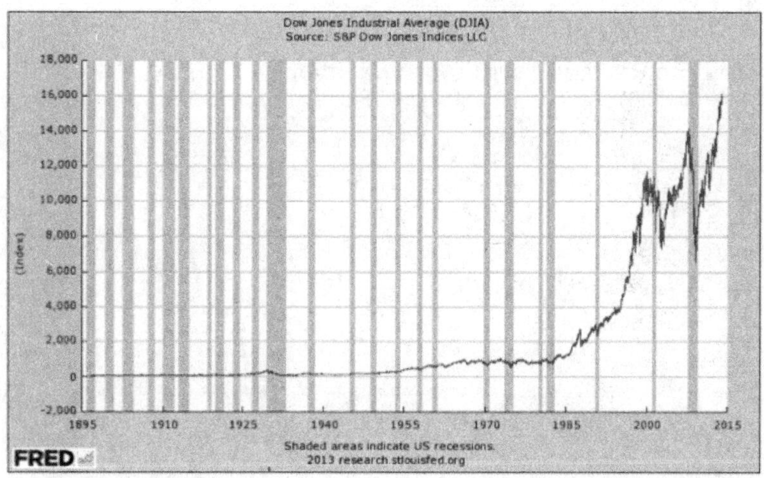

1895 - 2015 period

The first crash was the dotcom crash around the year 2000. The second and third crashes were the real estate crash of 2007, followed by the banking crash of 2008.

The Giant Crash of 1929

When you compare the first three crashes of the 21st century to the giant crash of 1929, you gain a perspective of how truly "giant" the first three crashes of this century were.

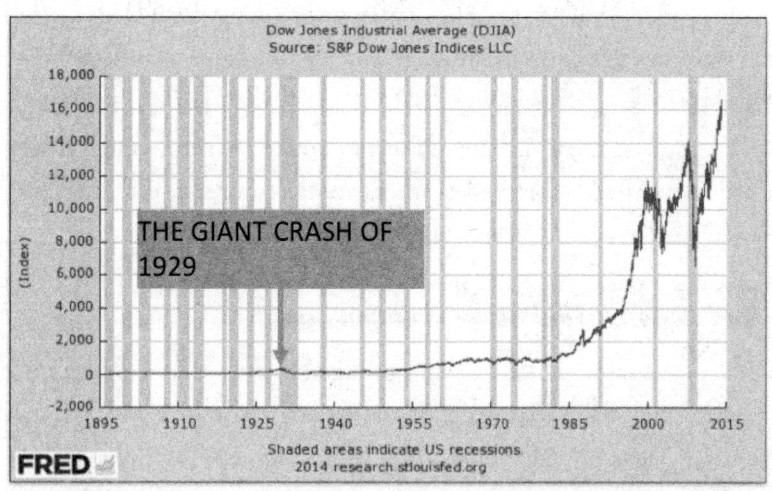

Printing Money

The chart below shows that after each crash, the U.S. government and the Federal Reserve Bank began "printing money."

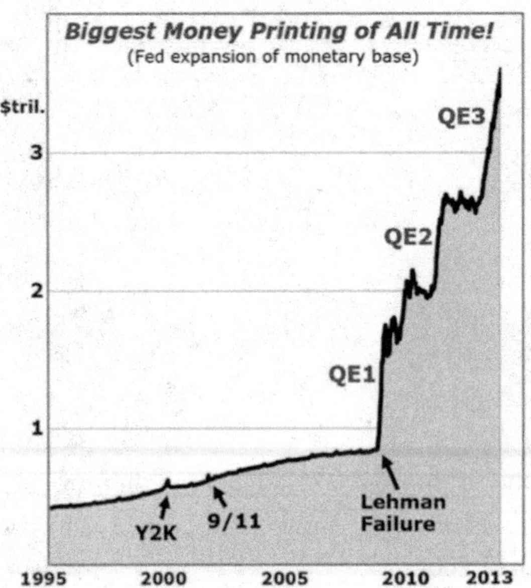

Saving the Rich

Between the years 2000 to 2016, in the name of saving the economy, the banks of the world kept cutting interest rates and printing money. While our leaders want us to believe they were saving the world, in reality, the rich were saving themselves and threw the poor and middle class under the bus.

Today, interest rates in many countries are below zero, which is why savers are losers. Today the biggest losers are the poor and middle class, the people who work for money and save money.

Rich Dad Lesson: "Your house is not an asset."

Twenty years ago, in 1997, every publisher who sent me a rejection slip criticized rich dad's lesson that "your house is not an asset."

Ten years later, in 2007 when subprime borrowers began to default on their subprime mortgages, the world's real estate bubble burst and millions of homeowners found out the truth in that lesson the hard way. Their house was not "an asset."

The Real Problem

Most people do not know that the real estate crash was not really a real estate crash.

Poor people did not cause the real estate crash. The rich caused the real estate crash. The rich created financially-engineered products known as derivatives—products Warren Buffett has called "weapons of mass financial destruction." When the financial weapons of mass destruction started to explode, the real estate market crashed… and poor, subprime borrowers were blamed.

In 2007 there were an estimated $700 trillion in financial derivatives.

Today, it is estimated there are $1.2 quadrillion in financial derivatives. In other words, the real problem has gotten bigger, not better.

Rich Dad Lesson: "Why the rich pay less in taxes."

Twenty years ago, a few publishers criticized *Rich Dad Poor Dad* for disclosing how and why the rich pay less in taxes. One stated that that lesson was illegal.

Ten years later, in 2007, President Barack Obama was running for re-election against former Governor Mitt Romney. When it was disclosed that President Obama paid approximately 30% of his income in taxes and Governor Romney paid less than 13% in taxes, Mitt Romney began the downhill slide that would cost him the election. Taxes, again, were a focal point in the 2016 U.S. Presidential election.

Rather than find out how people like Mitt Romney and President Donald Trump pay less in taxes *legally*, the poor and middle class get angry.

While President Trump promises to reduce taxes for the poor and middle class, the reality is the rich will always pay less in taxes. The reason the rich pay less in taxes goes back to rich dad's lesson number one: "The rich don't work for money." As long as a person works for money, they will pay taxes.

Even when Presidential candidate Hillary Clinton was promising to raise the taxes on the rich, she was promising to raise the taxes on those with high incomes—people like doctors, actors, and lawyers—not the real rich.

Twenty Years Ago

Although *Rich Dad Poor Dad* was not an immediate success, like The Beatles' *Sgt. Pepper's* album, *Rich Dad Poor Dad* did make *The New York Times* bestseller list by the year 2000 and stayed on that list for nearly seven years. Also in the year 2000, Oprah Winfrey called. I was on *Oprah!* for the entire hour, and, as they say, "the rest is history."

Rich Dad Poor Dad has become the number one personal finance book in history, with sales of the Rich Dad series of books estimated at nearly 40 million copies worldwide.

Was There Really a Rich Dad?

Millions have asked, "Was there really a rich dad?" To answer that question, you can listen to rich dad's son, Mike... when he was a guest on the Rich Dad Radio Show. You can listen to that program by going to Richdadradio.com

Rich Dad Graduate School

Rich Dad Poor Dad was written as simply as possible, so that almost everyone could understand my rich dad's lessons.

For those who want to learn more, as part of the 20-year celebration, I wrote, *Why the Rich Are Getting Richer — What Is Financial Education... Really?*

Why the Rich Are Getting Richer goes into greater, more specific detail on what rich dad really taught his son and me when it came to money and investing.

Why the Rich Are Getting Richer is *Rich Dad Poor Dad* for graduate students... it's Graduate School for Rich Dad students.

A Warning… and an Invitation

While I did my best to keep *Why the Rich Are Getting Richer* as simple as possible, what the rich really do is not easy. Or easy to explain. What the rich really do requires real financial education, financial education not taught in our schools.

I suggest reading *Rich Dad Poor Dad* first, then, if you want to learn more, *Why the Rich Are Getting Richer* may be for you.

Thank you… for 25 great years

To all our readers, past, present, and future…
all of us at The Rich Dad Company say,
"Thank you… for 25 amazing years."

It is our mission *to elevate the financial well-being of humanity…*
and that starts with one life and one person at a time.

Introduction

RICH DAD POOR DAD

Having two dads offered me the choice of contrasting points of view: one of a rich man and one of a poor man.

I had two fathers, a rich one and a poor one. One was highly educated and intelligent. He had a Ph.D. and completed four years of undergraduate work in less than two years. He then went on to Stanford University, the University of Chicago, and Northwestern University to do his advanced studies, all on full financial scholarships. The other father never finished the eighth grade.

Both men were successful in their careers, working hard all their lives. Both earned substantial incomes. Yet one always struggled financially. The other would become one of the richest men in Hawaii. One died leaving tens of millions of dollars to his family, charities, and his church. The other left bills to be paid when he died.

Both men were strong, charismatic, and influential. Both men offered me advice, but they did not advise the same things. Both men believed strongly in education but did not recommend the same course of study.

If I had had only one dad, I would have had to accept or reject his advice. Having two dads offered me the choice of contrasting points of view: one of a rich man and one of a poor man.

Instead of simply accepting or rejecting one or the other, I found myself thinking more, comparing, and then choosing for myself. The problem was that the rich man was not rich yet, and the poor man was not yet poor. Both were just starting out on their careers, and both were struggling with money and families. But they had very different points of view about money.

For example, one dad would say, "The love of money is the root of all evil." The other said, "The lack of money is the root of all evil."

As a young boy, having two strong fathers both influencing me was difficult. I wanted to be a good son and listen, but the two fathers did not say the same things. The contrast in their points of view, particularly about money, was so extreme that I grew curious and intrigued. I began to start thinking for long periods of time about what each was saying.

Much of my private time was spent reflecting, asking myself questions such as, "Why does he say that?" and then asking the same question of the other dad's statement. It would have been much easier to simply say, "Yeah, he's right. I agree with that." Or to simply reject the point of view by saying, "The old man doesn't know what he's talking about." Instead, having two dads whom I loved forced me to think and ultimately choose a way of thinking for myself. As a process, choosing for myself turned out to be much more valuable in the long run than simply accepting or rejecting a single point of view.

One of the reasons the rich get richer, the poor get poorer, and the middle class struggles in debt is that the subject of money is taught at home, not in school. Most of us learn about money from our parents. So what can poor parents tell their child about money? They simply say, "Stay in school and study hard." The child may graduate with excellent grades, but with a poor person's financial programming and mindset.

Sadly, money is not taught in schools. Schools focus on scholastic and professional skills, but not on financial skills. This explains why smart bankers,

25 YEARS LATER...

THE DEBT CLOCK

In 1997 when Rich Dad was first published, the U.S. national debt was just under $5.5 trillion. Today, 25 years later, it has topped a staggering $29 trillion. That's trillion... with a T.

doctors, and accountants who earned excellent grades may struggle financially all of their lives. Our staggering national debt is due in large part to highly educated politicians and government officials making financial decisions with little or no training in the subject of money.

Today I often wonder what will happen when we have millions of people who need financial and medical assistance. They will be dependent upon their families or the government for financial support. What will happen when Medicare and Social Security run out of money? How will a nation survive if teaching children about money continues to be left to parents — most of whom will be, or already are, poor?

Because I had two influential fathers, I learned from both of them. I had to think about each dad's advice and, in doing so, I gained valuable insight into the power and effect of one's thoughts on one's life. For example, one dad had a habit of saying, "I can't afford it." The other dad forbade those words to be used. He insisted I ask, "How can I afford it?" One is a statement, and the other is a question. One lets you off the hook, and the other forces you to think. My soon-to-be-rich dad would explain that by automatically saying the words "I can't afford it," your brain stops working. By asking the question "How can I afford it?" your brain is put to work. He did not mean that you should buy everything you want. He was fanatical about exercising your mind, the most powerful computer in the world. He'd say, "My brain gets stronger every day because I exercise it. The stronger it gets, the more money I can make." He believed that automatically saying "I can't afford it" was a sign of mental laziness.

Although both dads worked hard, I noticed that one dad had a habit of putting his brain to sleep when it came to finances, and the other had a habit of exercising his brain. The long-term result was that one dad grew stronger financially, and the other grew weaker. It is not much different from a person who goes to the gym to exercise on a regular basis versus someone who sits on the couch watching television. Proper physical exercise increases your chances for health, and proper mental exercise increases your chances for wealth.

My two dads had opposing attitudes and that affected the way they thought. One dad thought that the rich should pay more in taxes to take care of those less fortunate. The other said, "Taxes punish those who produce and reward those who don't produce."

One dad recommended, "Study hard so you can find a good company to work for." The other recommended, "Study hard so you can find a good company to buy."

One dad said, "The reason I'm not rich is because I have you kids." The other said, "The reason I must be rich is because I have you kids."

One encouraged talking about money and business at the dinner table, while the other forbade the subject of money to be discussed over a meal.

One said, "When it comes to money, play it safe. Don't take risks." The other said, "Learn to manage risk."

One believed, "Our home is our largest investment and our greatest asset." The other believed, "My house is a liability, and if your house is your largest investment, you're in trouble."

Both dads paid their bills on time, yet one paid his bills first while the other paid his bills last.

One dad believed in a company or the government taking care of you and your needs. He was always concerned about pay raises, retirement plans, medical benefits, sick leave, vacation days, and other perks. He was impressed with two of his uncles who joined the military

25 YEARS LATER...

YOUR HOUSE IS STILL NOT AN ASSET

The 2008 housing market crash was a clear message that your personal residence is not an asset. Not only does it not put money in your pocket, but we cannot count on the fact that it will go up in value. Today, many cities are seeing sky-high property values. Others are experiencing just the opposite. Your house ***can be an asset****... if you realize a profit when you sell it.*

and earned a retirement-and-entitlement package for life after 20 years of active service. He loved the idea of medical benefits and PX privileges the military provided its retirees. He also loved the tenure system available through the university. The idea of job protection for life and job benefits seemed more important, at times, than the job. He would often say, "I've worked hard for the government, and I'm entitled to these benefits."

The other believed in total financial self-reliance. He spoke out against the entitlement mentality and how it created weak and financially needy people. He was emphatic about being financially competent.

One dad struggled to save a few dollars. The other created investments. One dad taught me how to write an impressive résumé so I could find a good job. The other taught me how to write strong business and financial plans so I could create jobs.

Being a product of two strong dads allowed me the luxury of observing the effects different thoughts have on one's life. I noticed that people really do shape their lives through their thoughts.

For example, my poor dad always said, "I'll never be rich." And that prophecy became reality. My rich dad, on the other hand, always referred to himself as rich. He would say things like, "I'm a rich man, and rich people don't do this." Even when he was flat broke after a major financial setback, he continued to refer to himself as a rich man. He would cover himself by saying, "There is a difference between being poor and being broke. Broke is temporary. Poor is eternal."

My poor dad would say, "I'm not interested in money," or "Money doesn't matter." My rich dad always said, "Money is power."

The power of our thoughts may never be measured or appreciated, but it became obvious to me as a young boy that it was important to be aware of my thoughts and how I expressed myself. I noticed that my poor dad was poor, not because of the amount of money he earned, which was significant, but because of his thoughts and actions. As a young boy having two fathers, I became acutely aware of being careful about which thoughts I chose to adopt as my own. Should I listen to my rich dad or to my poor dad?

Although both men had tremendous respect for education and learning, they disagreed about what they thought was important to learn. One wanted me to study hard, earn a degree, and get a good job to earn money. He wanted me to study to become a professional, an attorney or an accountant, and to go to business school for my MBA. The other encouraged me to study to be rich, to understand how money works, and to learn how to have it work for me. "I don't work for money!" were words he would repeat over and over. "Money works for me!"

There is a difference between being poor and being broke. Broke is temporary. Poor is eternal.

At the age of nine, I decided to listen to and learn from my rich dad about money. In doing so, I chose not to listen to my poor dad, even though he was the one with all the college degrees.

A Lesson from Robert Frost

Robert Frost is my favorite poet. Although I love many of his poems, my favorite is "The Road Not Taken." I use its lesson almost daily.

The Road Not Taken

Two roads diverged in a yellow wood,
And sorry I could not travel both
And be one traveler, long I stood
And looked down one as far as I could
To where it bent in the undergrowth;
Then took the other, as just as fair,
And having perhaps the better claim,
Because it was grassy and wanted wear
Though as for that the passing there
Had worn them really about the same,
And both that morning equally lay
In leaves no step had trodden black.
Oh, I kept the first for another day!
Yet knowing how way leads onto way,
I doubted if I should ever come back.
I shall be telling this with a sigh
Somewhere ages and ages hence;
Two roads diverged in a wood, and I —
I took the one less traveled by,
And that has made all the difference.

And that has made all the difference.

Over the years, I have often reflected upon Robert Frost's poem. Choosing not to listen to my highly educated dad's advice and attitude about money was a painful decision, but it was a decision that shaped the rest of my life.

Once I made up my mind about whom to listen to, my education about money began. My rich dad taught me over a period of 30 years until I was 39 years old. He stopped once he realized that I knew and fully understood what he had been trying to drum into my often-thick skull.

Money is one form of power. But what is more powerful is financial education. Money comes and goes, but if you have the education about how money works, you gain power over it and can begin building wealth. The reason positive thinking alone does not work is because most people went to school and never learned how money works, so they spend their lives working for money.

Because I was only nine years old when I started, the lessons my rich dad taught me were simple. And when it was all said and done, there were only six main lessons, repeated over 30 years. This book is about those six lessons, put as simply as possible, just as simply as my rich dad put forth those lessons to me. The lessons are meant not to be answers, but guideposts that will assist you and your children and your families to grow wealthier no matter what happens in a world of increasing change and uncertainty.

Chapter One

LESSON 1: THE RICH DON'T WORK FOR MONEY

The poor and the middle class work for money. The rich have money work for them.

"Dad, can you tell me how to get rich?"

My dad put down the evening paper. "Why do you want to get rich, Son?"

"Because today Jimmy's mom drove up in their new Cadillac, and they were going to their beach house for the weekend. He took three of his friends, but Mike and I weren't invited. They told us we weren't invited because we were poor kids."

"They did?" my dad asked incredulously.

"Yeah, they did," I replied in a hurt tone.

My dad silently shook his head, pushed his glasses up the bridge of his nose, and went back to reading the paper. I stood waiting for an answer.

The year was 1956. I was nine years old. By some twist of fate, I attended the same public school where the rich people sent their kids. We were primarily a sugar-plantation town in Hawaii. The managers of the plantation and the other affluent people, such as doctors, business owners, and bankers, sent their children to this public elementary school. After grade six, their children were generally sent off to private schools. Because my family lived on one side of the street, I went to this school. Had I lived on the other side of the street, I would have gone to a different school with kids from families more like mine. After grade six, these kids and I would go on to the public intermediate and high school. There was no private school for them or for me.

My dad finally put down the paper. I could tell he was thinking.

"Well, Son…," he began slowly. "If you want to be rich, you have to learn to make money."

"How do I make money?" I asked.

"Well, use your head, Son," he said, smiling. Even then I knew that really meant, "That's all I'm going to tell you," or "I don't know the answer, so don't embarrass me."

A Partnership Is Formed

The next morning, I told my best friend, Mike, what my dad had said. As best as I could tell, Mike and I were the only poor kids in this school. Mike was also in this school by a twist of fate. Someone had drawn a jog in the line for the school district, and we wound up in school with the rich kids. We weren't really poor, but we felt as if we were because all the other boys had new baseball gloves, new bicycles, new everything.

Mom and Dad provided us with the basics, like food, shelter, and clothes. But that was about it. My dad used to say, "If you want something, work for it." We wanted things, but there was not much work available for nine-year-old boys.

"So what do we do to make money?" Mike asked.

"I don't know," I said. "But do you want to be my partner?"

He agreed, and so on that Saturday morning, Mike became my first business partner. We spent all morning coming up with ideas on how to make money. Occasionally we talked about all the "cool guys" at Jimmy's beach house having fun. It hurt a little, but that hurt was good, because it inspired us to keep thinking of a way to make money. Finally, that afternoon, a bolt of lightning struck. It was an idea Mike got from a science book he had read. Excitedly, we shook hands, and the partnership now had a business.

For the next several weeks, Mike and I ran around our neighborhood, knocking on doors and asking our neighbors if they would save their toothpaste tubes for us. With puzzled looks, most adults consented with a smile. Some asked us what we were doing, to which we replied, "We can't tell you. It's a business secret."

My mom grew distressed as the weeks wore on. We had selected a site next to her washing machine as the place we would stockpile our raw materials. In a brown cardboard box that at one time held catsup bottles, our little pile of used toothpaste tubes began to grow.

Finally my mom put her foot down. The sight of her neighbors' messy, crumpled, used toothpaste tubes had gotten to her. "What are you boys doing?" she asked. "And I don't want to hear again that it's a business secret. Do something with this mess, or I'm going to throw it out."

Mike and I pleaded and begged, explaining that we would soon have enough and then we would begin production. We informed her that we were waiting on a couple of neighbors to finish their toothpaste so we could have their tubes. Mom granted us a one-week extension.

The date to begin production was moved up, and the pressure was on. My first partnership was already being threatened with an eviction notice by my own mom! It became Mike's job to tell the neighbors to quickly use up their toothpaste, saying their dentist wanted them to brush more often anyway. I began to put together the production line.

One day my dad drove up with a friend to see two nine-year-old boys in the driveway with a production line operating at full speed. There was fine white powder everywhere. On a long table were small milk cartons from school, and our family's hibachi grill was glowing with red-hot coals at maximum heat.

Dad walked up cautiously, having to park the car at the base of the driveway since the production line blocked the carport. As he and his friend got closer, they saw a steel pot sitting on top of the coals in which the toothpaste tubes were being melted down. In those days, toothpaste did not come in plastic tubes. The tubes were made of lead. So once the paint was burned off, the tubes were dropped in the small steel pot. They melted until they became liquid, and with my mom's pot holders, we poured the lead through a small hole in the top of the milk cartons.

The milk cartons were filled with plaster of paris. White powder was everywhere. In my haste, I had knocked the bag over, and the entire area looked like it had been hit by a snowstorm. The milk cartons were the outer containers for plaster of paris molds.

My dad and his friend watched as we carefully poured the molten lead through a small hole in the top of the plaster of paris cube.

"Careful," my dad said.

I nodded without looking up.

Finally, once the pouring was through, I put the steel pot down and smiled at my dad.

"What are you boys doing?" he asked with a cautious smile.

"We're doing what you told me to do. We're going to be rich," I said.

"Yup," said Mike, grinning and nodding his head. "We're partners."

"And what is in those plaster molds?" my dad asked.

"Watch," I said. "This should be a good batch."

With a small hammer, I tapped at the seal that divided the cube in half. Cautiously, I pulled up the top half of the plaster mold and a lead nickel fell out.

"Oh, no!" my dad exclaimed. "You're casting nickels out of lead!"

"That's right," Mike said. "We're doing as you told us to do. We're making money."

My dad's friend turned and burst into laughter. My dad smiled and shook his head. Along with a fire and a box of spent toothpaste tubes, in front of him were two little boys covered with white dust smiling from ear to ear.

He asked us to put everything down and sit with him on the front step of our house. With a smile, he gently explained what the word "counterfeiting" meant.

Our dreams were dashed. "You mean this is illegal?" asked Mike in a quivering voice.

"Let them go," my dad's friend said. "They might be developing a natural talent."

My dad glared at him.

"Yes, it is illegal," my dad said gently. "But you boys have shown great creativity and original thought. Keep going. I'm really proud of you!"

Disappointed, Mike and I sat in silence for about twenty minutes before we began cleaning up our mess. The business was over on opening day. Sweeping the powder up, I looked at Mike and said, "I guess Jimmy and his friends are right. We are poor."

My father was just leaving as I said that. "Boys," he said. "You're only poor if you give up. The most important thing is that you did something. Most people only talk and dream of getting rich. You've done something. I'm very proud of the two of you. I will say it again: Keep going. Don't quit."

Mike and I stood there in silence. They were nice words, but we still did not know what to do.

"So how come you're not rich, Dad?" I asked.

"Because I chose to be a schoolteacher. Schoolteachers really don't think about being rich. We just like to teach. I wish I could help you, but I really don't know how to make money."

Mike and I turned and continued our cleanup.

"I know," said my dad. "If you boys want to learn how to be rich, don't ask me. Talk to your dad, Mike."

"My dad?" asked Mike with a scrunched-up face.

"Yeah, your dad," repeated my dad with a smile. "Your dad and I have the same banker, and he raves about your father. He's told me several times that your father is brilliant when it comes to making money."

"My dad?" Mike asked again in disbelief. "Then how come we don't have a nice car and a nice house like the rich kids at school?"

"A nice car and a nice house don't necessarily mean you're rich or you know how to make money," my dad replied. "Jimmy's dad works for the sugar plantation. He's not much different from me. He works for a company, and I work for the government. The company buys the car for him. The sugar company is in financial trouble, and Jimmy's dad may soon have nothing. Your dad is different, Mike. He seems to be building an empire, and I suspect in a few years he will be a very rich man."

With that, Mike and I got excited again. With new vigor, we began cleaning up the mess caused by our now-defunct first business. As we were cleaning, we made plans for how and when to talk to Mike's dad. The problem was that Mike's dad worked long hours and often did not come home until late. His father owned warehouses, a construction company, a chain of stores, and three restaurants. It was the restaurants that kept him out late.

Mike caught the bus home after we had finished cleaning up. He was going to talk to his dad when he got home that night and ask him if he would teach us how to become rich. Mike promised to call as soon as he had talked to his dad, even if it was late.

The phone rang at 8:30 p.m.

"Okay," I said. "Next Saturday." I put the phone down. Mike's dad had agreed to meet with us.

On Saturday I caught the 7:30 a.m. bus to the poor side of town.

The Lessons Begin

Mike and I met with his dad that morning at eight o'clock. He was already busy, having been at work for more than an hour. His construction supervisor was just leaving in his pickup truck as I walked up to his simple, small, and tidy home. Mike met me at the door.

"Dad's on the phone, and he said to wait on the back porch," Mike said as he opened the door.

The old wooden floor creaked as I stepped across the threshold of the aging house. There was a cheap mat just inside the door. The mat was there to hide the years of wear from countless footsteps that the floor had supported. Although clean, it needed to be replaced.

I felt claustrophobic as I entered the narrow living room that was filled with old musty overstuffed furniture that today would be collectors' items. Sitting on the couch were two women, both a little older than my mom. Across from the women sat a man in workman's clothes. He wore khaki slacks and a khaki shirt, neatly pressed but without starch, and polished work boots. He was about 10 years older than my dad. They smiled as Mike and I walked past them toward the back porch. I smiled back shyly.

"Who are those people?" I asked.

"Oh, they work for my dad. The older man runs his warehouses, and the women are the managers of the restaurants. And as you arrived, you saw the construction supervisor who is working on a road project about 50 miles from here. His other supervisor, who is building a track of houses, left before you got here."

"Does this go on all the time?" I asked.

"Not always, but quite often," said Mike, smiling as he pulled up a chair to sit down next to me.

"I asked my dad if he would teach us to make money," Mike said.

"Oh, and what did he say to that?" I asked with cautious curiosity.

"Well, he had a funny look on his face at first, and then he said he would make us an offer."

"Oh," I said, rocking my chair back against the wall. I sat there perched on two rear legs of the chair.

Mike did the same thing.

"Do you know what the offer is?" I asked.

"No, but we'll soon find out."

Suddenly, Mike's dad burst through the rickety screen door and onto the porch. Mike and I jumped to our feet, not out of respect, but because we were startled.

"Ready, boys?" he asked as he pulled up a chair to sit down with us.

We nodded our heads as we pulled our chairs away from the wall to sit in front of him.

He was a big man, about six feet tall and 200 pounds. My dad was taller, about the same weight, and five years older than Mike's dad. They sort of looked alike, though not of the same ethnic makeup. Maybe their energy was similar.

"Mike says you want to learn to make money? Is that correct, Robert?"

I nodded my head quickly, but with a little trepidation. He had a lot of power behind his words and smile.

"Okay, here's my offer. I'll teach you, but I won't do it classroom-style. You work for me, I'll teach you. You don't work for me, I won't teach you. I can teach you faster if you work, and I'm wasting my time if you just want to sit and listen like you do in school. That's my offer. Take it or leave it."

"Ah, may I ask a question first?" I asked.

"No. Take it or leave it. I've got too much work to do to waste my time. If you can't make up your mind decisively, then you'll never learn to make money anyway. Opportunities come and go. Being able to know when to make quick decisions is an important skill. You have the opportunity that you asked for. School is beginning, or it's over in 10 seconds," Mike's dad said with a teasing smile.

"Take it," I said.

"Take it," said Mike.

"Good," said Mike's dad. "Mrs. Martin will be by in 10 minutes. After I'm through with her, you'll ride with her to my superette and you can begin working. I'll pay you 10 cents an hour, and you'll work three hours every Saturday."

"But I have a softball game today," I said.

WISDOM THAT HAS STOOD THE TEST OF TIME…

DECISIVENESS

The world is moving faster and faster. Stock market trades are made in milliseconds. Deals come and go on the Internet in a matter of minutes. More and more people are competing for good deals. So the faster you can make a decision the more likely you'll be able to seize opportunities — before someone else does.

Mike's dad lowered his voice to a stern tone. "Take it, or leave it," he said.

"I'll take it," I replied, choosing to work and learn instead of playing.

Thirty Cents Later

By 9:00 a.m. that day, Mike and I were working for Mrs. Martin. She was a kind and patient woman. She always said that Mike and I reminded her of her two grown sons. Although kind, she believed in hard work and kept us moving. We spent three hours taking canned goods off the shelves, brushing each can with a feather duster to get the dust off, and then re-stacking them neatly. It was excruciatingly boring work.

Mike's dad, whom I call my rich dad, owned nine of these little superettes, each with a large parking lot. They were the early version of the 7-Eleven convenience stores, little neighborhood grocery stores where people bought items such as milk, bread, butter, and cigarettes. The problem was that this was Hawaii before air-conditioning was widely used, and the stores could not close their doors because of the heat. On two sides of the store, the doors had to be wide open to the road and parking lot. Every time a car drove by or pulled into the parking lot, dust would swirl and settle in the store. We knew we had a job as long as there was no air-conditioning.

For three weeks, Mike and I reported to Mrs. Martin and worked our three hours. By noon, our work was over, and she dropped three little dimes in each of our hands. Now, even at the age of nine in the mid-1950s, 30 cents was not too exciting. Comic books cost 10 cents back then, so I usually spent my money on comic books and went home.

By Wednesday of the fourth week, I was ready to quit. I had agreed to work only because I wanted to learn to make money from Mike's dad, and now I was a slave for 10 cents an hour. On top of that, I had not seen Mike's dad since that first Saturday.

"I'm quitting," I told Mike at lunchtime. School was boring, and now I did not even have my Saturdays to look forward to. But it was the 30 cents that really got to me.

This time Mike smiled.

"What are you laughing at?" I asked with anger and frustration.

"Dad said this would happen. He said to meet with him when you were ready to quit."

"What?" I said indignantly. "He's been waiting for me to get fed up?"

"Sort of," Mike said. "Dad's kind of different. He doesn't teach like your dad. Your mom and dad lecture a lot. My dad is quiet and a man of few words. You just wait till this Saturday. I'll tell him you're ready."

"You mean I've been set up?"

"No, not really, but maybe. Dad will explain on Saturday."

Waiting in Line on Saturday

I was ready to face Mike's dad. Even my real dad was angry with him. My real dad, the one I call the poor one, thought that my rich dad was violating child labor laws and should be investigated.

My educated, poor dad told me to demand what I deserve — at least 25 cents an hour. My poor dad told me that if I did not get a raise, I was to quit immediately.

"You don't need that damned job anyway," said my poor dad with indignation.

At eight o'clock Saturday morning, I walked through the door of Mike's house when Mike's dad opened it.

"Take a seat and wait in line," he said as I entered. He turned and disappeared into his little office next to a bedroom.

I looked around the room and didn't see Mike anywhere. Feeling awkward, I cautiously sat down next to the same two women who were there four weeks earlier. They smiled and slid down the couch to make room for me.

Forty-five minutes went by, and I was steaming. The two women had met with him and left 30 minutes earlier. An older gentleman was in there for 20 minutes and was also gone.

The house was empty, and here I sat in a musty, dark living room on a beautiful sunny Hawaiian day, waiting to talk to a cheapskate who exploited children. I could hear him rustling around the office, talking on the phone, and ignoring me. I was ready to walk out, but for some reason I stayed.

Finally, 15 minutes later, at exactly nine o'clock, rich dad walked out of his office, said nothing, and signaled with his hand for me to enter.

"I understand you want a raise, or you're going to quit," rich dad said as he swiveled in his office chair.

"Well, you're not keeping your end of the bargain," I blurted out, nearly in tears. It was really frightening for me to confront a grown-up.

"You said that you would teach me if I worked for you. Well, I've worked for you. I've worked hard. I've given up my baseball games to work for you, but you haven't kept your word, and you haven't taught me anything. You are a crook like everyone in town thinks you are. You're greedy. You want all the money and don't take care of your employees. You made me wait and don't show me any respect. I'm only a little boy, but I deserve to be treated better."

Rich dad rocked back in his swivel chair, hands up to his chin, and stared at me.

"Not bad," he said. "In less than a month, you sound like most of my employees."

"What?" I asked. Not understanding what he was saying, I continued with my grievance. "I thought you were going to keep your end of the bargain and teach me. Instead you want to torture me? That's cruel. That's really cruel."

"I am teaching you," rich dad said quietly.

"What have you taught me? Nothing!" I said angrily. "You haven't even talked to me once since I agreed to work for peanuts. Ten cents an hour. Hah! I should notify the government about you. We have child labor laws, you know. My dad works for the government, you know."

"Wow!" said rich dad. "Now you sound just like most of the people who used to work for me — people I've either fired or who have quit."

"So what do you have to say?" I demanded, feeling pretty brave for a little kid. "You lied to me. I've worked for you, and you have not kept your word. You haven't taught me anything."

"How do you know that I've not taught you anything?" asked rich dad calmly.

"Well, you've never talked to me. I've worked for three weeks and you have not taught me anything," I said with a pout.

"Does teaching mean talking or a lecture?" rich dad asked.

"Well, yes," I replied.

"That's how they teach you in school," he said, smiling. "But that is not how life teaches you, and I would say that life is the best teacher of all. Most of the time, life does not talk to you. It just sort of pushes you around. Each push is life saying, 'Wake up. There's something I want you to learn.'"

STILL TRUE TODAY...

THE CONE OF LEARNING

Edgar Dale gets credit for helping us to understand that we learn best through action — doing the real thing or a simulation. Sometimes it's called experiential learning. Dale and his Cone of Learning tell us that reading and lecture are the least effective ways to learn.

And yet we all know how most schools teach: reading and lecture.

Today, many are questioning — finally — what is being taught in our schools.

What is this man talking about? I asked myself. *Life pushing me around was life talking to me?* Now I knew I had to quit my job. I was talking to someone who needed to be locked up.

Cone of Learning

After 2 weeks we tend to remember		Nature of Involvement
90% of what we say and do	Doing the Real Thing	Active
	Simulating the Real Experience	
	Doing a Dramatic Presentation	
70% of what we say	Giving a Talk	
	Participating in a Discussion	
50% of what we hear and see	Seeing it Done on Location	Passive
	Watching a Demonstration	
	Looking at an Exhibit Watching a Demonstration	
	Watching a Movie	
30% of what we see	Looking at Pictures	
20% of what we hear	Hearing Words (Lecture)	
10% of what we read	Reading	

Source: From Dale. Audio-Visual Methods in Teaching, 1E. © 1969 South-Western, a part of Cengage, Inc. Reproduced by permission. www.cengage.com/permissions

"If you learn life's lessons, you will do well. If not, life will just continue to push you around. People do two things. Some just let life push them around. Others get angry and push back. But they push back against their boss, or their job, or their husband or wife. They do not know it's life that's pushing."

I had no idea what he was talking about.

"Life pushes all of us around. Some people give up and others fight. A few learn the lesson and move on. They welcome life pushing them around. To these few people, it means they need and want to learn something. They learn and move on. Most quit, and a few like you fight."

Rich dad stood and shut the creaky old wooden window that needed repair. "If you learn this lesson, you will grow into a wise, wealthy, and happy young man. If you don't, you will spend your life blaming a job, low pay, or your boss for your problems. You'll live life always hoping for that big break that will solve all your money problems."

Rich dad looked over at me to see if I was still listening. His eyes met mine. We stared at each other, communicating through our eyes. Finally, I looked away once I had absorbed his message. I knew he was right. I was blaming him, and I did ask to learn. I was fighting.

Rich dad continued, "Or if you're the kind of person who has no guts, you just give up every time life pushes you. If you're that kind of person, you'll live all your life playing it safe, doing the right things, saving yourself for some event that never happens. Then you die a boring old man. You'll have lots of friends who really like you because you were such a nice hardworking guy. But the truth is that you let life push you into submission. Deep down you were terrified of taking risks. You really wanted to win, but the fear of losing was greater than the excitement of winning.

STILL TRUE TODAY...

LIFE AS A TEACHER

Today's millennials and Gen X-ers are learning the hard facts of life. Jobs are harder to find. Robots are replacing workers by the millions. Learning by making mistakes through trial and error is more and more important. Book learning is proving to be less valuable in the real world. No longer does a college education guarantee a job.

Deep inside, you and only you will know you didn't go for it. You chose to play it safe."

Our eyes met again.

"You've been pushing me around?" I asked.

"Some people might say that," smiled rich dad. "I would say that I just gave you a taste of life."

"What taste of life?" I asked, still angry, but now curious and ready to learn.

"You boys are the first people who have ever asked me to teach them how to make money. I have more than 150 employees, and not one of them has asked me what I know about money. They ask me for a job and a paycheck, but never to teach them about money. So most will spend the best years of their lives working for money, not really understanding what it is they are working for."

I sat there listening intently.

"So when Mike told me you wanted to learn how to make money, I decided to design a course that mirrored real life. I could talk until I was blue in the face, but you wouldn't hear a thing. So I decided to let life push you around a bit so you could hear me. That's why I only paid you 10 cents."

STILL TRUE TODAY...

CHANGE WHAT YOU CAN

I've learned the truth and wisdom in rich dad's words. So much of life is out of our control. I've learned to focus on what I do have control over: myself. And for things to change, first I must change.

"So what is the lesson I learned from working for only 10 cents an hour?" I asked. "That you're cheap and exploit your workers?"

Rich dad rocked back and laughed heartily. Finally he said, "You'd best change your point of view. Stop blaming me and thinking I'm the problem. If you think I'm the problem, then you have to change me. If you realize that you're the problem, then you can change yourself, learn something, and grow wiser. Most people want everyone else in the world to change but themselves. Let me tell you, it's easier to change yourself than everyone else."

"I don't understand," I said.

"Don't blame me for your problems," rich dad said, growing impatient.

"But you only pay me 10 cents."

"So what are you learning?" rich dad asked, smiling.

"That you're cheap," I said with a sly grin.

"See, you think I'm the problem," said rich dad.

"But you are."

"Well, keep that attitude and you'll learn nothing. Keep the attitude that I'm the problem and what choices do you have?"

"Well, if you don't pay me more or show me more respect and teach me, I'll quit."

"Well put," rich dad said. "And that's exactly what most people do. They quit and go looking for another job, a better opportunity, and higher pay, actually thinking that this will solve the problem. In most cases, it won't."

"So what should I do?" I asked. "Just take this measly 10 cents an hour and smile?"

Rich dad smiled. "That's what the other people do. But that's all they do, waiting for a raise thinking that more money will solve their problems. Most just accept it, and some take a second job working harder, but again accepting a small paycheck."

I sat staring at the floor, beginning to understand the lesson rich dad was presenting. I could sense it was a taste of life. Finally, I looked up and asked, "So what will solve the problem?"

"This," he said, leaning forward in his chair and tapping me gently on the head. "This stuff between your ears."

It was at that moment that rich dad shared the pivotal point of view that separated him from his employees and my poor dad — and led him to eventually become one of the richest men in Hawaii, while my highly educated but poor dad struggled financially all his life. It was a singular point of view that made all the difference over a lifetime.

Rich dad explained this point of view over and over, which I call lesson number one: *The poor and the middle class work for money. The rich have money work for them.*

On that bright Saturday morning, I learned a completely different point of view from what I had been taught by my poor dad. At the age of nine, I understood that both dads wanted me to learn. Both dads encouraged me to study, but not the same things.

My highly educated dad recommended that I do what he did. "Son, I want you to study hard, get good grades, so you can find a safe, secure job with a big company. And make sure it has excellent benefits." My rich dad wanted me to learn how money works so I could make it work for me.

TIMELESS RICH DAD WISDOM

ASSETS OVER INCOME

Buying or building assets that deliver cash flow is putting your money to work for you. High-paying jobs mean two things: you're working for money and the taxes you pay will probably increase. I've learned to put my money to work for me and enjoy the tax benefits of generating income that doesn't come from a paycheck.

These lessons I would learn through life with his guidance, not because of a classroom.

My rich dad continued my first lesson, "I'm glad you got angry about working for 10 cents an hour. If you hadn't got angry and had simply accepted it, I would have to tell you that I could not teach you. You see, true learning takes energy, passion, and a burning desire. Anger is a big part of that formula, for passion is anger and love combined. When it comes to money, most people want to play it safe and feel secure. So passion does not direct them. Fear does."

"So is that why they'll take jobs with low pay?" I asked.

"Yes," said rich dad. "Some people say I exploit people because I don't pay as much as the sugar plantation or the government. I say the people exploit themselves. It's their fear, not mine."

"But don't you feel you should pay them more?" I asked.

"I don't have to. And besides, more money will not solve their problems. Just look at your dad. He makes a lot of money, and he still can't pay his bills. Most people, given more money, only get into more debt."

"So that's why the 10 cents an hour," I said, smiling. "It's a part of the lesson."

"That's right," smiled rich dad. "You see, your dad went to school and got an excellent education, so he could get a high-paying job. But he still has money problems because he never learned anything about money in school. On top of that, he believes in working for money."

"And you don't?" I asked.

"No, not really," said rich dad. "If you want to learn to work for money, then stay in school. That is a great place to learn to do that. But if you want to learn how to have money work for you, then I will teach you that. But only if you want to learn."

QUESTIONS STILL PERSIST...

GO TO SCHOOL?

While I am a huge supporter of education and life-long learning, "going to school" — especially college — has become a financial nightmare. Student loan debt is at another record high with 44.7 million Americans owing nearly $1.71 trillion. Again: that's trillion... with a T.

"Wouldn't everyone want to learn that?" I asked.

"No," said rich dad, "simply because it's easier to learn to work for money, especially if fear is your primary emotion when the subject of money is discussed."

"I don't understand," I said with a frown.

"Don't worry about that for now. Just know that it's fear that keeps most people working at a job: the fear of not paying their bills, the fear of being fired, the fear of not having enough money, and the fear of starting over. That's the price of studying to learn a profession or trade, and then working for money. Most people become a slave to money — and then get angry at their boss."

"Learning to have money work for you is a completely different course of study?" I asked.

"Absolutely," rich dad answered. "Absolutely."

We sat in silence on that beautiful Hawaiian Saturday morning. My friends had just started their Little League baseball game, but for some reason I was now thankful I had decided to work for 10 cents an hour. I sensed that I was about to learn something my friends wouldn't learn in school.

"Ready to learn?" asked rich dad.

"Absolutely," I said with a grin.

"I have kept my promise. I've been teaching you from afar," my rich dad said. "At nine years old, you've gotten a taste of what it feels like to work for money. Just multiply your last month by fifty years and you will have an idea of what most people spend their life doing."

"I don't understand," I said.

"How did you feel waiting in line to see me, once to get hired and once to ask for more money?"

"Terrible," I said.

"If you choose to work for money, that is what life will be like," said rich dad.

"And how did you feel when Mrs. Martin dropped three dimes in your hand for three hours of work?"

"I felt like it wasn't enough. It seemed like nothing. I was disappointed," I said.

"And that is how most employees feel when they look at their paychecks — especially after all the tax and other deductions are taken out. At least you got 100 percent."

"You mean most workers don't get paid everything?" I asked with amazement.

"Heavens no!" said rich dad. "The government always takes its share first."

"How do they do that?" I asked.

"Taxes," said rich dad. "You're taxed when you earn.

You're taxed when you spend. You're taxed when you save. You're taxed when you die."

"Why do people let the government do that to them?"

"The rich don't," said rich dad with a smile. "The poor and the middle class do. I'll bet you that I earn more than your dad, yet he pays more in taxes."

"How can that be?" I asked. At my age, that made no sense to me. "Why would someone let the government do that to them?"

Rich dad rocked slowly and silently in his chair, just looking at me.

"Ready to learn?" he asked.

STILL TRUE TODAY...

TAXES... TAXES... TAXES

As governments expand and need more and more money, the only place to get it is the middle class. That means the workers. Every government now favors the professional investor and business owners. Workers pay tax; investors and business owners pay very little tax, if they use the tax law as intended — as a tool to build the economy.

I nodded my head slowly.

"As I said, there is a lot to learn. Learning how to have money work for you is a lifetime study. Most people go to college for four years, and their education ends. I already know that my study of money will continue over my lifetime, simply because the more I find out, the more I find out I need to know. Most people never study the subject. They go to work, get their paycheck, balance their checkbooks, and that's it. Then they wonder why they have money problems. They think that more money will solve the problem and don't realize that it's their lack of financial education that is the problem."

"So my dad has tax problems because he doesn't understand money?" I asked, confused.

"Look," said rich dad, "taxes are just one small section on learning how to have money work for you. Today, I just wanted to find out if you still have the passion to learn about money. Most people don't.

They want to go to school, learn a profession, have fun at their work, and earn lots of money. One day they wake up with big money problems, and then they can't stop working. That's the price of only knowing how to work for money instead of studying how to have money work for you. So do you still have the passion to learn?" asked rich dad.

I nodded my head.

"Good," said rich dad. "Now get back to work. This time, I will pay you nothing."

"What?" I asked in amazement.

"You heard me. Nothing. You will work the same three hours every Saturday, but this time you will not be paid 10 cents per hour. You said you wanted to learn to not work for money, so I'm not going to pay you anything."

I couldn't believe what I was hearing.

"I've already had this conversation with Mike and he's already working, dusting and stacking canned goods for free. You'd better hurry and get back there."

"That's not fair," I shouted. "You've got to pay something!"

"You said you wanted to learn. If you don't learn this now, you'll grow up to be like the two women and the older man sitting in my living room, working for money and hoping I don't fire them. Or like your dad, earning lots of money only to be in debt up to his eyeballs, hoping more money will solve the problem. If that's what you want, I'll go back to our original deal of 10 cents an hour. Or you can do what most adults do: Complain that there is not enough pay, quit, and go looking for another job."

"But what do I do?" I asked.

Rich dad tapped me on the head. "Use this," he said. "If you use it well, you will soon thank me for giving you an opportunity and you will grow into a rich man."

I stood there, still not believing what a raw deal I was handed. I came to ask for a raise, and somehow I was instead working for nothing.

Rich dad tapped me on the head again and said, "Use this. Now get out of here and get back to work."

Lesson #1: The Rich Don't Work for Money

I didn't tell my poor dad I wasn't being paid. He wouldn't have understood, and I didn't want to try to explain something I didn't understand myself.

For three more weeks, Mike and I worked three hours every Saturday for nothing. The work didn't bother me, and the routine got easier, but it was the missed baseball games and not being able to afford to buy a few comic books that got to me.

Rich dad stopped by at noon on the third week. We heard his truck pull up in the parking lot and sputter when the engine was turned off. He entered the store and greeted Mrs. Martin with a hug. After finding out how things were going in the store, he reached into the ice-cream freezer, pulled out two bars, paid for them, and signaled to Mike and me.

"Let's go for a walk, boys."

We crossed the street, dodging a few cars, and walked across a large grassy field where a few adults were playing softball. Sitting down at a lone picnic table, he handed Mike and me the treats.

"How's it going, boys?"

"Okay," Mike said.

I nodded in agreement.

"Learn anything yet?" rich dad asked.

Mike and I looked at each other, shrugged our shoulders, and shook our heads in unison.

Avoiding One of Life's Biggest Traps

"Well, you boys had better start thinking. You're staring at one of life's biggest lessons. If you learn it, you'll enjoy a life of great freedom and security. If you don't, you'll wind up like Mrs. Martin and most of the people playing softball in this park. They work very hard for little money, clinging to the illusion of job security and looking forward to a three-week vacation each year and maybe a skimpy pension after forty-five years of service. If that excites you, I'll give you a raise to 25 cents an hour."

"But these are good hardworking people. Are you making fun of them?" I demanded.

A smile came over rich dad's face.

"Mrs. Martin is like a mother to me. I would never be that cruel. I may sound unkind because I'm doing my best to point something out to the two of you. I want to expand your point of view so you can see something most people never have the benefit of seeing because their vision is too narrow. Most people never see the trap they are in."

Mike and I sat there, uncertain of his message. He sounded cruel, yet we could sense he was trying to drive home a point.

With a smile, rich dad said, "Doesn't that 25 cents an hour sound good? Doesn't it make your heart beat a little faster?"

I shook my head no, but it really did. Twenty-five cents an hour would be big bucks to me.

"Okay, I'll pay you a dollar an hour," rich dad said, with a sly grin.

Now my heart started to race. My brain was screaming, "Take it. Take it." I could not believe what I was hearing. Still, I said nothing.

"Okay, two dollars an hour."

My little brain and heart nearly exploded. After all, it was 1956 and being paid $2 an hour would have made me the richest kid in the world. I couldn't imagine earning that kind of money. I wanted to say yes. I wanted the deal. I could picture a new bicycle, new baseball glove, and the adoration of my friends when I flashed some cash. On top of that, Jimmy and his rich friends could never call me poor again. But somehow my mouth stayed shut.

The ice cream had melted and was running down my hand. Rich dad was looking at two boys staring back at him, eyes wide open and brains empty. He was testing us, and he knew there was a part of our emotions that wanted to take the deal. He understood that every person has a weak and needy part of their soul that can be bought, and he knew that every individual also had a part of their soul that was resilient and could never be bought. It was only a question of which one was stronger.

"Okay, five dollars an hour."

Suddenly I was silent. Something had changed. The offer was too big and ridiculous. Not many grown-ups in 1956 made more than that, but quickly my temptation disappeared, and calm set in. Slowly, I turned to my left to look at Mike. He looked back at me. The part of my soul that was weak and needy was silenced. The part of me that had no price took over. I knew Mike had gotten to that point too.

People's lives are forever controlled by two emotions: fear and greed.

"Good," rich dad said softly. "Most people have a price. And they have a price because of human emotions named fear and greed. First, the fear of being without money motivates us to work hard, and then once we get that paycheck, greed or desire starts us thinking about all the wonderful things money can buy. The pattern is then set."

"What pattern?" I asked.

"The pattern of get up, go to work, pay bills; get up, go to work, pay bills. People's lives are forever controlled by two emotions: fear and greed. Offer them more money and they continue the cycle by increasing their spending. This is what I call the Rat Race."

"There is another way?" Mike asked.

"Yes," said rich dad slowly. "But only a few people find it."

"And what is that way?" Mike asked.

"That's what I hope you boys will learn as you work and study with me. That is why I took away all forms of pay."

"Any hints?" Mike asked. "We're kind of tired of working hard, especially for nothing."

"Well, the first step is telling the truth," said rich dad.

"We haven't been lying," I said.

"I did not say you were lying. I said to tell the truth," rich dad retorted.

"The truth about what?" I asked.

"How you're feeling," rich dad said. "You don't have to say it to anyone else. Just admit it to yourself."

"You mean the people in this park, the people who work for you, Mrs. Martin, they don't do that?" I asked.

"I doubt it," said rich dad. "Instead, they feel the fear of not having money. They don't confront it logically. They react emotionally instead of using their heads," rich dad said. "Then, they get a few bucks in their hands and again, the emotions of joy, desire, and greed take over. And again they react, instead of think."

"So their emotions control their brain," Mike said.

"That's correct," said rich dad. "Instead of admitting the truth about how they feel, they react to their feelings and fail to think. They feel the fear so they go to work, hoping that money will soothe the fear, but it doesn't. It continues to haunt them and they return to work, hoping again that money will calm their fears, and again it doesn't. Fear keeps them in this trap of working, earning money, working, earning money, hoping the fear will go away. But every day they get up, and that old fear wakes up with them. For millions of people that old fear keeps them awake all night, causing a night of turmoil and worry. So they get up and go to work, hoping that a paycheck will kill that fear gnawing at their soul. Money is running their lives, and they refuse to tell the truth about that. Money is in control of their emotions and their souls."

STILL TRUE TODAY...

THE #1 FEAR

As the world population ages and more and more people move toward retirement, it's been reported that the #1 fear is tied to money. Nearly 50% of those surveyed fear that they will outlive their money... running out of money in their "golden years."

Rich dad sat quietly, letting his words sink in. Mike and I heard what he said but didn't understand fully what he was talking about. I just knew that I often wondered why grown-ups hurried off to work. It did not seem like much fun, and they never looked that happy, but something kept them going.

Realizing we had absorbed as much as possible of what he was talking about, rich dad said, "I want you boys to avoid that trap. That is really what I want to teach you. Not just to be rich, because being rich does not solve the problem."

"It doesn't?" I asked, surprised.

"No, it doesn't. Let me explain the other emotion: desire. Some call it greed, but I prefer desire. It's perfectly normal to desire something better, prettier, more fun, or exciting. So people also work for money because of desire. They desire money for the joy they think it can buy. But the joy that money brings is often short-lived, and they soon need more money for more joy, more pleasure, more comfort, and more security. So they keep working, thinking money will soothe their souls that are troubled by fear and desire. But money can't do that."

"Even rich people do this?" Mike asked.

"Rich people included," said rich dad. "In fact, the reason many rich people are rich isn't because of desire, but because of fear. They believe that money can eliminate the fear of being poor, so they amass tons of it, only to find the fear gets worse. Now they fear losing the money. I have friends who keep working even though they have plenty. I know people who have millions who are more afraid now than when they were poor. They're terrified of losing it all. The fears that drove them to get rich got worse. That weak and needy part of their soul is actually screaming louder. They don't want to lose the big houses, the cars and the high life money has bought them. They worry about what their friends would say if they lost all their money. Many are emotionally desperate and neurotic, although they look rich and have more money."

"So is a poor man happier?" I asked.

"No, I don't think so," replied rich dad. "The avoidance of money is just as psychotic as being attached to money."

As if on cue, the town derelict went past our table, stopping by the large rubbish can and rummaging around in it. The three of us watched him with great interest, when before we probably would have just ignored him.

Rich dad pulled a dollar out of his wallet and gestured to the older man. Seeing the money, the derelict came over immediately, took the bill, thanked rich dad profusely, and hurried off, ecstatic with his good fortune.

"He's not much different from most of my employees," said rich dad. "I've met so many people who say, 'Oh, I'm not interested in money.' Yet they'll work at a job for eight hours a day. That's a denial of truth. If they weren't interested in money, then why are they working? That kind of thinking is probably more psychotic than a person who hoards money."

As I sat there listening to my rich dad, my mind flashed back to the countless times my own dad said, "I'm not interested in money." He said those words often. He also covered himself by always saying, "I work because I love my job."

So many people say, "Oh, I'm not interested in money." Yet they'll work at a job for eight hours a day.

"So what do we do?" I asked. "Not work for money until all traces of fear and greed are gone?"

"No, that would be a waste of time," said rich dad. "Emotions are what make us human. The word 'emotion' stands for 'energy in motion.' Be truthful about your emotions and use your mind and emotions in your favor, not against yourself."

"Whoa!" said Mike.

"Don't worry about what I just said. It will make more sense in years to come. Just be an observer, not a reactor, to your emotions. Most people do not know that it's their emotions that are doing the thinking. Your emotions are your emotions, but you have got to learn to do your own thinking."

"Can you give me an example?" I asked.

"Sure," replied rich dad. "When a person says, 'I need to find a job,' it's most likely an emotion doing the thinking. Fear of not having money generates that thought."

"But people do need money if they have bills to pay," I said.

"Sure they do," smiled rich dad. "All I'm saying is that it's fear that is all too often doing the thinking."

"I don't understand," said Mike.

"For example," said rich dad. "If the fear of not having enough money arises, instead of immediately running out to get a job, they instead might ask themselves this question: 'Will a job be the best solution to this fear over the long run?' In my opinion, the answer is no. A job is really a short-term solution to a long-term problem."

"But my dad is always saying, 'Stay in school and get good grades, so you can find a safe, secure job,'" I interjected, somewhat confused.

"Yes, I understand he says that," said rich dad, smiling. "Most people recommend that, and it's a good path for most people. But people make that recommendation primarily out of fear."

"You mean my dad says that because he's afraid?"

"Yes," said rich dad. "He's terrified that you won't earn enough money and won't fit into society. Don't get me wrong. He loves you and wants the best for you. I too believe an education and a job are important, but it won't handle the fear. You see, that same fear that makes him get up in the morning to earn a few bucks is the fear that is causing him to be so fanatical about your going to school."

"So what do you recommend?" I asked.

"I want to teach you to master the power of money, instead of being afraid of it.

25 YEARS LATER...

MASTERING MONEY

With mastering money has become essential to surviving in the world economy. With low interest rates and an uncertain stock market, the old adages of saving and investing for the long term make no sense.

They don't teach that in school and, if you don't learn it, you become a slave to money."

It was finally making sense. He wanted us to widen our views and to see what the Mrs. Martins of this world couldn't see. He used examples that sounded cruel at the time, but I've never forgotten them. My vision widened that day, and I began to see the trap that lay ahead for most people.

"You see, we're all employees ultimately. We just work at different levels," said rich dad. "I just want you boys to have a chance to avoid the trap caused by those two emotions, fear and desire. Use them in your favor, not against you. That's what I want to teach you. I'm not interested in just teaching you to make a pile of money. That won't handle the fear or desire. If you don't first handle fear and desire, and you get rich, you'll only be a highly paid slave."

"So how do we avoid the trap?" I asked.

"The main cause of poverty or financial struggle is fear and ignorance, not the economy or the government or the rich. It's self-inflicted fear and ignorance that keep people trapped. So you boys go to school and get your college degrees, and I'll teach you how to stay out of the trap."

The pieces of the puzzle were appearing. My highly educated dad had a great education and a great career, but school never told him how to handle money or his fear of it. It became clear that I could learn different and important things from two fathers.

"So you've been talking about the fear of not having money. How does the desire for money affect our thinking?" Mike asked.

"How did you feel when I tempted you with a pay raise? Did you notice your desires rising?"

We nodded our heads.

"By not giving in to your emotions, you were able to delay your reactions and think. That is important. We will always have emotions of fear and greed. From here on in, it's imperative for you to use those emotions to your advantage, and for the long term to not let your emotions control your thinking. Most people use fear and greed against themselves. That's the start of ignorance. Most people live their lives chasing paychecks, pay raises and job security because of the emotions of desire and fear, not really questioning where those emotion-driven thoughts are leading them. It's just like the picture of a donkey dragging a cart with its owner dangling a carrot just in front of its nose. The donkey's owner may be going where he wants to, but the donkey is chasing an illusion. Tomorrow there will only be another carrot for the donkey."

"You mean the moment I picture a new baseball glove, candy and toys, that's like a carrot to a donkey?" Mike asked.

"Yes, and as you get older, your toys get more expensive — a new car, a boat, and a big house to impress your friends," said rich dad with a smile. "Fear pushes you out the door, and desire calls to you. That's the trap."

"So what's the answer?" Mike asked.

"What intensifies fear and desire is ignorance. That is why rich people with lots of money often have more fear the richer they get. Money is the carrot, the illusion. If the donkey could see the whole picture, it might rethink its choice to chase the carrot."

Rich dad went on to explain that a human's life is a struggle between ignorance and illumination.

He explained that once a person stops searching for information and self-knowledge, ignorance sets in. That struggle is a moment-to-moment decision — to learn to open or close one's mind.

"Look, school is very important. You go to school to learn a skill or profession to become a contributing member of society. Every culture needs teachers, doctors, mechanics, artists, cooks, businesspeople, police officers, firefighters, and soldiers. Schools train them so society can thrive and flourish," said rich dad. "Unfortunately, for many people school is the end, not the beginning."

There was a long silence. Rich dad was smiling. I didn't comprehend everything he said that day. But as with most great teachers, his words continued to teach for years.

"I've been a little cruel today," said rich dad. "But I want you to always remember this talk. I want you to always think of Mrs. Martin. And I want you always to remember that donkey. Never forget that fear and desire can lead you into life's biggest trap if you're not aware of them controlling your thinking. To spend your life living in fear, never exploring your dreams, is cruel. To work hard for money, thinking that it will buy you things that will make you happy is also cruel. To wake up in the middle of the night terrified about paying bills is a horrible way to live. To live a life dictated by the size of a paycheck is not really living a life. Thinking that a job makes you secure is lying to yourself. That's cruel, and that's the trap I want you to avoid. I've seen how money runs people's lives. Don't let that happen to you. Please don't let money run your life."

A softball rolled under our table. Rich dad picked it up and threw it back.

"So what does ignorance have to do with greed and fear?" I asked.

"Because it is ignorance about money that causes so much greed and fear," said rich dad. "Let me give you some examples. A doctor, wanting more money to better provide for his family, raises his fees. By raising his fees, it makes health care more expensive for everyone.

It hurts the poor people the most, so they have worse health than those with money. Because the doctors raise their fees, the attorneys raise their fees. Because the attorneys' fees have gone up, schoolteachers want a raise, which raises our taxes, and on and on and on. Soon there will be such a horrifying gap between the rich and the poor that chaos will break out and another great civilization will collapse. History proves that great civilizations collapse when the gap between the haves and have-nots is too great.

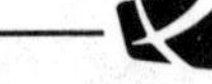

25 YEARS LATER...

INCOME INEQUALITY

In his 2016 U.S. Presidential bid, Senator Bernie Sanders stated: "Wealth and income inequality is the biggest moral crisis facing Americans today." Today income inequality is still a hotly debated issue... in a world of abundance.

Sadly, America is on that same course because we haven't learned from history. We only memorize historical dates and names, not the lesson."

"Aren't prices supposed to go up?" I asked.

"In an educated society with a well-run government, prices should actually come down. Of course, that is often only true in theory. Prices go up because of greed and fear caused by ignorance. If schools taught people about money, there would be more money and lower prices. But schools focus only on teaching people to work for money, not how to harness money's power."

"But don't we have business schools?" Mike asked. "And haven't you encouraged me to go for my MBA?"

"Yes," said rich dad. "But all too often business schools train employees to become sophisticated bean-counters. Heaven forbid a bean-counter takes over a business. All they do is look at the numbers, fire people, and kill the business. I know this because I hire bean-counters. All they think about is cutting costs and raising prices, which cause more problems. Bean-counting is important. I wish more people knew it, but it, too, is not the whole picture," added rich dad angrily.

"So is there an answer?" asked Mike.

"Yes," said rich dad. "Learn to use your emotions to think, not think with your emotions. When you boys mastered your emotions by agreeing to work for free, I knew there was hope. When you again resisted your emotions when I tempted you with more money, you were again learning to think in spite of being emotionally charged. That's the first step."

"Why is that step so important?" I asked.

"Well, that's up to you to find out. If you want to learn, I'll take you boys into the briar patch, a place almost everyone else avoids. If you go with me, you'll let go of the idea of working for money and instead learn to have money work for you."

"And what will we get if we go with you. What if we agree to learn from you? What will we get?" I asked.

"The same thing Brer Rabbit got," said rich dad, referring to the classic children's story.

"Is there a briar patch?" I asked.

"Yes," said rich dad. "The briar patch is our fear and greed. Confronting fear, weaknesses, and neediness by choosing our own thoughts is the way out."

"Choosing our thoughts?" Mike asked, puzzled.

"Yes. Choosing what we think rather than reacting to our emotions. Instead of just getting up and going to work because not having the money to pay your bills is scaring you, ask yourself, 'Is working harder at this the best solution to this problem?' Most people are too afraid to rationally think things through and instead run out the door to a job they hate. The Tar Baby is in control. That's what I mean by choosing your thoughts."

"And how do we do that?" Mike asked.

"That's what I will teach you. I'll teach you to have a choice of thoughts rather than a knee-jerk reaction, like gulping down your morning coffee and running out the door.

"Remember what I said before: A job is only a short-term solution to a long-term problem. Most people have only one problem in mind, and it's short-term. It's the bills at the end of the month, the Tar Baby. Money controls their lives, or should I say the fear and ignorance about money controls it. So they do as their parents did. They get up every day and go work for money, not taking the time to ask the question, 'Is there another way?' Their emotions now control their thinking, not their heads."

TIMELESS RICH DAD WISDOM

EMOTIONS... AND INTELLIGENCE

I constantly work to control my thoughts and my emotions.

I've seen this play out over and over in my life: When emotion goes up, intelligence goes down.

"Can you tell the difference between emotions thinking and the head thinking?" Mike asked.

"Oh, yes. I hear it all the time," said rich dad. "I hear things like, 'Well, everyone has to work.' Or 'The rich are crooks.' Or 'I'll get another job. I deserve this raise. You can't push me around.' Or 'I like this job because it's secure.' No one asks, 'Is there something I'm missing here?' which would break through the emotional thought and give you time to think clearly."

As we headed back to the store, rich dad explained that the rich really did "make money." They did not work for it. He went on to explain that when Mike and I were casting five-cent pieces out of lead, thinking we were making money, we were very close to thinking the way the rich think. The problem was that creating money is legal for the government and banks to do, but illegal for us to do. There are legal ways to create money from nothing, he told us.

Rich dad went on to explain that the rich know that money is an illusion, truly like the carrot for the donkey. It's only out of fear and greed that the illusion of money is held together by billions of people who believe that money is real. It's not. Money is really made up. It is only because of the illusion of confidence and the ignorance of the masses that this house of cards stands.

He talked about the gold standard that America was on, and that each dollar bill was actually a silver certificate. What concerned him was the rumor that we would someday go off the gold standard and our dollars would no longer be backed by something tangible.

"If that happens, boys, all hell will break loose. The poor, the middle class, and the ignorant will have their lives ruined simply because they will continue to believe that money is real and that the company they work for, or the government, will look after them."

We really did not understand what he was saying that day, but over the years, it made more and more sense.

Seeing What Others Miss

As he climbed into his pickup truck outside his convenience store, rich dad said, "Keep working boys, but the sooner you forget about needing a paycheck, the easier your adult life will be. Keep using your brain, work for free, and soon your mind will show you ways of making money far beyond what I could ever pay you. You will see things that other people never see. Most people never see these opportunities because they're looking for money and security, so that's all they get. The moment you see one opportunity, you'll see them for the rest of your life. The moment you do that, I'll teach you something else. Learn this, and you'll avoid one of life's biggest traps.

Mike and I picked up our things from the store and waved goodbye to Mrs. Martin. We went back to the park, to the same picnic bench, and spent several more hours thinking and talking.

We spent the next week at school thinking and talking, too. For two more weeks, we kept thinking, talking, and working for free.

At the end of the second Saturday, I was again saying goodbye to Mrs. Martin and looking at the comic-book stand with a longing gaze. The hard thing about not even getting 30 cents every Saturday was that I didn't have any money to buy comic books. Suddenly, as Mrs. Martin said goodbye to Mike and me, I saw her do something I'd never seen her do before.

Mrs. Martin was cutting the front page of the comic book in half. She kept the top half of the comic book cover and threw the rest of the book into a large cardboard box. When I asked her what she did with the comic books, she said, "I throw them away. I give the top half of the cover back to the comic-book distributor for credit when he brings in the new comics. He's coming in an hour."

Mike and I waited for an hour. Soon the distributor arrived, and I asked him if we could have the comic books. To my delight, he said, "You can have them if you work for this store and do not resell them."

Remember our old business partnership? Well, Mike and I revived it. Using a spare room in Mike's basement, we began piling hundreds of comic books in that room. Soon our comic-book library was open to the public. We hired Mike's younger sister, who loved to study, to be head librarian. She charged each child 10 cents admission to the library, which was open from 2:30 p.m. to 4:30 p.m. every day after school. The customers, the children of the neighborhood, could read as many comics as they wanted in two hours. It was a bargain for them since a comic cost 10 cents each, and they could read five or six in two hours.

Mike's sister would check the kids as they left to make sure they weren't borrowing any comic books. She also kept the books, logging in how many kids showed up each day, who they were, and any comments they might have. Mike and I averaged $9.50 per week over a three-month period. We paid his sister one dollar a week and allowed her to read the comics for free, which she rarely did since she was always studying.

Mike and I kept our agreement by working in the store every Saturday and collecting all the comic books from the different stores. We kept our agreement to the distributor by not selling any comic books. We burned them once they got too tattered. We tried opening a branch office, but we could never quite find someone as trustworthy and dedicated as Mike's sister. At an early age, we found out how hard it was to find good staff.

25 YEARS LATER...

THE POWER OF IMAGINATION

In the Information Age and the age of the Internet, millions of people of all ages are getting rich using their imaginations to create products, platforms, and apps that change the world — from TikTok to Reddit to Rumble and Gemini, for cryptocurrency, and others. Those with imaginations thrive while those without it are still looking for a job... a job that may soon be replaced by robots and technology.

Three months after the library first opened, a fight broke out in the room. Some bullies from another neighborhood pushed their way in, and Mike's dad suggested we shut down the business. So our comic-book business shut down, and we stopped working on

Saturdays at the convenience store. But rich dad was excited because he had new things he wanted to teach us. He was happy because we had learned our first lesson so well: We learned to make money work for us. By not getting paid for our work at the store, we were forced to use our imaginations to identify an opportunity to make money. By starting our own business, the comic-book library, we were in control of our own finances, not dependent on an employer. The best part was that our business generated money for us, even when we weren't physically there. Our money worked for us.

Instead of paying us money, rich dad had given us so much more.

STUDY SESSION

Chapter One

LESSON 1: THE RICH DON'T WORK FOR MONEY

Chapter One

LESSON 1: THE RICH DON'T WORK FOR MONEY

Summary

When he was 9 years old, Robert Kiyosaki and his childhood friend weren't invited to a classmate's beach house because they were "poor kids" in an affluent school. After being told by his poor dad — his father who was a teacher and made a good living but always struggled to make ends meet — to simply go and "make money," he and his friend, Mike, did just that: They collected empty toothpaste tubes, which at that time were made of lead. They melted them down and used plaster molds to make counterfeit nickels.

They were soon set straight by Robert's dad, who told them they should talk to Mike's dad, who never finished eighth grade but ran multiple successful businesses.

Mike's dad, the "rich dad" of the book title, agreed to teach them, but on his terms. He had them work three hours every Saturday morning at one of his convenience stores, dusting the food packaging and cleaning. He paid them 10 cents an hour, which Robert usually spent on 10-cent comic books.

Fairly quickly, Robert grew disenchanted with the boring work and low pay. When he told his friend he was going to quit, Mike told him that his dad said that would happen and that Robert needed to meet with him. Robert's dad as a schoolteacher used lectures, but Mike's dad was a man of few words and taught in a very different way, which Robert was about to find out.

The next Saturday morning, Robert went to meet Mike's dad but was kept waiting in a dusty, dark living room for an hour. He was fed up and emotional by the time he got to complain to Mike's dad, accusing him of being greedy and not showing him respect. When he said Mike's dad hadn't taught him anything despite their agreement, the business owner calmly disagreed.

His rich dad explained that life doesn't teach you with words, but by pushing you around. Some people let life push them around; others get angry and push back against their boss or their loved ones. But some people learn a lesson from it, and in fact welcome life pushing them around because it means they need to learn something.

Those who don't learn that lesson spend their lives blaming everyone else and waiting for a big break — or decide to play it safe and never risk, or win, big.

He told Robert that he and Mike were the first people who had ever asked him to teach them how to make money. He had more than 150 employees, and though they had asked for a job, they had never asked for the knowledge that Robert and Mike wanted.

So the rich dad decided to create a course that mirrored life and pushed the boys around a little. Robert asked what lesson he'd learned, other than that his rich dad was cheap and exploited his workers. The rich dad challenged him on this, saying that most people blamed others when in fact their attitude was the problem.

What would solve the problem? His brain, Mike's dad told him. He wanted Robert to learn how money worked so he could make it work for him. He was also glad that Robert was angry, because anger combines with love to create passion — a key component of learning.

Money wouldn't solve people's problems, he went on. Many people who have a high-paying job still struggle with money problems — like Robert's poor dad — because they didn't know how to make money work for them.

He said that the emotions Robert had felt working for those 10 cents an hour — disappointment and feeling like it wasn't enough — was what he'd feel like his whole life if he didn't learn this lesson now. He introduced Robert to the concept of taxes, explaining that the poor and middle class allow the government to tax them, but the rich don't.

He asked if Robert still had a passion to learn. When he said yes, his rich dad told him he was going to stop paying him for the work at the store. He told Robert to use his head to figure it out.

Robert and Mike worked for free for three weeks. Mike's dad

showed up and took them outside for a talk, asking if they'd learned anything yet. They hadn't. The rich dad told them if they didn't learn this lesson, they'd be like most people who work hard for little money their whole lives. He offered them 25 cents an hour, which they resisted. He upped it to $1 an hour, then $2. But Robert stayed silent. A final offer of $5 an hour — a princely sum at that time — solidified for Robert that he wouldn't be bought.

The rich dad said it was good they didn't have a price. Most people did, because their lives are controlled by fear and greed. Fear of being without makes them work hard and earn a paycheck, but once they have that money, greed gets them thinking about all the things they could buy. Which makes them need more money, which makes them spend more. It's what the rich dad called the Rat Race.

He told the boys that the first step was admitting to themselves what they were feeling. Too often people reacted to their emotions instead of thinking logically. They're afraid to admit money is running their lives, and so money controls them.

It's not just the poor who face that fear; the rich often operate from a place of fear. He wanted to teach the boys to not just be rich because money doesn't solve the problem.

School is important, he told them, but for most people it's the end, not the beginning. And the key for the boys was to learn to use their emotions to think, not to think with their emotions. They must learn to choose their thoughts.

He told them to keep an eye out for ways to make money, saying, "The moment you see one opportunity, you'll see them for the rest of your life."

The boys did, and soon they saw an opportunity in creating a library where kids could pay an admission fee and read as many comic books as they could in two hours — unsold comic books that otherwise would've been thrown away from the convenience store.

They made a great profit, and the business did well for about three months until a fight in the library shut it down. But they'd learned the first lesson of making money work for them, even when they weren't physically present. They were ready to learn more, and Mike's dad was ready to teach them.

Left-hemisphere moment: Despite having a high-paying job, people like Robert's poor dad struggled to make ends meet.

Right-hemisphere moment: Looking at the discarded comic books in a new, creative way led to a business opportunity.

Subconscious moment: People let the emotions of fear and greed rule their lives.

What Was Robert Saying

Now it's time to reflect. Ask yourself, "*What* is Robert saying in this quote?" And, "*Why* does he say that?" In this section you do not need to agree or disagree with Robert. The goal is to *understand* what Robert is saying.

Remember, this curriculum is designed to be cooperative and supportive. Two minds are better than one. If you do not understand what Robert is saying, do not shy away from it. Ask for help in understanding. Take the time discuss each quote until you understand it:

"The poor and the middle class work for money. The rich have money work for them."

"Life pushes all of us around. Some people give up and others fight. A few learn the lesson and move on. They welcome life pushing them around."

"Stop blaming me and thinking I'm the problem. If you think I'm the problem, then you have to change me. If you realize that you're the problem, then you can change yourself, learn something, and grow wiser."

"When it comes to money, most people want to play it safe and feel secure. So passion does not direct them. Fear does."

"Most people, given more money, only get into more debt."

"It's fear that keeps most people working at a job: the fear of not paying their bills, the fear of being fired, the fear of not having enough money, and the fear of starting over. That's the price of studying to learn a profession or trade, and then working for money. Most people become a slave to money — and then get angry at their boss."

"Most people do not know that it's their emotions that are doing the thinking."

"A job is really a short-term solution to a long-term problem."

"It's just like the picture of a donkey dragging a cart with its owner dangling a carrot just in front of its nose. The donkey's owner may be going where he wants to, but the donkey is chasing an illusion. Tomorrow there will only be another carrot for the donkey."

Additional Questions

Now it's time to take the stories in this chapter along with the understanding of what Robert was saying and apply them to you and your life. Ask yourself the questions below and discuss them with your study partner. Be honest with yourself and your partner. If you do not like some of the answers you are giving, ask yourself if you are willing to change and accept the challenge to change your thoughts and mindset:

1. How common is the approach to money taken by Robert's poor dad?
2. Robert's rich dad said true learning takes energy, passion, and a burning desire. What are examples of when this has proven true in your life? What's one lesson you never forgot, and why?
3. Would the pay rate of 10 cents an hour — and then nothing an hour — have stirred in you the same reaction as Robert?
4. Is it fear that drives most people to work? Are there other factors at play?
5. Is the temptation strong to think that more money will soothe that fear? Why is that such a common reaction?
6. What's an example from your life when you reacted with your emotions? What's a time when you were able to observe your emotions instead and choose your thoughts?

7. Are the rich or the poor more susceptible to those controlling emotions of fear and greed? Why do you think that is?
8. Do you think most people realize they are stuck in the Rat Race? Why or why not?

NOTES

Chapter Two

LESSON 2: WHY TEACH FINANCIAL LITERACY?

It's not how much money you make. It's how much money you keep.

In 1990, Mike took over his father's empire and is, in fact, doing a better job than his dad did. We see each other once or twice a year on the golf course. He and his wife are wealthier than you could imagine. Rich dad's empire is in great hands, and Mike is now grooming his son to take his place, as his dad had groomed us.

In 1994, I retired. I was 47, and Kim was 37. Retirement does not mean not working. For us, it means that, barring unforeseen cataclysmic changes, we can work or not work, and our wealth grows automatically, staying ahead of inflation. Our assets are large enough to grow by themselves. It's like planting a tree. You water it for years, and then one day it doesn't need you anymore. Its roots are implanted deep enough. Then the tree provides shade for your enjoyment.

Mike chose to run the empire, and I chose to retire.

Whenever I speak to groups of people, they often ask what I would recommend that they do. "How do I get started?" "Is there a book you would recommend?" "What should I do to prepare my children?" "What is your secret to success?" "How do I make millions?"

Whenever I hear one of these questions, I'm reminded of the following story:

The Richest Businessmen

In 1923 a group of our greatest leaders and richest businessmen held a meeting at the Edgewater Beach hotel in Chicago. Among them were Charles Schwab, head of the largest independent steel company; Samuel Insull, president of the world's largest utility; Howard Hopson, head of the largest gas company; Ivar Kreuger, president of International Match Co., one of the world's largest companies at that time; Leon Frazier, president of the Bank of International Settlements; Richard Whitney, president of the New York Stock Exchange; Arthur Cotton and Jesse Livermore, two of the biggest stock speculators; and Albert Fall, a member of President Harding's cabinet. Twenty-five years later, nine of these titans ended their lives as follows: Schwab died penniless after living for five years on borrowed money. Insull died broke in a foreign land, and Kreuger and Cotton also died broke. Hopson went insane. Whitney and Albert Fall were released from prison, and Fraser and Livermore committed suicide.

I doubt if anyone can say what really happened to these men. If you look at the date, 1923, it was just before the 1929 market crash and the Great Depression, which I suspect had a great impact on these men and their lives. The point is this: Today we live in times of greater and faster change than these men did. I suspect there will be many booms and busts in the coming years that will parallel the ups and downs these men faced. I am concerned that too many people are too focused on money and not on their greatest wealth, their education. If people are prepared to be flexible, keep an open mind and learn, they will grow richer and richer despite tough changes. If they think money will solve problems, they will have a rough ride. Intelligence solves problems and produces money. Money without financial intelligence is money soon gone.

Most people fail to realize that in life, it's not how much money you make. It's how much money you keep. We've all heard stories of lottery winners who are poor, then suddenly rich, and then poor again. They win millions, yet are soon back where they started. Or stories of professional athletes, who at the age of 24 are earning millions, but are sleeping under a bridge 10 years later.

I remember a story of a young basketball player who a year ago had millions. Today, at just 29, he claims his friends, attorney, and accountant took his money, and he was forced to work at a car wash for minimum wage. He was fired from the car wash because he refused to take off his championship ring as he was wiping off the cars. His story made national news and he is appealing his termination, claiming hardship and discrimination. He claims that the ring is all he has left and if it was stripped away, he'll crumble.

I know so many people who became instant millionaires. And while I am glad some people have become richer and richer, I caution them that in the long run, it's not how much money you make. It's how much you keep, and for how many generations you keep it.

So when people ask, "Where do I get started?" or "Tell me how to get rich quick," they often are greatly disappointed with my answer. I simply say to them what my rich dad said to me when I was a little kid. "If you want to be rich, you need to be financially literate."

That idea was drummed into my head every time we were together. As I said, my educated dad stressed the importance of reading books, while my rich dad stressed the need to master financial literacy.

If you are going to build the Empire State Building, the first thing you need to do is dig a deep hole and pour a strong foundation. If you are going to build a home in the suburbs, all you need to do is pour a six-inch slab of concrete. Most people, in their drive to get rich, are trying to build an Empire State Building on a six-inch slab.

Our school system, created in the Agrarian Age, still believes in homes with no foundation. Dirt floors are still the rage. So kids graduate from school with virtually no financial foundation. One day, sleepless and deep in debt in suburbia, living the American Dream, they decide that the answer to their financial problems is to find a way to get rich quick.

Construction on the skyscraper begins. It goes up quickly, and soon, instead of the Empire State Building, we have the Leaning Tower of Suburbia. The sleepless nights return.

As for Mike and me in our adult years, both of our choices were possible because we were taught to pour a strong financial foundation when we were just kids.

Accounting is possibly the most confusing, boring subject in the world, but if you want to be rich long-term, it could be the most important subject. For rich dad, the question was how to take a boring and confusing subject and teach it to kids. The answer he found was to make it simple by teaching it in pictures.

Rich people acquire assets. The poor and middle class acquire liabilities that they think are assets.

My rich dad poured a strong financial foundation for Mike and me. Since we were just kids, he created a simple way to teach us.

For years he only drew pictures and used few words. Mike and I understood the simple drawings, the jargon, the movement of money, and then in later years, rich dad began adding numbers. Today, Mike has gone on to master much more complex and sophisticated accounting analysis because he had to in order to run his empire. I am not as sophisticated because my empire is smaller, yet we come from the same simple foundation. Over the following pages, I offer to you the same simple line drawings Mike's dad created for us. Though basic, those drawings helped guide two little boys in building great sums of wealth on a solid and deep foundation.

Rule #1: You must know the difference between an asset and a liability, and buy assets.

If you want to be rich, this is all you need to know. It is rule number one. It is the only rule. This may sound absurdly simple, but most people have no idea how profound this rule is. Most people struggle financially because they do not know the difference between an asset and a liability.

"Rich people acquire assets. The poor and middle class acquire liabilities that they think are assets," said rich dad.

When rich dad explained this to Mike and me, we thought he was kidding. Here we were, nearly teenagers and waiting for the secret to getting rich, and this was his answer. It was so simple that we stopped for a long time to think about it.

"What is an asset?" asked Mike.

"Don't worry right now," said rich dad. "Just let the idea sink in. If you can comprehend the simplicity, your life will have a plan and be financially easy. It is simple. That is why the idea is missed."

"You mean all we need to know is what an asset is, acquire them, and we'll be rich?" I asked.

Rich dad nodded his head. "It's that simple."

"If it's that simple, how come everyone is not rich?" I asked.

Rich dad smiled. "Because people do not know the difference between an asset and a liability."

I remember asking, "How could adults be so misguided? If it is that simple, if it is that important, why would everyone not want to find out?"

It took rich dad only a few minutes to explain what assets and liabilities were.

As an adult, I have difficulty explaining it to other adults. The simplicity of the idea escapes them because they have been educated differently. They were taught by other educated professionals, such as bankers, accountants, real estate agents, financial planners, and so forth. The difficulty comes in asking adults to unlearn, or become children again. An intelligent adult often feels it is demeaning to pay attention to simplistic definitions.

Rich dad believed in the KISS principle — Keep It Simple, Stupid (or Keep It Super Simple) — so he kept it simple for us, and that made our financial foundation strong.

So what causes the confusion? How could something so simple be so screwed up? Why would someone buy an asset that was really a liability? The answer is found in basic education.

We focus on the word "literacy" and not "financial literacy." What defines something to be an asset or a liability are not words. In fact, if you really want to be confused, look up the words "asset" and "liability" in the dictionary. I know the definition may sound good to a trained accountant, but for the average person, it makes no sense. But we adults are often too proud to admit that something does not make sense.

An asset puts money in my pocket. A liability takes money out of my pocket.

To us young boys, rich dad said, "What defines an asset are not words, but numbers. And if you can't read the numbers, you can't tell an asset from a hole in the ground. In accounting," rich dad would say, "it's not the numbers, but what the numbers are telling you. It's just like words. It's not the words, but the story the words are telling you."

"If you want to be rich, you've got to read and understand numbers." If I heard that once, I heard it a thousand times from my rich dad. And I also heard, "The rich acquire assets, and the poor and middle class acquire liabilities."

TIMELESS RICH DAD WISDOM

LEARN... UNLEARN... RELEARN

This quote from futurist Alvin Toffler mirrors what rich dad told me two decades ago: "The illiterate of the 21st century will not be those who cannot read and write, but those who cannot learn, unlearn, and relearn."

Here is how to tell the difference between an asset and a liability. Most accountants and financial professionals do not agree with the definitions, but these simple drawings were the start of strong financial foundations for two young boys.

This is the cash-flow pattern of an asset:

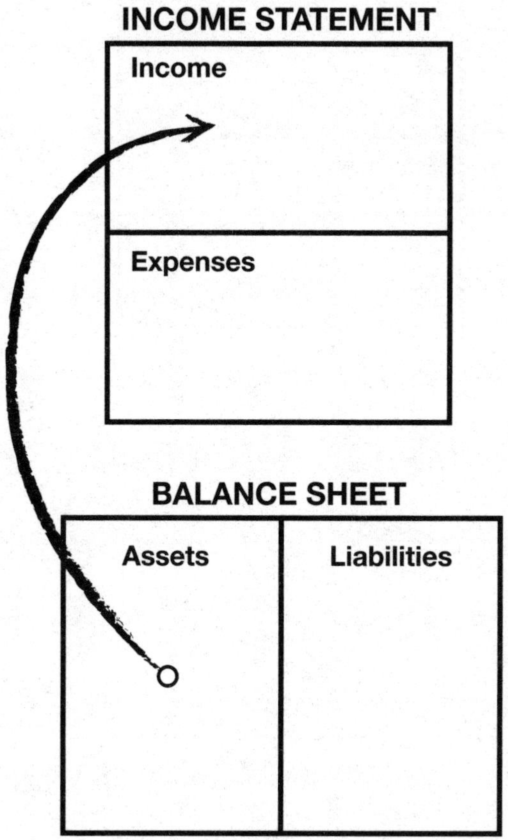

The top part of the diagram is an Income Statement, often called a Profit-and-Loss Statement. It measures income and expenses: money in and money out. The lower part of the diagram is a Balance Sheet. It's called that because it's supposed to balance assets against liabilities. Many financial novices do not know the relationship between the Income Statement and the Balance Sheet, and it is vital to understand that relationship.

So as I said earlier, my rich dad simply told two young boys that "assets put money in your pocket." Nice, simple, and usable.

This is the cash-flow pattern of a liability:

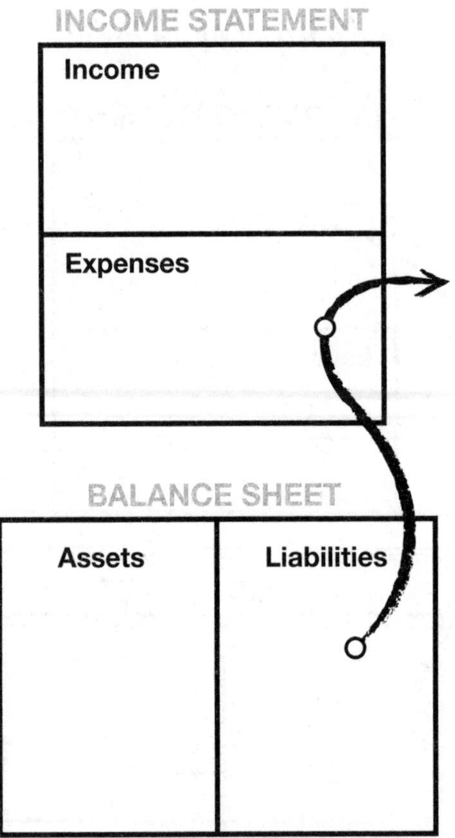

Now that assets and liabilities have been defined through pictures, it may be easier to understand my definitions in words. An asset is something that puts money in my pocket whether I work or not. A liability is something that takes money out of my pocket. This is really all you need to know. If you want to be rich, simply spend your life buying or building assets. If you want to be poor or middle class, spend your life buying liabilities.

Illiteracy, both in words and numbers, is the foundation of financial struggle. If people are having difficulties financially, there is something that they don't understand, either in words or numbers. The rich are rich because they are more literate in different areas than people who struggle financially. So if you want to be rich and maintain your wealth, it's important to be financially literate, in words as well as numbers.

The arrows in the diagrams represent the flow of cash, or "cash flow." Numbers alone mean little, just as words out of context mean little. It's the story that counts. In financial reporting, reading numbers is looking for the plot, the story of where the cash is flowing. In 80 percent of most families, the financial story paints a picture of hard work to get ahead. However, this effort is for naught because they spend their lives buying liabilities instead of assets.

This is the cash-flow pattern of a poor person:

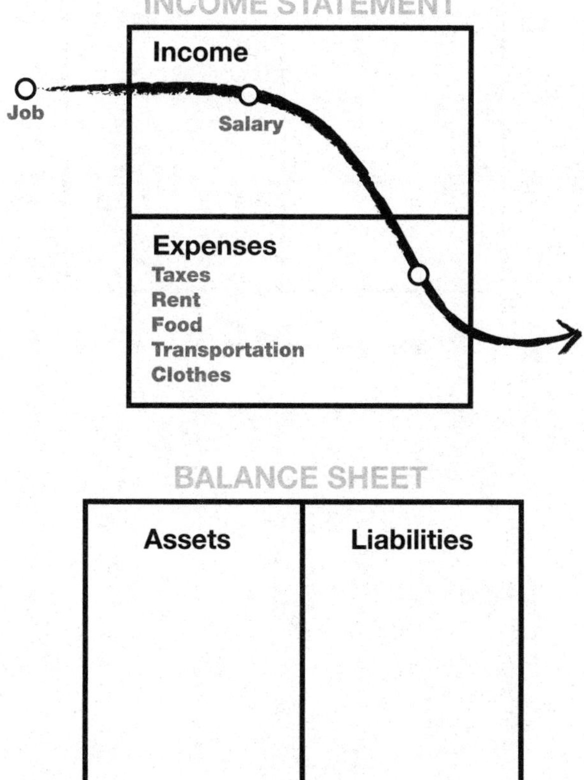

This is the cash-flow pattern of a person in the middle class:

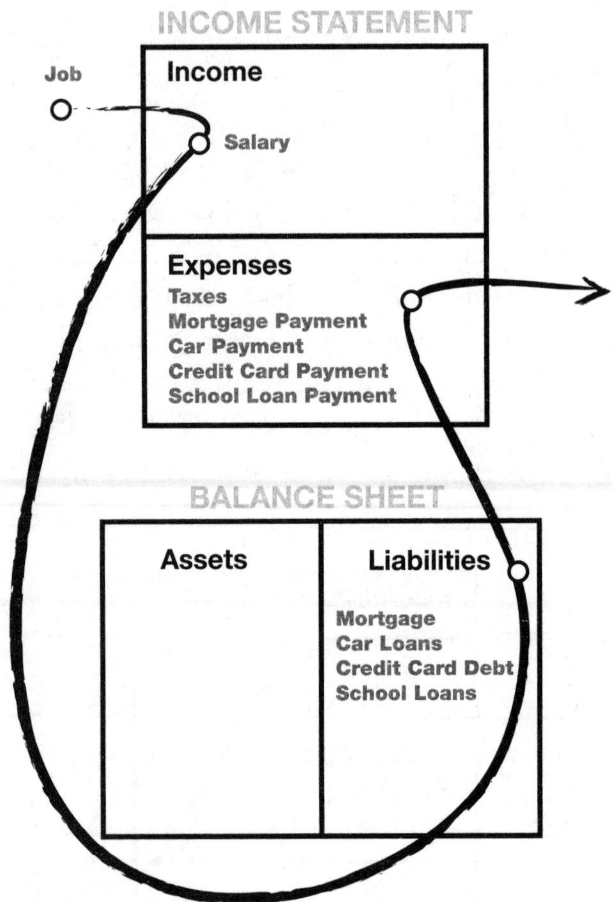

This is the cash-flow pattern of a rich person:

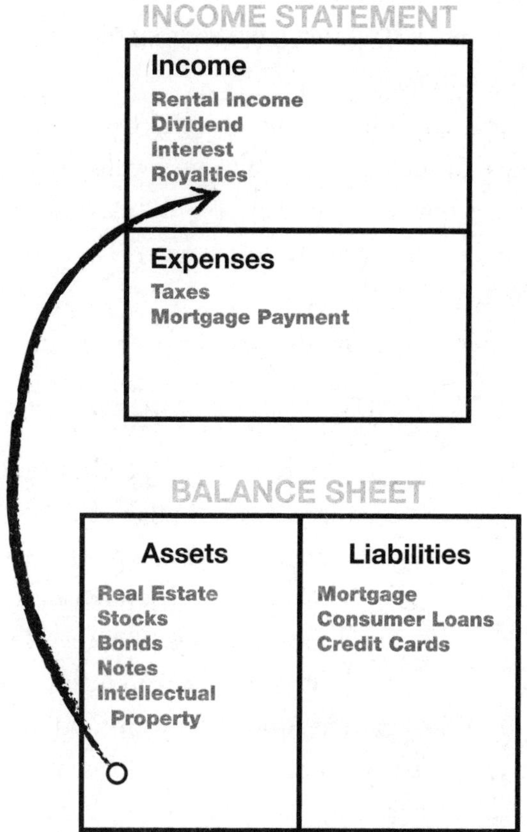

All of these diagrams are obviously oversimplified. Everyone has living expenses, the need for food, shelter, and clothing. The diagrams show the flow of cash through a poor, middle-class, and wealthy person's life. It is the cash flow that tells the story of how a person handles his or her money.

The reason I started with the story of the richest men in America is to illustrate the flaw in believing that money will solve all problems. That is why I cringe whenever I hear people ask me how to get rich quicker, or where they should start. I often hear, "I'm in debt, so I need to make more money."

But more money will often not solve the problem. In fact, it may compound the problem. Money often makes obvious our tragic human flaws, putting a spotlight on what we don't know. That is why, all too often, a person who comes into a sudden windfall of cash — let's say an inheritance, a pay raise, or lottery winnings — soon returns to the same financial mess, if not worse, than the mess they were in before. Money only accentuates the cash-flow pattern running in your head. If your pattern is to spend everything you get, most likely an increase in cash will just result in an increase in spending. Thus, the saying, "A fool and his money is one big party."

Cash flow tells the story of how a person handles money.

I have said many times that we go to school to gain scholastic and professional skills, both of which are important. We learn to make money with our professional skills. In the 1960s when I was in high school, if someone did well academically, people assumed this bright student would go on to be a medical doctor because it was the profession with the promise of the greatest financial reward.

Today, doctors face financial challenges I wouldn't wish on my worst enemy: insurance companies taking control of the business, managed health care, government intervention, and malpractice lawsuits. Today, kids want to be famous athletes, movie stars, rock stars, beauty queens, or CEOs because that is where the fame, money, and prestige are. That is the reason it is so hard to motivate kids in school today. They know that professional success is no longer solely linked to academic success, as it once was.

Because students leave school without financial skills, millions of educated people pursue their profession successfully, but later find themselves struggling financially. They work harder but don't get ahead. What is missing from their education is not how to make money, but how to manage money. It's called financial aptitude — what you do with the money once you make it, how to keep people from taking it from you, how to keep it longer, and how to make that money work hard for you. Most people don't understand why they struggle financially because they don't understand cash flow. A person can be highly educated, professionally successful, and financially illiterate. These people often work harder than they need to because they learned how to work hard, but not how to have their money work hard for them.

How the Quest for a Financial Dream Turns into a Financial Nightmare

The classic story of hardworking people has a set pattern. Recently married, the happy, highly educated young couple now share a cramped rented apartment. Immediately, they realize that they are saving money because two can live as cheaply as one.

The problem is the apartment is cramped. They decide to save money to buy their dream home so they can have kids. They now have two incomes, and they begin to focus on their careers. Their incomes begin to increase.

As their incomes go up, their expenses go up as well.

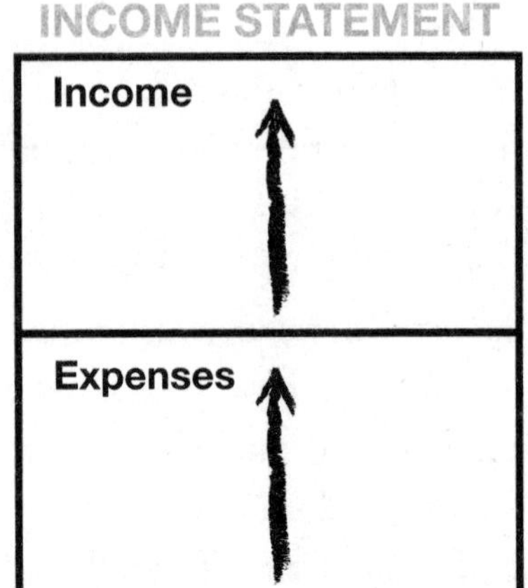

BALANCE SHEET

Assets	Liabilities

The number-one expense for most people is taxes. Many people think it's income tax, but for most Americans, their highest tax is Social Security. As an employee, it appears as if the Social Security tax combined with the Medicare tax rate is roughly 7.5 percent, but it's really 15 percent since the employer must match the Social Security amount. In essence, it is money the employer can't pay you. On top of that, you still have to pay income tax on the amount deducted from your wages for Social Security tax, income you never received because it went directly to Social Security through withholding.

Going back to the young couple, as a result of their incomes increasing, they decide to buy the house of their dreams. Once in their house with a mortgage, they have a new tax, called property tax. Then they buy a new car, new furniture, and new appliances to match their new house. All of a sudden, they wake up and their liabilities column is full of mortgage and credit-card debt. Their liabilities go up.

Fast Forward... to Today

TAXES AND ENTITLEMENT PROGRAMS

Taxes around the world are getting higher and higher as social demands for tax dollars require higher property, income, and sales (or value-added) taxes. Higher incomes create even more of a 'bracket creep' as tax rates become more progressive (steeper) to pay for social services (also called entitlements). Today the government faces serious challenges as entitlement programs like Social Security and Medicare face insolvency.

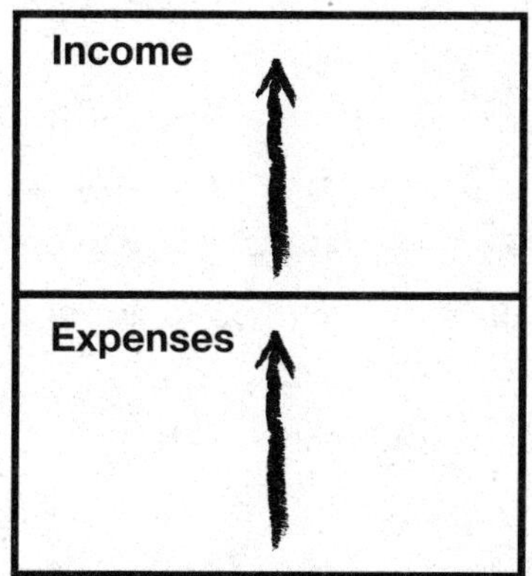

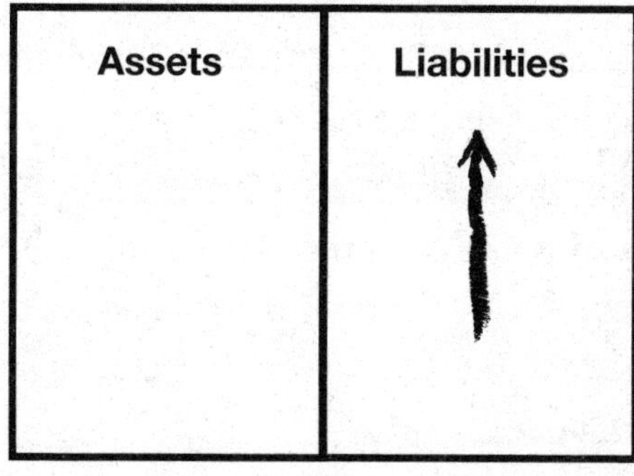

STILL TRUE TODAY...

CREDIT CARD DEBT

Today, based on 2021 stats, U.S. consumer credit card debt is at an all-time high: $998.4 billion. Is it all bad debt... or good debt? Do you know the difference?

They're now trapped in the Rat Race. Pretty soon a baby comes along and they work harder. The process repeats itself: Higher incomes cause higher taxes, also called "bracket creep." A credit card comes in the mail. They use it and max it out. A loan company calls and says their greatest "asset," their home, has appreciated in value. Because their credit is so good, the company offers a bill-consolidation loan and tells them the intelligent thing to do is clear off the high-interest consumer debt by paying off their credit card. And besides, mortgage interest is a tax deduction. They go for it, and pay off those high-interest credit cards. They breathe a sigh of relief. Their credit cards are paid off. They've now folded their consumer debt into their home mortgage. Their payments go down because they extend their debt over 30 years. It is the smart thing to do.

Their neighbor calls to invite them to go shopping. The Memorial Day sale is on. They promise themselves they'll just window shop, but they take a credit card, just in case.

I run into this young couple all the time. Their names change, but their financial dilemma is the same. They come to one of my talks to hear what I have to say. They ask me, "Can you tell us how to make more money?"

They don't understand that their trouble is really how they choose to spend the money they do have. It is caused by financial illiteracy and not understanding the difference between an asset and a liability.

More money seldom solves someone's money problems. Intelligence solves problems. There is a saying a friend of mine uses over and over to people in debt: "If you find you have dug yourself into a hole... stop digging."

As a child, my dad often told us that the Japanese were aware of three powers: the power of the sword, the jewel, and the mirror.

The sword symbolizes the power of weapons. America has spent trillions of dollars on weapons and, because of this, is a powerful military presence in the world.

The jewel symbolizes the power of money. There is some degree of truth to the saying, "Remember the Golden Rule. He who has the gold makes the rules."

The mirror symbolizes the power of self-knowledge. This self-knowledge, according to Japanese legend, was the most treasured of the three.

All too often, the poor and middle class allow the power of money to control them. By simply getting up and working harder, failing to ask themselves if what they do makes sense, they shoot themselves in the foot as they leave for work every morning. By not fully understanding money, the vast majority of people allow its awesome power to control them.

If they used the power of the mirror, they would have asked themselves, "Does this make sense?" All too often, instead of trusting their inner wisdom, that genius inside, most people follow the crowd. They do things because everybody else does them. They conform, rather than question. Often, they mindlessly repeat what they have been told: "Diversify." "Your home is an asset." "Your home is your biggest investment." "You get a tax break for going into greater debt." "Get a safe job." "Don't make mistakes." "Don't take risks."

A person can be highly educated, professionally successful, and financially illiterate.

It is said that the fear of public speaking is a fear greater than death for most people. According to psychiatrists, the fear of public speaking is caused by the fear of ostracism, the fear of standing out, the fear of criticism, the fear of ridicule, and the fear of being an outcast. The fear of being different prevents most people from seeking new ways to solve their problems.

That is why my educated dad said the Japanese valued the power of the mirror the most, for it is only when we look into it that we find truth. Fear is the main reason that people say, "Play it safe." That goes for anything, be it sports, relationships, careers, or money.

It is that same fear, the fear of ostracism, that causes people to conform to, and not question, commonly accepted opinions or popular trends: "Your home is an asset." "Get a bill-consolidation loan, and get out of debt." "Work harder." "It's a promotion." "Someday I'll be a vice president." "Save money." "When I get a raise, I'll buy us a bigger house." "Mutual funds are safe."

Many financial problems are caused by trying to keep up with the Joneses. Occasionally, we all need to look in the mirror and be true to our inner wisdom rather than our fears.

By the time Mike and I were 16 years old, we began to have problems in school. We were not bad kids. We just began to separate from the crowd. We worked for Mike's dad after school and on weekends. Mike and I often spent hours after work just sitting at a table with his dad while he held meetings with his bankers, attorneys, accountants, brokers, investors, managers, and employees. Here was a man who had left school at 13 who was now directing, instructing, ordering, and asking questions of educated people. They came at his beck and call, and cringed when he didn't approve of them.

TIMELESS RICH DAD WISDOM

WHO'S ON YOUR TEAM?

Rich dad surrounded himself with men and women who were specialists: attorneys, accountants, brokers, and bankers... and Kim and I have done the same. Today, our team of Advisors is among our greatest assets.

What's more important than money?

An entrepreneur's team...

Who's on yours?

Here was a man who had not gone along with the crowd. He was a man who did his own thinking and detested the words, "We have to do it this way because that's the way everyone else does it." He also hated the word "can't." If you wanted him to do something, just say, "I don't think you can do it."

Mike and I learned more sitting in on his meetings than we did in all our years of school, college included. Mike's dad was not book-smart, but he was financially educated and successful as a result. He told us over and over again, "An intelligent person hires people who are more intelligent than he is." So Mike and I had the benefit of spending hours listening to and learning from intelligent people.

But because of this, Mike and I couldn't go along with the standard dogma our teachers preached, and that caused problems. Whenever the teacher said, "If you don't get good grades, you won't do well in the real world," Mike and I just raised our eyebrows. When we were told to follow set procedures and not deviate from the rules, we could see how school discouraged creativity. We started to understand why our rich dad told us that schools were designed to produce good employees, instead of employers. Occasionally, Mike or I would ask our teachers how what we studied was applicable in the real world, or why we never studied money and how it worked. To the latter question, we often got the answer that money was not important, that if we excelled in our education, the money would follow. The more we knew about the power of money, the more distant we grew from the teachers and our classmates.

My highly educated dad never pressured me about my grades, but we did begin to argue about money. By the time I was 16, I probably had a far better foundation with money than both my parents. I could keep books, I listened to tax accountants, corporate attorneys, bankers, real estate brokers, investors, and so forth. By contrast, my dad talked only to other teachers.

One day my dad told me that our home was his greatest investment. A not-too-pleasant argument took place when I showed him why I thought a house was not a good investment.

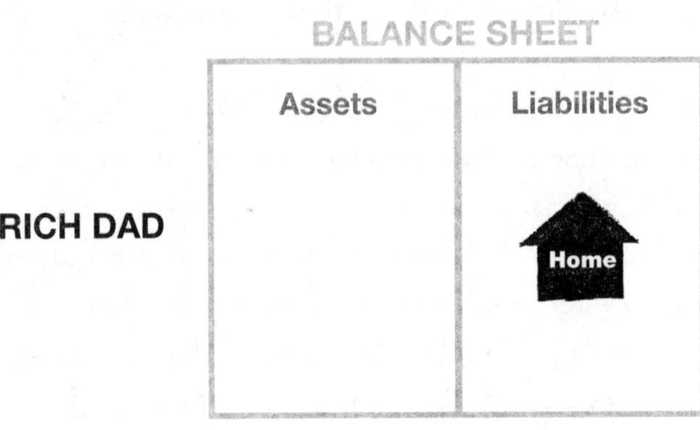

BALANCE SHEET

Assets

Liabilities

POOR DAD

Home

The diagram above illustrates the difference in perception between my rich dad and my poor dad when it came to their homes. One dad thought his house was an asset, and the other dad thought it was a liability.

I remember when I drew the following diagram for my dad, showing him the direction of cash flow. I also showed him the ancillary expenses that went along with owning the home. A bigger home meant bigger expenses, and the cash flow kept going out through the expense column.

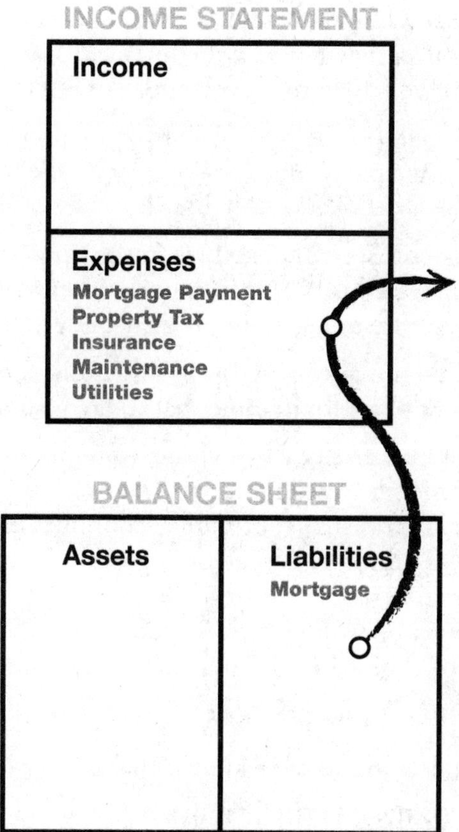

Today, people still challenge me on the idea of a house not being an asset. I know that for many people, it is their dream as well as their largest investment. And owning your own home is better than nothing. I simply offer an alternate way of looking at this popular dogma. If Kim and I were to buy a bigger, flashier house, we realize it wouldn't be an asset. It would be a liability since it would take money out of our pocket.

So here is the argument I put forth. I really don't expect most people to agree with it because your home is an emotional thing and when it comes to money, high emotions tend to lower financial intelligence. I know from personal experience that money has a way of making every decision emotional.

- When it comes to houses, most people work all their lives paying for a home they never own. In other words, most people buy a new house every few years, each time incurring a new 30-year loan to pay off the previous one.
- Even though people receive a tax deduction for interest on mortgage payments, they pay for all their other expenses with after-tax dollars, even after they pay off their mortgage.
- Kim's parents were shocked when the property taxes on their home increased to $1,000 a month. They had already retired, so the increase put a strain on their budget.
- Houses do not always go up in value. I have friends who owe a million dollars for a home that today would sell for far less.
- The greatest losses of all are those from missed opportunities. If all your money is tied up in your house, you may be forced to work harder because your money continues blowing out of the expense column, instead of adding to the asset column — the classic middle-class cash-flow pattern. If a young couple would put more money into their asset column early on, their later years would be easier. Their assets would have grown and would be available to help cover expenses.

Making a decision to own a house that is too expensive in lieu of starting an investment portfolio impacts an individual in at least the following three ways:

1. *Loss of time,* during which other assets could have grown in value.
2. *Loss of additional capital,* which could have been invested instead of paying high home maintenance expenses.
3. *Loss of education.* Too often, people count their house and savings and retirement plans as all they have in their asset column. Because they have no money to invest, they simply don't invest. This costs them investment experience. Most never become what the investment world calls "a sophisticated investor." And the best investments are usually first sold to sophisticated investors, who then turn around and sell them to the people playing it safe.

I am not saying don't buy a house. What I am saying is that you should understand the difference between an asset and a liability. When I want a bigger house, I first buy assets that will generate the cash flow to pay for the house.

My educated dad's personal financial statement best demonstrates the life of someone caught in the Rat Race. His expenses match his income, never allowing him enough left over to invest in assets. As a result, his liabilities are larger than his assets.

TIMELESS RICH DAD WISDOM

YOUR SCORECARD

Without a financial statement you don't really know where you are in life's financial game. Like it or not, money tells the score of your "game," and a financial statement is your scorecard. Banks want financial statements — Income Statement and Balance Sheet — to know how well you're scoring in your life's financial game.

The following diagram on the left shows my poor dad's income statement. It is worth a thousand words. It shows that his income and expenses are equal while his liabilities are larger than his assets.

My rich dad's personal financial statement on the right reflects the results of a life dedicated to investing and minimizing liabilities.

Poor Dad's Financial Statement

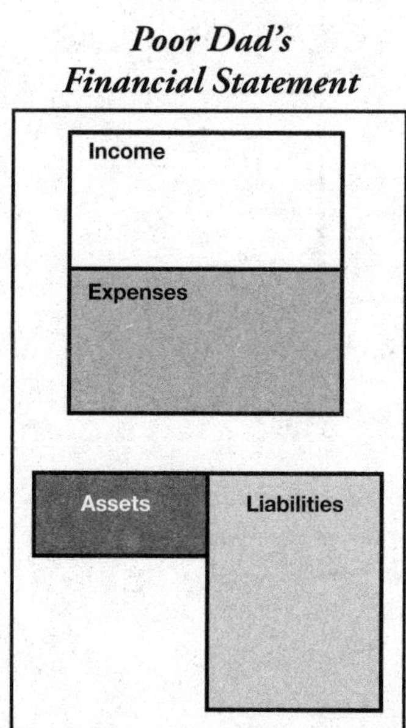

Rich Dad's Financial Statement

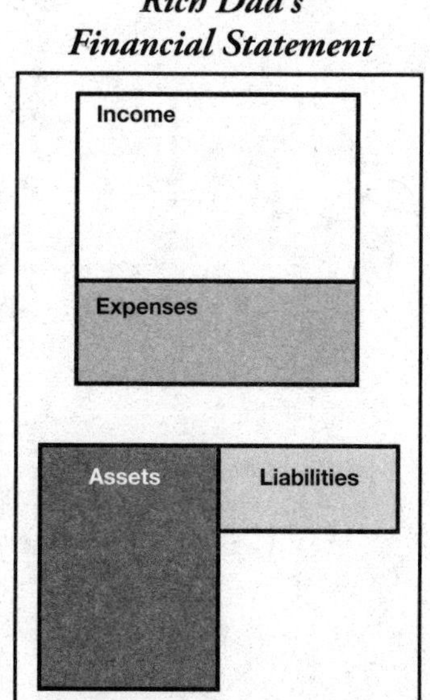

Why the Rich Get Richer

A review of my rich dad's financial statement shows why the rich get richer. The asset column generates more than enough income to cover expenses, with the balance reinvested into the asset column. The asset column continues to grow and, therefore, the income it produces grows with it. The result is that the rich get richer!

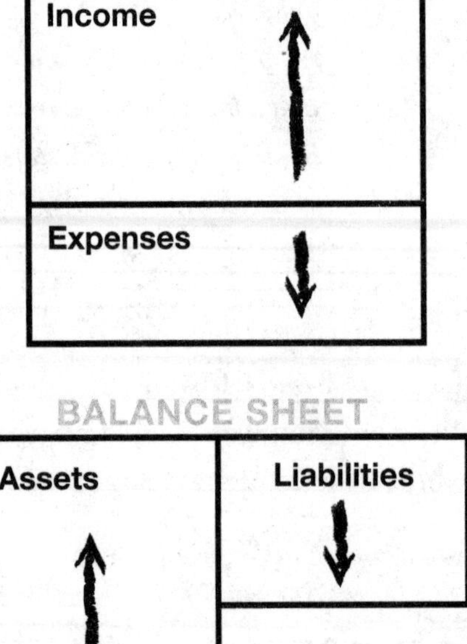

Why the Middle Class Struggle

The middle class finds itself in a constant state of financial struggle. Their primary income is through their salary. As their wages increase, so do their taxes. Their expenses tend to increase in proportion to their salary increase: hence, the phrase "the Rat Race." They treat their home as their primary asset, instead of investing in income-producing assets.

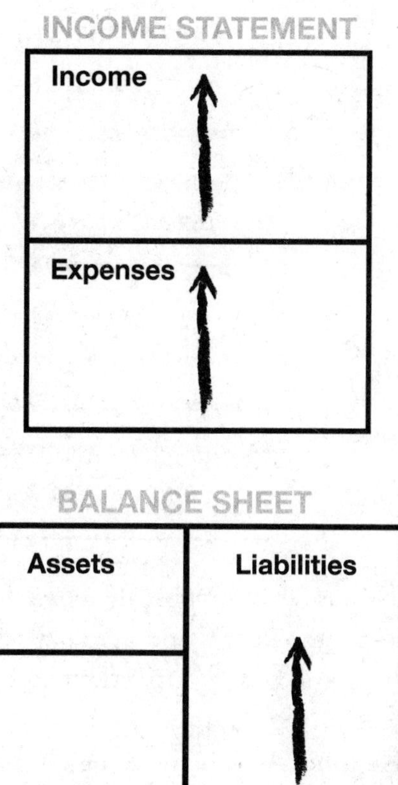

This pattern of treating your home as an investment, and the philosophy that a pay raise means you can buy a larger home or spend more, is the foundation of today's debt-ridden society. Increased spending throws families into greater debt and into more financial uncertainty, even though they may be advancing in their jobs and receiving pay raises. This is high-risk living caused by weak financial education.

The massive loss of jobs in recent times proves how shaky the middle class really is financially. Company pension plans are being replaced by 401(k) plans. Social Security is obviously in trouble and can't be relied upon as a source for retirement. Panic has set in for the middle class.

FAST FORWARD... TO TODAY

PENSION PLANS

Since Enron, it has become clear that pension plans are in trouble. Even government pension plans, such as those in Greece, Italy, and California, cannot pay out what is owed to retirees. So a retirement plan is no longer the guarantee it once was of security for old age and retirement. Today pension plans continue to be plagued by poor or inept management, marginal investment strategies, and volatile markets.

Today, mutual funds are popular because they supposedly represent safety. Average mutual-fund buyers are too busy working to pay taxes and mortgages, save for their children's college, and pay off credit cards. They do not have time to study investing, so they rely on the expertise of the manager of a mutual fund. Also, because the mutual fund includes many different types of investments, they feel their money is safer because it is "diversified." This educated middle class subscribes to the dogma put out by mutual-fund brokers and financial planners: "Play it safe. Avoid risk."

The real tragedy is that the lack of early financial education is what creates the risk faced by average middle-class people. The reason they have to play it safe is because their financial positions are tenuous at best. Their balance sheets are not balanced. Instead, they are loaded with liabilities and have no real assets that generate income. Typically, their only source of income is their paycheck. Their livelihood becomes entirely dependent on their employer. So when genuine "deals of a lifetime" come along, these people can't take advantage of them because they are working so hard, are taxed to the max, and are loaded with debt.

As I said at the start of this section, the most important rule is to know the difference between an asset and a liability. Once you understand the difference, concentrate your efforts on buying income-generating assets. That's the best way to get started on a path to becoming rich. Keep doing that, and your asset column will grow. Keep liabilities and expenses down so more money is available to continue pouring into the asset column. Soon the asset base will be so deep that you can afford to look at more speculative investments: investments that may have returns of 100 percent to infinity; $5,000 investments that are soon turned into $1 million or more; investments that the middle class calls "too risky." The investment is not risky for the financially literate.

If you do what the masses do, you get the following picture:

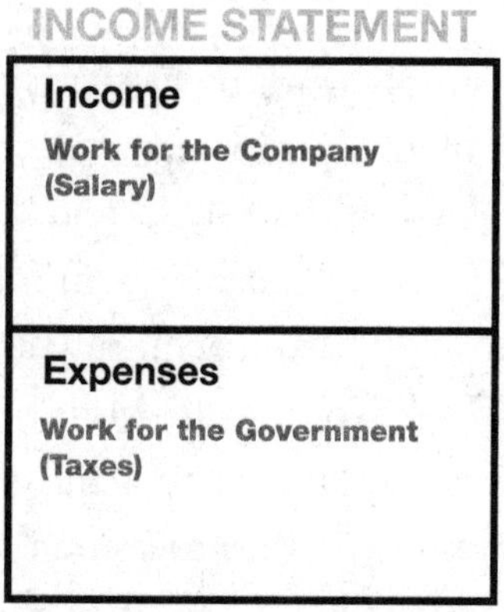

INCOME STATEMENT

Income
Work for the Company (Salary)
Expenses
Work for the Government (Taxes)

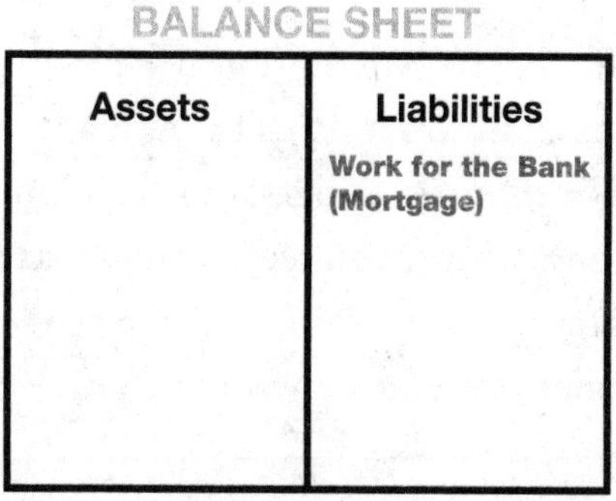

BALANCE SHEET

Assets	Liabilities
	Work for the Bank (Mortgage)

As an employee who is also a homeowner, your working efforts are generally as follows:

1. ***You work for the company.***
   Employees make their business owner or the shareholders rich, not themselves. Your efforts and success will help provide for the owner's success and retirement.

2. ***You work for the government.***
   The government takes its share from your paycheck before you even see it. By working harder, you simply increase the amount of taxes taken by the government. Most people work from January to May just for the government.

3. ***You work for the bank.***
   After taxes, your next largest expense is usually your mortgage and credit-card debt.

The problem with simply working harder is that each of these three levels takes a greater share of your increased efforts. You need to learn how to have your increased efforts benefit you and your family directly.

Once you have decided to concentrate on minding your own business — focusing your efforts on acquiring assets instead of a bigger paycheck — how do you set your goals? Most people must keep their job and rely on their wages to fund their acquisition of assets.

As their assets grow, how do they measure the extent of their success? When does someone know that they are rich, that they have wealth?

As well as having my own definitions for assets and liabilities, I also have my own definition for wealth. Actually, I borrowed it from a man named R. Buckminster Fuller. Some call him a quack, and others call him a genius. Years ago he got architects buzzing because he applied for a patent for something called a geodesic dome. But in the application, Fuller also said something about wealth.

It was pretty confusing at first, but after reading it, it began to make some sense:

> *Wealth is a person's ability to survive so many number of days forward — or, if I stopped working today, how long could I survive?*

Unlike net worth — which is the difference between your assets and liabilities, and is often filled with a person's expensive junk and opinions of what things are worth — this definition creates the possibility for developing a truly accurate measurement. I could now measure and know where I was in terms of my goal to become financially independent.

Although net worth often includes non-cash-producing assets, like stuff you bought that now sits in your garage, wealth measures how much money your money is making and, therefore, your financial survivability.

Wealth is the measure of the cash flow from the asset column compared with the expense column.

Let's use an example. Let's say I have cash flow from my asset column of $1,000 a month. And I have monthly expenses of $2,000. What is my wealth?

Let's go back to Buckminster Fuller's definition. Using his definition, how many days forward can I survive? Assuming a 30-day month, I have enough cash flow for half a month.

When I achieve $2,000 a month cash flow from my assets, then I will be wealthy.

So while I'm not yet rich, I am wealthy. I now have income generated from assets each month that fully cover my monthly expenses. If I want to increase my expenses, I first must increase my cash flow to maintain this level of wealth. Also note that it is at this

STILL TRUE TODAY...

WEALTH AND CASH RESERVES

Today, more and more people are living paycheck to paycheck — with little buffer for emergencies or unplanned expenses. Another staggering statistic reported in a 2019 GOBankingRates survey: 45% of Americans have no savings at all. More and more people count on government assistance... which often leads to dependency.

point that I'm no longer dependent on my wages. I have focused on, and been successful in, building an asset column that has made me financially independent. If I quit my job today, I would be able to cover my monthly expenses with the cash flow from my assets.

My next goal would be to have the excess cash flow from my assets reinvested into the asset column. The more money that goes into my asset column, the more my asset column grows. The more my assets grow, the more my cash flow grows. And as long as I keep my expenses less than the cash flow from these assets, I grow richer with more and more income from sources other than my physical labor.

As this reinvestment process continues, I am well on my way to becoming rich. Just remember this simple observation:

- **The rich buy assets.**
- **The poor only have expenses.**
- **The middle class buy liabilities they think are assets.**

So how do I start minding my own business? What is the answer? Listen to the founder of McDonald's in the next chapter.

STUDY SESSION

Chapter Two

LESSON 2: WHY TEACH FINANCIAL LITERACY?

Chapter Two

LESSON 2: WHY TEACH FINANCIAL LITERACY?

Summary

We revisit Robert and Mike some three and a half decades later. Mike has taken over his father's company and is doing an even better job than the rich dad did.

As for Robert, he retired in 1994 at the age of 47. His and his wife's wealth is growing automatically, like a well-established tree.

He shares a story of the 1923 meeting of some of our greatest leaders and richest businessmen — men who owned the largest steel and gas company, who ran the New York Stock Exchange, and who sat on President Harding's cabinet. Twenty-five years later, most of their lives had ended tragically, with the men either broke, exiled, or in prison.

The 1929 stock crash and Great Depression likely played a part in their fates, but today we live in a time of even more turmoil and change than they did. More important than money to our survival is our education and the ability to learn.

It's not how much you make but how much you keep — and how many generations you keep it.

So when people ask Robert where to start getting rich, he gives them the same answer his rich dad gave him: "If you want to be rich, you need to be financially literate."

Robert compares the way many people act to building a skyscraper on a slab made for a small home. Because kids graduate school with little financial education, they launch into their adults lives chasing the American Dream but find themselves deep in debt. The only way out that they can see is a get-rich strategy.

But without having that financial-literacy background, their efforts are like building a skyscraper on a weak foundation, and instead of creating the Empire State Building, they end up with the Leaning Tower of Suburbia.

Robert and his childhood friend Mike, however, were given a strong foundation worthy of a skyscraper thanks to the teaching of the rich dad.

Accounting as a subject is boring, confusing — and absolutely crucial to financial success. To make it accessible to kids, rich dad used pictures to teach it to the two boys. Only later did he start adding numbers to guide the boys through key concepts.

Rule No. 1, Robert says, is that you must know the difference between an asset and a liability, and only buy assets. That's all you need to know. But despite it being so simple, it's something that many people don't understand.

When rich dad first explained it to the two now-teenagers, they thought he was kidding. How could adults not understand this? Shouldn't everyone be rich?

The problem is that most people have been educated differently by bankers, financial planners and others, so they must unlearn what they think they know. Some find this demeaning to return to such a basic introduction.

The true definitions of "asset" and "liability" lie not in words, but in numbers.

Robert uses drawings to help readers the same way rich dad used them to help him.

This is the cash-flow pattern of an asset:

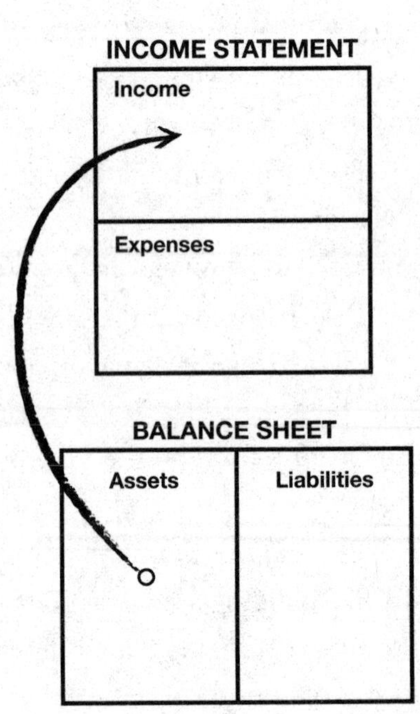

The top part of the diagram is an Income Statement, often called a Profit-and-Loss Statement. It measures income and expenses: money in and money out. The lower part of the diagram is a Balance Sheet. It's called that because it's supposed to balance assets against liabilities.

Assets add to your income. They put money in your pocket.

This is the cash-flow pattern of a liability:

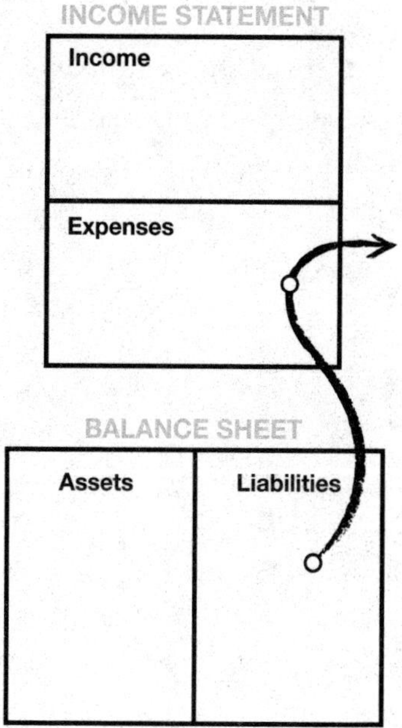

A liability takes money out of your pocket.

Want to be rich? Buy assets. It seems simple, but so many people struggle because they buy liabilities. If you want to gain and maintain wealth, you must build your understanding.

It's not just straight numbers; it's how the numbers tell a story. Follow the arrows in each of these diagrams to see where the money is flowing, or "cash flow." It will tell you the story, the plot of that financial situation.

This is the cash-flow pattern of a poor person:

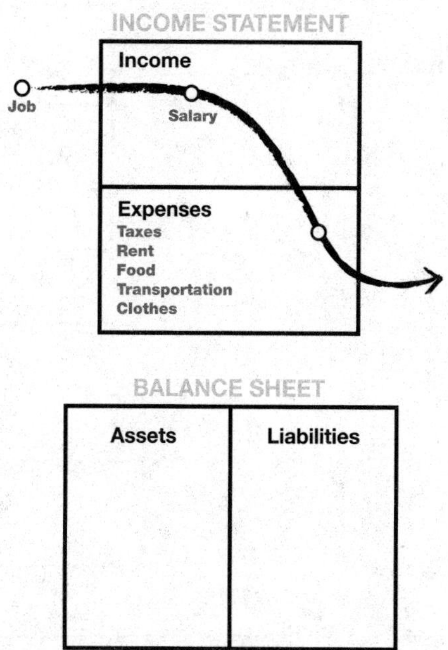

This is the cash-flow pattern of a person in the middle class:

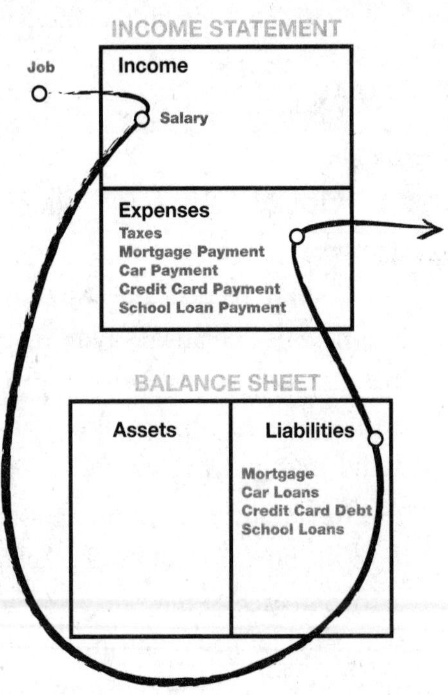

This is the cash-flow pattern of a wealthy person:

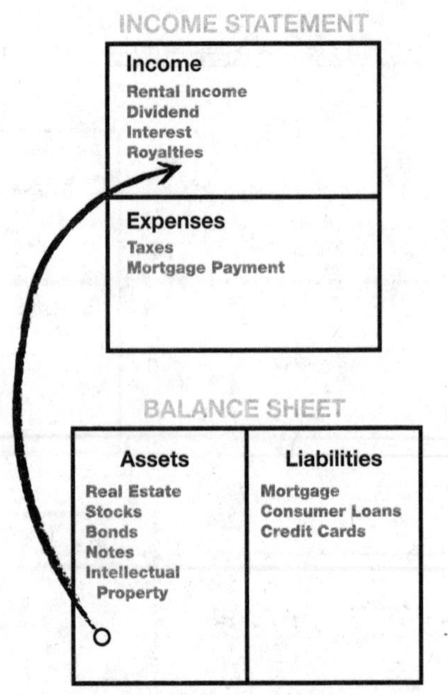

Through these simplified diagrams, the cash flow tells the story of how each person handles money.

Often, those in debt think the answer is to make more money. But not only will more money not always solve their problems, it may compound them. It's why many people who get a sudden windfall — through the lottery or an inheritance, for instance — so quickly burn through it. An increase in cash only results in an increase in spending.

What is missing for so many people is a financial education. It's why they might end up successful in their professions but still struggling with money. They may have learned how to make money, but not how to manage it. People can be very intelligent and still be illiterate when it comes to finances. They learned how to work hard for money, but not how to make their money work hard for them.

Robert tells the story of a young couple who get married and start their lives together. Their incomes begin to increase, but so do their expenses.

The couple is hit with the No. 1 expense for most people: taxes. And for many people, it's not income tax that gives the biggest hit but Social Security. It's roughly 15 percent (Social Security tax combined with the Medicare tax rate, all of which must be matched by the employer, funds that the employer now can't pay the worker). And the employee is charged income tax on that amount, too.

The young couple is faced with those taxes and, when they buy a house, property tax. And to go with the new house is a new car, new furniture, and new appliances. Suddenly, their liabilities go up, filling with mortgage and credit-card debt.

The couple is trapped in the Rat Race. Add a baby to the mix, and they work harder: higher incomes that lead to higher taxes. They continue to rack up debt, eventually rolling it into their mortgage in a consolidation loan. But their habits haven't changed, so the credit-card debt continues — not to mention they extended their home loan.

For this couple and so many like them, their true problem is not knowing how to handle the money they have. It's caused by financial illiteracy and not understanding the true difference between an asset and a liability.

So many people don't take the time to question whether something makes sense and simply follow the crowd. Often, they mindlessly repeat what they have been told: "Diversify." "Your home is an asset." "You get a tax break for going into greater debt." "Get a safe job." "Don't make mistakes." "Don't take risks."

Because of the large amount of time Robert and Mike spent sitting in on meetings with rich dad and learning from the intelligent people he surrounded himself with, they learned a lot — and learned to question the standard dogma taught at their school. It began to cause problems and made them grow distant from their teachers.

Robert also began disagreeing with his own father over money matters, especially when it came to his poor dad's view that his home was his greatest investment. In contrast, rich dad saw his home as a liability.

Many people still believe that their home is an asset. But Robert teaches that a home is a liability, because it takes money out of your pocket — not only with taxes and expenses, but because of its loss in value and the opportunities missed when all your money is tied up in your house. And that causes you to lose out on the education of investment experience.

That doesn't mean you can't ever buy a bigger house. But make sure to first buy assets that will generate the cash flow to pay for the house.

When there are enough assets to generate more than enough income to cover expenses, the balance is reinvested into assets. Which grows the asset column on a balance sheet. Which produces more income. The result is that the rich who understand the difference between assets and liabilities, get richer.

The middle class get stuck in the Rat Race because they treat their home as an asset instead of investing in income-producing assets. They are also stuck because their salary is their primary source of income — and thus when their income increases, so do their taxes.

Many invest in mutual funds, paying a manager to handle their accounts, because they don't have the time or the expertise to do it themselves. They feel like a mutual fund is playing it safe, and they have to play it safe because their balance sheets are not balanced. They can't take advantage of opportunities because they are maxed out on debt and only have their salary bringing money in.

Want to grow rich? Concentrate your efforts on buying income-producing assets — when you truly understand what an asset is. Keep liabilities and expenses low. You'll deepen your asset column.

So how do you know when you're wealthy? Robert uses a definition by R. Buckminster Fuller: "Wealth is a person's ability to survive so many number of days forward — or, if I stopped working today, how long could I survive?"

Another way of stating it: Wealth is the measure of the cash flow from the asset column compared with the expense column. When your assets generate enough income to cover your expenses, you are wealthy, even if you are not yet rich.

Left-hemisphere moment: Look at the numbers and learn to read the story they are telling. Assets put money in your pocket. If something takes money out of your pocket, it's not an asset; it's a liability.

Right-hemisphere moment: The balance sheet drawings help explain the movement of money through different people's lives.

Subconscious moment: The fear of ostracism causes people to conform to, and not question, commonly-accepted opinions or popular trends, often to their financial detriment.

What Was Robert Saying

Now it's time to reflect. Ask yourself, "*What* is Robert saying in this quote?" And, "*Why* does he say that?" In this section you do not need to agree or disagree with Robert. The goal is to *understand* what Robert is saying.

Remember, this curriculum is designed to be cooperative and supportive. Two minds are better than one. If you do not understand what Robert is saying, do not shy away from it. Ask for help in understanding. Take the time discuss each quote until you understand it:

"It's not how much money you make. It's how much money you keep."

"Intelligence solves problems and produces money. Money without financial intelligence is money soon gone."

"If you are going to build the Empire State Building, the first thing you need to do is dig a deep hole and pour a strong foundation. If you are going to build a home in the suburbs, all you need to do is pour a six-inch slab of concrete. Most people, in their drive to get rich, are trying to build an Empire State Building on a six-inch slab."

"Rich people acquire assets. The poor and middle class acquire liabilities that they think are assets."

"If your pattern is to spend everything you get, most likely an increase in cash will just result in an increase in spending."

"In 80 percent of most families, the financial story paints a picture of hard work to get ahead. However, this effort is for naught because they spend their lives buying liabilities instead of assets."

"By not fully understanding money, the vast majority of people allow its awesome power to control them."

Additional Questions

Now it's time to take the stories in this chapter along with the understanding of what Robert was saying and apply them to you and your life. Ask yourself the questions below and discuss them with your study partner. Be honest with yourself and your partner. If you do not like some of the answers you are giving, ask yourself if you are willing to change and accept the challenge to change your thoughts and mindset:

1. When did your financial education begin? Was it with this book, or from another source?
2. How did you react when you first read Robert's definition of assets and liabilities?
3. How did you react when he stated that a home is not an asset? Had you viewed yours as one? After he fully laid out his argument, did he change your mind?
4. Which cash-flow situation looks most like your life?
5. Other than your home, is there something that you thought was an asset that later revealed itself to be a liability?
6. Would you agree with this statement: "What is missing from most people's education is not how to make money, but how to manage money." Why or why not?
7. Rich dad told the boys that it's not the numbers that matter in accounting, but what the numbers are telling you. What story do the numbers in your life tell?
8. When was a time in your life that a seemingly positive accomplishment, such as a promotion or raise, didn't lead to the balance-sheet result you expected?
9. How many days forward could you survive if you stopped working today? Does that number surprise or frighten you?

Term definitions:

401(k): A U.S. retirement plan developed by the ERISA Act of 1974 when companies realized they could not provide for retirees' health care.

ASSET: Something that puts money "in your pocket" with minimum labor.

BALANCE SHEET: The lower part of an income-statement diagram, so called because it's supposed to balance assets against liabilities.

CASH FLOW: Cash coming in (as income) and cash going out (as expenses). It is the direction of cash flow that determines whether something is income, expense, asset, or liability. Cash flow tells the story.

FINANCIAL APTITUDE: What you do with the money once you make it, how to keep people from taking it from you, how to keep it longer, and how to make that money work hard for you.

GOLDEN RULE: He who has the gold makes the rules.

INCOME: The money that is received as a result of the normal business activities of an individual or business.

INCOME STATEMENT, OR PROFIT-AND-LOSS STATEMENT: It measures income and expenses: money in and money out.

LIABILITY: Something that takes money "out of your pocket."

MUTUAL FUND: A variety of stocks, bonds, or securities grouped together, managed by a professional investment company and purchased by individual investors through shares. The shares possess no direct ownership value in the various companies.

SOCIAL SECURITY: A social welfare or social insurance program commonly funded through automatic payroll deductions to subsidize persons in their old age and with disabilities.

NOTES

Chapter Three

LESSON 3: MIND YOUR OWN BUSINESS

The rich focus on their asset columns while everyone else focuses on their income statements.

In 1974, Ray Kroc, the founder of McDonald's, was asked to speak to the MBA class at the University of Texas at Austin. A friend of mine was a student in that MBA class. After a powerful and inspiring talk, the class adjourned and the students asked Ray if he would join them at their favorite hangout to have a few beers. Ray graciously accepted.

"What business am I in?" Ray asked, once the group had all their beers in hand.

"Everyone laughed," my friend said. "Most of the MBA students thought Ray was just fooling around."

No one answered, so Ray asked again, "What business do you think I'm in?"

The students laughed again, and finally one brave soul yelled out, "Ray, who in the world doesn't know that you're in the hamburger business?"

Ray chuckled. "That's what I thought you would say." He paused and then quickly added, "Ladies and gentlemen, I'm not in the hamburger business. My business is real estate."

As my friend tells the story, Ray spent a good amount of time explaining his viewpoint. In his business plan, Ray knew that the primary business focus was to sell hamburger franchises, but what he never lost sight of was the location of each franchise. He knew that the land and its location were the most significant factors in the success of each franchise. Basically, the person who bought the franchise was also buying the real estate under the franchise for Ray Kroc's organization.

Today, McDonald's is the largest single owner of real estate in the world, owning even more than the Catholic church. McDonald's owns some of the most valuable intersections and street corners in America and around the globe.

My friend considers this as one of the most important lessons in his life. Today he owns car washes, but his business is the real estate under those car washes.

25 YEARS LATER...

FAST FORWARD: 2022

McDonald's, KFC, and Burger King hold the spots as the three largest global franchised brands... with Subway and Starbucks in the hunt. In 2021, McDonald's alone posted global sales of $89 billion... and industry-wide sales growth is consistently in the double digits.

The previous chapter presented diagrams illustrating that most people work for everyone but themselves. They work first for the owners of the company, then for the government through taxes, and finally for the bank that owns their mortgage.

When I was a young boy, we did not have a McDonald's nearby. Yet my rich dad was responsible for teaching Mike and me the same lesson that Ray Kroc talked about at the University of Texas. It is secret number three of the rich. That secret is: Mind your own business. Financial struggle is often directly the result of people working all their lives for someone else. Many people will simply have nothing at the end of their working days to show for their efforts.

Our current educational system focuses on preparing today's youth to get good jobs by developing scholastic skills. Their lives will revolve around their wages or, as described earlier, their income column. Many will study further to become engineers, scientists, cooks, police officers, artists, writers, and so on. These professional skills allow them to enter the workforce and work for money.

But there is a big difference between your profession and your business. Often I ask people, "What is your business?" And they will say, "Oh, I'm a banker." Then I ask them if they own the bank. And they usually respond, "No, I work there." In that instance, they have confused their profession with their business. Their profession may be a banker, but they still need their own business.

A problem with school is that you often become what you study. So if you study cooking, you become a chef. If you study the law, you become an attorney, and a study of auto mechanics makes you a mechanic. The mistake in becoming what you study is that too many people forget to mind their own business. They spend their lives minding someone else's business and making that person rich.

To become financially secure, a person needs to mind their own business. Your business revolves around your asset column, not your income column. As stated earlier, the number-one rule is to know the difference between an asset and a liability, and to buy assets. The rich focus on their asset columns, while everyone else focuses on their income statements.

That is why we hear so often: "I need a raise." "If only I had a promotion." "I am going back to school to get more training so I can get a better job." "I am going to work overtime." "Maybe I can get a second job."

Financial struggle is often the result of people working all their lives for someone else.

In some circles, these are sensible ideas. But you are still not minding your own business. These ideas all still focus on the income column and will only help a person become more financially secure if the additional money is used to purchase income-generating assets.

The primary reason the majority of the poor and middle class are fiscally conservative — which means, "I can't afford to take risks" — is that they have no financial foundation. They have to cling to their jobs and play it safe.

When downsizing became the "in" thing to do, millions of workers found out their largest so-called asset, their home, was eating them alive. Their "asset" was costing them money every month. Their car, another "asset," was eating them alive. The golf clubs in the garage that cost $1,000 were not worth $1,000 anymore. Without job security, they had nothing to fall back on. What they thought were assets could not help them survive in a time of financial crisis.

I assume most of us have filled out a credit application to buy a house or a car. It's always interesting to look at the "net-worth" section because of what accepted banking and accounting practices allow a person to count as assets.

FAST FORWARD... TO TODAY

JOBS, JOBS, JOBS!

Unemployment continues to be a hot topic — in election cycles and throughout the pandemic. Hikes in the minimum wage, government initiatives that pay people not to work, and automation are all realities in today's world. "Reports" often reflect different formulas and statistics... oftentimes by design. Another sobering thought: The Rise of Robots...

One day when I wanted a loan, my financial position did not look too good. So I added my new golf clubs, my art collection, books, electronics, Armani suits, wristwatches, shoes, and other personal effects to boost the number in the asset column.

But I was turned down because I had too much investment real estate. The loan committee didn't like that I made so much money from rent. They wanted to know why I did not have a normal job with a salary. They did not question the Armani suits, golf clubs, or art collection. Life is sometimes tough when you do not fit the standard profile.

I cringe every time I hear someone say to me that their net worth is a million dollars or $100,000 dollars or whatever. One of the main reasons net worth is not accurate is simply because, the moment you begin selling your assets, you are taxed for any gains.

So many people have put themselves in deep financial trouble when they run short of income. To raise cash, they sell their assets. But their personal assets can generally be sold for only a fraction of the value that is listed on their personal balance sheet. Or if there is a gain on the sale of the assets, they are taxed on the gain. So again, the government takes its share, thus reducing the amount available to help them out of debt. That is why I say someone's net worth is often "worth less" than they think.

Start minding your own business. Keep your daytime job, but start buying real assets, not liabilities or personal effects that have no real value once you get them home. A new car loses nearly 25 percent of the price you pay for it the moment you drive it off the lot. It is not a true asset even if your banker lets you list it as one. My $400 new titanium driver was worth $150 the moment I teed off.

Keep expenses low, reduce liabilities, and diligently build a base of solid assets. For young people who have not yet left home, it is important for parents to teach them the difference between an asset and a liability. Get them to start building a solid asset column before they leave home, get married, buy a house, have kids, and get stuck in a risky financial position, clinging to a job, and buying everything on credit. I see so many young couples who get married and trap themselves into a lifestyle that will not let them get out of debt for most of their working years.

For many people, just as the last child leaves home, the parents realize they have not adequately prepared for retirement and they begin to scramble to put some money away. Then their own parents become ill and they find themselves with new responsibilities.

So what kind of assets am I suggesting that you or your children acquire? In my world, real assets fall into the following categories:

- *Businesses that do not require my presence* I own them, but they are managed or run by other people. If I have to work there, it's not a business. It becomes my job.
- *Stocks*
- *Bonds*
- *Income-generating real estate*
- *Notes (IOUs)*
- *Royalties from intellectual property such as music, scripts, and patents*
- *Anything else that has value, produces income or appreciates, and has a ready market*

As a young boy, my educated dad encouraged me to find a safe job. But my rich dad encouraged me to begin acquiring assets that I loved. "If you don't love it, you won't take care of it." I collect real estate simply because I love buildings and land. I love shopping for them, and I could look at them all day long. When problems arise, the problems aren't so bad that it changes my love for real estate. For people who hate real estate, they shouldn't buy it.

I also love stocks of small companies, especially start-ups, because I am an entrepreneur, not a corporate person. In my early years, I worked in large organizations, such as Standard Oil of California, the U.S. Marine Corps, and Xerox Corp. I enjoyed my time with those organizations and have fond memories, but I know deep down I am not a company man. I like starting companies, not running them. So my stock buys are usually of small companies. Sometimes I even start the company and take it public. Fortunes are made in new stock issues, and I love the game. Many people are afraid of small-cap companies and call them risky, and they are. But that risk is diminished if you love what

Start minding your own business. Keep your daytime job, but start buying real assets, not liabilities.

the investment is, understand it, and know the game. With small companies, my investment strategy is to be out of the stock in a year. On the other hand, my real estate strategy is to start small and keep trading up for bigger properties and, therefore, delay paying taxes on the gain. This allows the value to increase dramatically. I generally hold real estate less than seven years.

For years, even while I was with the Marine Corps and Xerox, I did what my rich dad recommended. I kept my day job, but I still minded my own business. I was active in my asset column trading real estate and small stocks. Rich dad always stressed the importance of financial literacy. The better I was at understanding the accounting and cash management, the better I would be at analyzing investments and eventually starting and building my own company.

I don't encourage anyone to start a company unless they really want to. Knowing what I know about running a company, I wouldn't wish that task on anyone. There are times when people can't find employment and starting a company seems like the best solution. But the odds are against success: Nine out of ten companies fail in five years. Of those that survive the first five years, nine out of every ten of those eventually fail as well. So only if you really have the desire to own your own company do I recommend it. Otherwise, keep your day job and mind your own business.

When I say mind your own business, I mean to build and keep your asset column strong. Once a dollar goes into it, never let it come out. Think of it this way: Once a dollar goes into your asset column, it becomes your employee. The best thing about money is that it works 24 hours a day and can work for generations. Keep your day job, be a great hardworking employee, but keep building that asset column.

As your cash flow grows, you can indulge in some luxuries. An important distinction is that rich people buy luxuries last, while the poor and middle class tend to buy luxuries first. The poor and the middle class often buy luxury items like big houses, diamonds, furs, jewelry, or boats because they want to look rich. They look rich, but in reality they just get deeper in debt on credit. The old-money people, the long-term rich, build their asset column first. Then the income generated from the asset column buys their luxuries. The poor and middle class buy luxuries with their own sweat, blood, and children's inheritance.

A true luxury is a reward for investing in and developing a real asset. For example, when Kim and I had extra money coming from our apartment houses, she went out and bought her Mercedes. It didn't take any extra work or risk on her part because the apartment house bought the car. She did, however, have to wait four years while the real estate investment portfolio grew and began generating enough extra cash flow to pay for the car. But the luxury, the Mercedes, was a true reward because she proved she knew how to grow her asset column. That car now means a lot more to her than simply another pretty car. It means she used her financial intelligence to afford it.

Instead, most people impulsively go out and buy a new car, or some other luxury, on credit. They may feel bored and just want a new toy. Buying a luxury on credit often causes a person to eventually resent that luxury because the debt becomes a financial burden.

After you've taken the time and invested in and built your own business, you are now ready to learn the biggest secret of the rich — the secret that puts the rich way ahead of the pack.

STUDY SESSION

Chapter Three

LESSON 3: MIND YOUR OWN BUSINESS

Chapter Three

LESSON 3: MIND YOUR OWN BUSINESS

Summary

A friend of Robert's got to hear Ray Kroc of McDonald's fame speak in 1974 at the University of Texas at Austin. Afterward, Ray agreed to join the students at their favorite hangout for a few beers.

He asked the students what business he was in. At first they laughed, and then they answered that he was in the business of selling hamburgers, of course.

But Ray told them he was not in the hamburger business, but in the real estate business. He knew that the land and location of each franchise were the most significant factors in its success. Today, McDonald's is the largest single owner of real estate in the world, owning some of the most valuable intersections and street corners around the globe.

Robert's friend took that lesson to heart, and today owns car washes — but his business is the real estate under those car washes.

So many people work for everyone else: their employer, the government (taxes), and the bank (mortgage). What Ray Kroc and rich dad knew was secret No. 3 of the rich: Mind your business. Don't spend your whole life working for someone else.

There is a big difference between your profession and your business. Often Robert will ask people, "What is your business?" And they will say, "Oh, I'm a banker." Then he asks them if they own the bank. And they usually respond, "No, I work there." In that instance, they have confused their profession with their business. Their profession may be a banker, but they still need their own business.

Too many people spend their lives minding someone else's business and making them rich.

Minding your business doesn't mean starting a company, though for some people it will. Instead, your business revolves around your asset column, not your income column.

Promotions or a better job will only help you become more financially secure if the additional money is used to purchase income-generating assets.

The primary reason the majority of the poor and middle class are fiscally conservative is that they have no financial foundation. They have to cling to their jobs and play it safe. They can't afford to take risks.

And when hard times come, what many people thought were assets will not help them survive a financial crisis. That car has lost much of its value. Those golf clubs? The same.

Too often what a bank will allow a person to list as assets on a financial statement are not true assets.

Robert was once turned down for a loan because the bank didn't like how much money he made from rent and was concerned he didn't have a normal job. But they were fine with him listing suits, an art collection, and other personal effects as assets.

Net worth isn't the measure that people think it is. Most so-called assets that people base their net worth on either aren't as valuable as they think or, if they have gained value, will trigger taxes on the gain if they're sold.

So Robert tells people to start minding your own business. Keep your daytime job, but start buying real assets, not liabilities or personal effects that have no real value once you get them home. Keep expenses low, reduce liabilities, and diligently build a base of solid assets.

Parents need to teach young people this before they leave home, so that they understand what a true asset is and won't find themselves trapped in a lifestyle of debt.

Robert says real assets fall into the following categories:

1. *Businesses that do not require his presence:* He owns them, but they are managed or run by other people. If he has to work there, it's not a business. It becomes his job.
2. *Stocks*
3. *Bonds*
4. *Income-generating real estate*

5. *Notes (IOUs)*
6. *Royalties from intellectual property such as music, scripts, and patents*
7. *Anything else that has value, produces income or appreciates, and has a ready market*

Acquire assets that you love. Robert loves real estate and thus spends much of his time thinking about and shopping for it. If you don't like real estate, don't invest in it.

Robert also loves the stocks of small startup companies, because he himself is an entrepreneur. Some are afraid of the risk of such small-cap companies, but he sees these as the place to make fortunes. His strategy is to be out of the stock in a year. His real estate strategy, on the other hand, is to start small and keep trading up for bigger properties (and delaying taxes on the gain), holding real estate less than seven years.

Even while working for the Marines and Xerox, Robert minded is own business. He kept his day job but was active in his asset column, trading real estate and small stocks.

The more he understood accounting and cash management, the better he was at analyzing investments and eventually building his own company.

He doesn't recommend people start a company unless they really have the desire to. Otherwise, he advises them to keep their day job and mind their business: building and keeping their asset column strong.

As cash flow grows, people can indulge in luxuries — but only if the cash flow supports them. Build the asset column and let the income generated by those assets pay for the luxuries.

Left-hemisphere moment: When assets generate enough income to cover luxuries, that's when you can buy them.

Right-hemisphere moment: Think creatively about what your business is. It's not your profession.

Subconscious moment: Acquire the type of assets you love, because you will take better care of them and enjoy learning about them.

What Was Robert Saying

Now it's time to reflect. Ask yourself, "*What* is Robert saying in this quote?" And, "*Why* does he say that?" In this section you do not need to agree or disagree with Robert. The goal is to *understand* what Robert is saying.

Remember, this curriculum is designed to be cooperative and supportive. Two minds are better than one. If you do not understand what Robert is saying, do not shy away from it. Ask for help in understanding. Take the time discuss each quote until you understand it:

"To become financially secure, a person needs to mind their own business."

"The rich focus on their asset columns while everyone else focuses on their income statements."

"Financial struggle is often directly the result of people working all their lives for someone else. Many people will simply have nothing at the end of their working days to show for their efforts."

"One of the main reasons net worth is not accurate is simply because, the moment you begin selling your assets, you are taxed for any gains."

"Once a dollar goes into it, never let it come out. Think of it this way: Once a dollar goes into your asset column, it becomes your employee. The best thing about money is that it works 24 hours a day and can work for generations."

"An important distinction is that rich people buy luxuries last, while the poor and middle class tend to buy luxuries first."

"The poor and middle class buy luxuries with their own sweat, blood, and children's inheritance."

Additional Questions

Now it's time to take the stories in this chapter along with the understanding of what Robert was saying and apply them to you and your life. Ask yourself the questions below and discuss them with your study partner. Be honest with yourself and your partner. If you do not like some of the answers you are giving, ask yourself if you are willing to change and accept the challenge to change your thoughts and mindset:

1. What is your profession, and what is your business? How do they differ?
2. What are things you might have counted in your net worth before reading this chapter? How do you view them now?
3. Are the assets you're acquiring the type that you love? If not, how can you change that?
4. What is a time you bought a luxury that your cash flow couldn't justify? What is a time you did so when it could justify the purchase? Compare how you felt in the two situations, both at the moment of purchase and later.
5. Have there been people in your family who have spent their whole lives working for someone else, only to end up with nothing? What would you have advised them if you could?

Term definitions:

BOND: A debt security in which the authorized issuer owes the holders a debt and is obliged to repay the principal and interest at a later date, termed maturity.

ENTREPRENEUR: Someone who creates a system to offer a product or service in order to obtain a profit. Entrepreneurs are willing to accept a level of risk to pursue opportunity and are viewed as fundamentally important in the capitalistic society.

FINANCIAL STATEMENT: A statement of your income, expenses, assets, and liabilities. Your "report card" when you leave school and what your banker wants to see before lending you money.

STOCK: The capital raised by a corporation through the distribution of shares.

NOTES

Chapter Four

LESSON 4: THE HISTORY OF TAXES AND THE POWER OF CORPORATIONS

My rich dad just played the game smart, and he did it through corporations — the biggest secret of the rich.

I remember in school being told the story of Robin Hood and his Merry Men. My teacher thought it was a wonderful story of a romantic hero who robbed from the rich and gave to the poor. My rich dad did not see Robin Hood as a hero. He called Robin Hood a crook.

Robin Hood may be long gone, but his followers live on. I often still hear people say, "Why don't the rich pay for it?" or "The rich should pay more in taxes and give it to the poor."

It is this Robin Hood fantasy, or taking from the rich to give to the poor, that has caused the most pain for the poor and the middle class. The reason the middle class is so heavily taxed is because of the Robin Hood ideal. The reality is that the rich are not taxed. It's the middle class, especially the educated upper-income middle class, who pays for the poor.

Again, to understand fully how things happen, we need to look at the history of taxes. Although my highly educated dad was an expert on the history of education, my rich dad fashioned himself as an expert on the history of taxes.

Rich dad explained to Mike and me that originally, in England and America, there were no taxes. Occasionally, there were temporary taxes levied in order to pay for wars. The king or the president would put the word out and ask everyone to "chip in." Taxes were levied in Britain for the fight against Napoleon from 1799 to 1816, and in America to pay for the Civil War from 1861 to 1865.

In 1874, England made income tax a permanent levy on its citizens. In 1913, an income tax became permanent in the United States with the adoption of the 16th Amendment to the U.S. Constitution. At one time, Americans were anti-tax. It had been the tax on tea that led to the famous Tea Party in Boston Harbor, an incident that helped ignite the Revolutionary War. It took approximately 50 years in both England and the United States to sell the idea of a regular income tax.

What these historical dates fail to reveal is that both of these taxes were initially levied against only the rich. It was this point that rich dad wanted Mike and me to understand. He explained that the idea of taxes was made popular, and accepted by the majority, by telling the poor and the middle class that taxes were created only to punish the rich. This is how the masses voted for the law, and it became constitutionally legal. Although it was intended to punish the rich, in reality it wound up punishing the very people who voted for it, the poor and middle class.

"Once government got a taste of money, its appetite grew," said rich dad. "Your dad and I are exactly opposite. He's a government bureaucrat, and I am a capitalist. We get paid, and our success is measured on opposite behaviors. He gets paid to spend money and hire people. The more he spends and the more people he hires, the larger his organization becomes. In the government, a large organization is a respected organization. On the other hand, within my organization, the fewer people I hire and the less money I spend, the more I am respected by my investors. That's why I don't like government people. They have different objectives than most business people. As the government grows, more and more tax dollars are needed to support it."

My educated dad sincerely believed that government should help people. He loved John F. Kennedy and especially the idea of the Peace

Corps. He loved the idea so much that both he and my mom worked for the Peace Corps, training volunteers to go to Malaysia, Thailand, and the Philippines. He always strived for additional grants and budget increases so he could hire more people, both in his job with the Education Department and in the Peace Corps.

From the time I was about 10 years old, I would hear from my rich dad that government workers were a pack of lazy thieves, and from my poor dad I would hear how the rich were greedy crooks who should be made to pay more taxes. Both sides had valid points. It was difficult to go to work for one of the biggest capitalists in town and come home to a father who was a prominent government leader. It was not easy to know which dad to believe.

My rich dad did not see Robin Hood as a hero. He called Robin Hood a crook.

Yet when you study the history of taxes, an interesting perspective emerges. As I said, the passage of taxes was only possible because the masses believed in the Robin Hood theory of economics: Take from the rich, and give to everyone else. The problem was that the government's appetite for money was so great that taxes soon needed to be levied on the middle class, and from there it kept trickling down.

FAST FORWARD 25 YEARS...

TAXES... AND TAX INCENTIVES

We continue to see governments use the tax laws to provide incentives to business owners and investors to create jobs and housing — as well as other work the government needs done. These incentives reduce the taxes of the rich. And this pushes the government to drive tax revenue from the middle class.

However, the rich saw an opportunity because they don't play by the same set of rules. The rich knew about corporations, which became popular in the days of sailing ships. The rich created the corporation as a vehicle to limit their risk to the assets of each voyage. The rich put their money into a corporation to finance the voyage. The corporation would then hire a crew to sail to the New World to look for treasure. If the ship was lost, the crew lost their lives, but the loss to the rich would be limited only to the money they invested for that particular voyage.

The diagram that follows shows how the corporate structure sits outside your personal income statement and balance sheet.

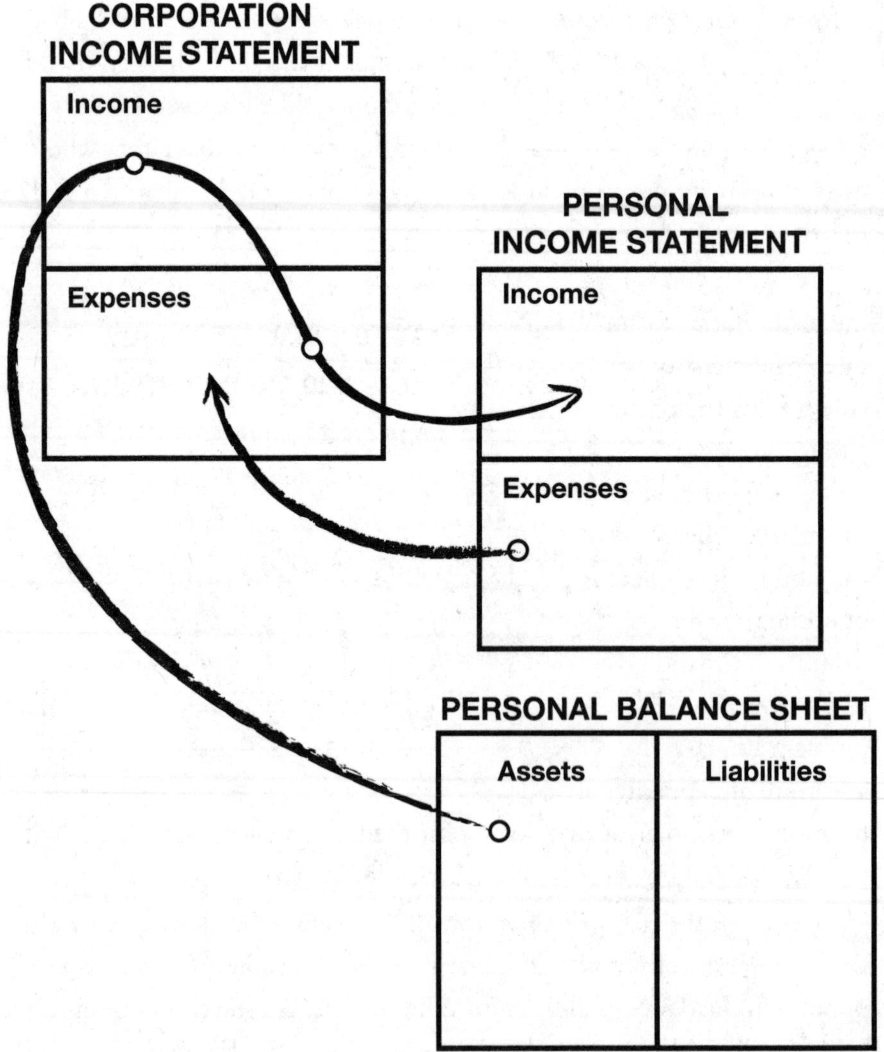

It is the knowledge of the legal corporate structure that really gives the rich a vast advantage over the poor and the middle class. Having two fathers teaching me, one a socialist and the other a capitalist, I quickly began to realize that the philosophy of the capitalist made more financial sense to me. It seemed to me that the socialists ultimately penalized themselves due to their lack of financial education. No matter what the "take-from-the-rich" crowd came up with, the rich always found a way to outsmart them. That is how taxes were eventually levied on the middle class. The rich outsmarted the intellectuals solely because they understood the power of money, a subject not taught in schools.

How did the rich outsmart the intellectuals? Once the "take-from-the-rich" tax was passed, cash started flowing into government coffers. Initially, people were happy. Money was handed out to government workers and the rich. It went to government workers in the form of jobs and pensions, and it went to the rich via their factories receiving government contracts. The government received a large pool of money, but the problem was the fiscal management of that money. The government ideal is to avoid having excess money. If you fail to spend your allotted funds, you risk losing it in the next budget. You would certainly not be recognized for being efficient. Business people, on the other hand, are rewarded for having excess money and are applauded for their efficiency. As this cycle of growing government spending continued, the demand for money increased, and the "tax-the-rich" idea was adjusted to include lower-income levels, down to the very people who voted it in, the poor and the middle class.

True capitalists used their financial knowledge to simply find an escape. They headed back to the protection of a corporation. But what many people who have never formed a corporation don't know is that a corporation is not really a thing. A corporation is merely a file folder with some legal documents in it, sitting in some attorney's office and registered with a state government agency. It's not a big building or a factory or a group of people. A corporation is merely a legal document that creates a legal body without a soul. Using it, the wealth of the rich was once again protected. It was popular because the income-tax rate of a corporation is less than the individual income-tax rates. In addition, certain expenses could be paid by a corporation with pre-tax dollars.

This war between the haves and have-nots has raged for hundreds of years. The battle is waged whenever and wherever laws are made, and it will go on forever. The problem is that the people who lose are the uninformed: the ones who get up every day and diligently go to work and pay taxes. If they only understood the way the rich play the game, they could play it too. Then they would be on their way to their own financial independence. This is why I cringe every time I hear a parent advise their children to go to school so they can find a safe, secure job. An employee with a safe, secure job, without financial aptitude, has no escape.

Average Americans today work four to five months for the government just to cover their taxes. In my opinion, that is simply too long. The harder you work, the more you pay the government. That is why I believe that the idea of "take-from-the-rich" backfired on the very people who voted it in.

Every time people try to punish the rich, the rich don't simply comply. They react. They have the money, power, and intent to change things. They don't just sit there and voluntarily pay more taxes. Instead, they search for ways to minimize their tax burden. They hire smart attorneys and accountants, and persuade politicians to change laws or create legal loopholes. They use their resources to effect change.

The Tax Code of the United States also allows other ways to reduce taxes. Most of these vehicles are available to anyone, but it is the rich who find them because they are minding their own business. For example, "1031" is jargon for Section 1031 of the Internal Revenue Code which allows a seller to delay paying taxes on a piece of real estate that is sold for a capital gain through an exchange for a more expensive piece of real estate. Real estate is one investment vehicle that has a great tax advantage. As long as you keep trading up in value, you will not be taxed on the gains until you liquidate. People who don't take advantage of these legal tax savings are missing a great opportunity to build their asset columns.

The poor and middle class don't have the same resources. They sit there and let the government's needles enter their arm and allow the blood donation to begin.

STILL TRUE TODAY...

THE TAX MAN

The tax man will take as much as you let him. The tax system is ultimately fair in that it works the same for everyone who has the same situation. If you are willing to invest, the tax laws will work in your favor. If you want to just spend money and buy liabilities, the tax law won't give you any breaks — and it's likely you will pay the most tax possible.

Today, I am constantly shocked at the number of people who pay more taxes, or take fewer deductions, simply because they are afraid of the government. I have friends who have had their businesses shut down and destroyed, only to find out it was a mistake on the part of the government. I realize all that. But the price of working from January to May is a high price to pay for that intimidation. My poor dad never fought back. My rich dad didn't either. He just played the game smarter, and he did it through corporations — the biggest secret of the rich.

You may remember the first lesson I learned from my rich dad. I was a little boy of nine who had to sit and wait for him to choose to talk to me. I sat in his office waiting for him to get to me. He was ignoring me on purpose. He wanted me to recognize his power and to desire to have that power for myself one day. During all the years I studied and learned from him, he always reminded me that knowledge is power. And with money comes great power that requires the right knowledge to keep it and make it multiply. Without that knowledge, the world pushes you around. Rich dad constantly reminded Mike and me that the biggest bully was not the boss or the supervisor, but the tax man. The tax man will always take more if you let him.

If you work for money, you give the power to your employer. If money works for you, you keep the power and control it.

The first lesson of having money work for you, as opposed to you working for money, is all about power. If you work for money, you give the power to your employer. If money works for you, you keep the power and control it.

Once we had this knowledge of the power of money working for us, he wanted us to be financially smart and not let anyone or anything push us around. If you're ignorant, it's easy to be bullied. If you know what you're talking about, you have a fighting chance. That is why he paid so much for smart tax accountants and attorneys. It was less expensive to pay them than to pay the government. His best lesson to me was: "Be smart and you won't be pushed around as much." He knew the law because he was a law-abiding citizen and because it was expensive to not know the law. "If you know you're right, you're not afraid of fighting back." Even if you are taking on Robin Hood and his band of Merry Men.

My highly educated dad always encouraged me to land a good job with a strong corporation. He spoke of the virtues of "working your way up the corporate ladder." He didn't understand that, by relying solely on a paycheck from a corporate employer, I would be a docile cow ready for milking.

Each dollar in my asset column was a great employee, working hard to make more employees and buy the boss a new Porsche.

When I told my rich dad of my father's advice, he only chuckled. "Why not own the ladder?" was all he said.

As a young boy, I did not understand what rich dad meant by owning my own corporation. It was an idea that seemed impossible and intimidating. Although I was excited by the idea, my inexperience wouldn't let me envision the possibility that grown-ups would someday work for a company I would own.

The point is that, if not for my rich dad, I would have probably followed my educated dad's advice. It was merely the occasional reminder of my rich dad that kept the idea of owning my own corporation alive and kept me on a different path. By the time I was 15 or 16, I knew I wasn't going to continue down the path my educated dad recommended. I didn't know how I was going to do it, but I was determined not to head in the direction most of my classmates were heading. That decision changed my life.

TIMELESS RICH DAD WISDOM

OWN THE LADDER

As technology continues to change the way we work and do business, I talk with more and more people who ask themselves: "How can I own the ladder?" Capitalism is thriving and the free-market system means that entrepreneurs who can offer a better product at a better price have a good chance of success.

It was not until my mid-twenties that my rich dad's advice began to make more sense to me. I was just out of the Marine Corps and working for Xerox. I was making a lot of money, but every time I looked at my paycheck, I was disappointed. The deductions were so large and, the more I worked, the greater they became. As I became more successful, my bosses talked about promotions and raises. It was flattering, but I could hear my rich dad asking in my ear: "Who are you working for? Who are you making rich?"

In 1974, while still an employee for Xerox, I formed my first corporation and began minding my own business. There were already a few assets in my asset column, but now I was determined to focus on making it bigger. Those paychecks, with all the deductions, made all the years of my rich dad's advice make total sense. I could see the future if I followed my educated dad's advice.

Many employers feel that advising their workers to mind their own business is bad for business. But for me, focusing on my own business and developing assets made me a better employee because I now had a purpose. I came in early and worked diligently, amassing as much money as possible so I could invest in real estate. Hawaii was just set to boom, and there were fortunes to be made. The more I realized that we were in the beginning stages of a boom, the more Xerox machines I sold. The more I sold, the more money I made and, of course, the more deductions came out of my paycheck. It was inspiring. I wanted out of the employee trap so badly that I worked even harder so I could invest more. By 1978, I was consistently one of the top five sales people at the company. I badly wanted out of the Rat Race.

In less than three years, I was making more in my real estate holding corporation than I was making at Xerox. And the money I was making in my asset column in my own corporation was money working for me, not me pounding on doors selling copiers. My rich dad's advice made much more sense. Soon the cash flow from my properties was so strong that my company bought me my first Porsche. My fellow Xerox salespeople thought I was spending my commissions. I wasn't. I was investing my commissions in assets.

My money was working hard to make more money. Each dollar in my asset column was a great employee, working hard to make more employees and buy the boss a new Porsche with before-tax dollars. I began to work harder for Xerox. The plan was working, and my Porsche was the proof. By using the lessons I learned from my rich dad, I was able to get out of the proverbial Rat Race at an early age. It was made possible because of the strong financial knowledge I had acquired through rich dad's lessons.

Without this financial knowledge, which I call financial intelligence or financial IQ, my road to financial independence would have been much more difficult. I now teach others in the hope that I may share my knowledge with them.

I remind people that financial IQ is made up of knowledge from four broad areas of expertise:

1. ***Accounting***
   Accounting is financial literacy or the ability to read numbers. This is a vital skill if you want to build an empire. The more money you are responsible for, the more accuracy is required,

or the house comes tumbling down. This is the left-brain side, or the details. Financial literacy is the ability to read and understand financial statements which allows you to identify the strengths and weaknesses of any business.

2. ***Investing***
   Investing is the science of "money making money." This involves strategies and formulas that use the creative right-brain side.

3. ***Understanding markets***
   Understanding markets is the science of supply and demand. You need to know the technical aspects of the market, which are emotion-driven, in addition to the fundamental or economic aspects of an investment. Does an investment make sense or does it not make sense based on current market conditions?

4. ***The law***
   A corporation wrapped around the technical skills of accounting, investing, and markets can contribute to explosive growth. A person who understands the tax advantages and protections provided by a corporation can get rich so much faster than someone who is an employee or a small-business sole proprietor. It's like the difference between someone walking and someone flying. The difference is profound when it comes to long-term wealth.

   - **Tax advantages**
     A corporation can do many things that an employee cannot, like pay expenses before paying taxes. That is a whole area of expertise that is very exciting. Employees earn and get taxed, and they try to live on what is left. A corporation earns, spends everything it can, and is taxed on anything that is left. It's one of the biggest legal tax loopholes that the rich use. They're easy to set up and are not expensive if you own investments that are producing good cashflow. For example, by owning your own corporation, your vacations can be board meetings in Hawaii. Car payments, insurance, repairs, and health-club memberships are company expenses. Most

restaurant meals are partial expenses, and on and on. But it's done legally with pre-tax dollars.

- **Protection from lawsuits**
  We live in a litigious society. Everybody wants a piece of your action. The rich hide much of their wealth using vehicles such as corporations and trusts to protect their assets from creditors. When someone sues a wealthy individual, they are often met with layers of legal protection and often find that the wealthy person actually owns nothing. They control everything, but own nothing. The poor and middle class try to own everything and lose it to the government or to fellow citizens who like to sue the rich. They learned it from the Robin Hood story: Take from the rich, and give it to the poor.

It is not the purpose of this book to go into the specifics of owning a corporation. But I will say that if you own any kind of legitimate assets, I would consider finding out more about the benefits and protection offered by a corporation as soon as possible. There are many books written on the subject that will detail the benefits and even walk you through the steps necessary to set up a corporation. Garret Sutton's books on corporations provide wonderful insight into the power of personal corporations.

Financial IQ is actually the synergy of many skills and talents. I would say it is the combination of the four technical skills listed above that make up basic financial intelligence. If you aspire to great wealth, it is the combination of these skills that will greatly amplify your financial intelligence.

In summary:

Business Owners with Corporations	**Employees Who Work for Corporations**
1. Earn	1. Earn
2. Spend	2. Pay Taxes
3. Pay Taxes	3. Spend

As part of your overall financial strategy, I recommend that you learn about the protection that legal entities can provide for businesses and assets.

STUDY SESSION

Chapter Four

LESSON 4: THE HISTORY OF TAXES AND THE POWER OF CORPORATIONS

Chapter Four

LESSON 4: THE HISTORY OF TAXES AND THE POWER OF CORPORATIONS

Summary

Many people see Robin Hood as a hero, taking from the rich and giving to the poor. Rich dad did not share that opinion. He called Robin Hood a crook.

Though the popular sentiment is that the rich should pay more in taxes and give to the poor, in reality it is the middle class that is heavily taxed, especially the educated upper-income middle class.

To understand how this happens, Robert gives a brief history of taxes. In England and America, originally there were no taxes, only occasional temporary levies to pay for such things as wars.

In 1874, England made income tax a permanent levy on its citizens. In America — the land where a tax on tea led to the Boston Tea Party protest and helped ignite the Revolutionary War — the adoption of the 16th Amendment in 1913 made an income tax permanent.

These countries were able to get taxes accepted by the majority because they were first levied only against the rich. However, although income tax was designed to punish the rich, it wound up punishing those who had voted for it, the poor and middle class.

Rich dad explained that he and poor dad were opposite. Poor dad, as a government employee, was rewarded if he spent money and hired people, making his organization larger. But for rich dad, the fewer people he hired and the less money he spent, the more he was respected by his investors.

And as the government grows, so does the amount of tax dollars needed to support it.

Poor dad sincerely believed the government should help people. He and Robert's mom worked for the Peace Corps, training volunteers to go to Malaysia, Thailand, and the Philippines. They were always seeking more grants and budget increases so they could hire more people.

For Robert, it was a challenge to work for one of the biggest capitalists in town and go home to a prominent government leader. It wasn't easy to know which dad to believe.

But over time, as Robert studied the history of taxes, he saw an interesting perspective: As the government's appetite for money grew, taxes soon needed to be levied on the middle class, and from there it kept trickling down.

But the rich saw an opportunity because they don't play by the same set of rules. Corporations — which became popular in the days of sailing ships — offered a way around taxes. Understanding the legal corporate structure gave the rich a steep advantage and allowed them to outsmart the intellectuals.

The government ideal is to avoid having excess money. If you fail to spend your allotted funds, you risk losing it in the next budget. Business people, on the other hand, are rewarded for having excess money and are applauded for their efficiency. And as the government continued its ideal and spent more and more money, more taxes — this time on the middle class, and eventually the poor — were needed.

A corporation is simply a legal document that creates a legal entity. It is not really a thing, not a factory or a group of people. But it offers a lower income-tax rate than individuals have, and certain expenses can be paid by a corporation with pre-tax dollars.

If those who get up and go to work at their jobs and pay taxes could only understand the way the rich play the game, they could too.

The problem is, the harder you work in a job, the more you must pay the government. Taxes end up punishing the very people who voted them in.

Attempts to punish the rich rarely work, because the rich find ways to minimize their tax burden. One such way is Section 1031 of the Internal Revenue Code, which allows a seller to delay paying taxes on a piece of real estate that is sold for a capital gain through an exchange for a more expensive piece of real estate. As long as you keep trading up in value, you won't be taxed on the gains until you liquidate. Those who don't take advantage of these savings are missing a chance to build their asset column.

In all the years rich dad was guiding Robert, he was trying to teach him that knowledge is power. And with money comes great power that requires the right knowledge to keep it and make it multiply. Without that knowledge, the world pushes you around.

The tax man is a bully who will always take more if you let him. Don't let him by making your money work for you.

Smart tax consultants and attorneys are worth their cost, as it's still cheaper than paying the government. It's expensive to not know the law.

In his mid-20s, when he was just out of the Marine Corps and working for Xerox, Robert was disappointed by how much was taken out of his paychecks. It motivated him to form his first corporation in 1974 and work harder at his day job to amass as much money as possible to invest in real estate.

He became one of the top salesmen at Xerox and in less than three years was making more in his real estate holding corporation than he was at Xerox. His company bought him his first Porsche, proof that the plan was working.

The lessons he learned from rich dad helped him break out of the proverbial Rat Race at an early age, and he wants to help others do the same.

Financial IQ, or financial intelligence, is what makes that possible. It's made up of four things: accounting (financial literacy, or the ability to read numbers and evaluate the strengths and weaknesses of any business), investing (the science and strategies of money making money), understanding markets (the science of supply and demand, and market conditions), and the law (tax advantages and protections).

Understanding those legal advantages is profound when it comes to long-term wealth. For instance, a corporation can pay expenses before paying taxes, whereas an employee gets taxed first and must try to pay expenses on what is left. Board meetings in Hawaii, car payments and insurance and health-club memberships can be pre-tax expenses for a corporation.

Corporations also offer legal protection from lawsuits. When someone sues a wealthy individual, they are often met with layers of legal protection and often find that the wealthy person actually owns nothing. They control everything, but own nothing.

Robert urges those who own legitimate assets to find out more about corporations' benefits and protections. Garret Sutton's books are among many that can help.

In summary:

Business Owners with Corporations

1. Earn
2. Spend
3. Pay Taxes

Employees Who Work for Corporations

1. Earn
2. Pay Taxes
3. Spend

Left-hemisphere moment: Accounting is financial literacy or the ability to read numbers. This is a vital skill if you want to build an empire. The more money you are responsible for, the more accuracy is required, or the house comes tumbling down.

Right-hemisphere moment: Investing is the science of "money making money." This involves strategies and formulas, which use the creative side of the brain.

Subconscious moment: Understanding markets is the science of supply and demand. You need to know the technical aspects of the market, which are emotion-driven, in addition to the fundamental or economic aspects of an investment.

What Was Robert Saying

Now it's time to reflect. Ask yourself, "*What* is Robert saying in this quote?" And, "*Why* does he say that?" In this section you do not need to agree or disagree with Robert. The goal is to *understand* what Robert is saying.

Remember, this curriculum is designed to be cooperative and supportive. Two minds are better than one. If you do not understand what Robert is saying, do not shy away from it. Ask for help in understanding. Take the time discuss each quote until you understand it:

> "My rich dad just played the game smart, and he did it through corporations — the biggest secret of the rich."
>
> "The reality is that the rich are not taxed. It's the middle class who pays for the poor, especially the educated upper-income middle class."
>
> "Every time people try to punish the rich, the rich don't simply comply. They react. They have the money, power, and intent to change things. They don't just sit there and voluntarily pay more taxes."
>
> "If you work for money, you give the power to your employer. If money works for you, you keep the power and control it."
>
> "A person who understands the tax advantages and protections provided by a corporation can get rich so much faster than someone who is an employee or a small-business sole proprietor. It's like the difference between someone walking and someone flying."
>
> "Employees earn and get taxed, and they try to live on what is left. A corporation earns, spends everything it can, and is taxed on anything that is left. It's one of the biggest legal tax loopholes that the rich use."

Additional Questions

Now it's time to take the stories in this chapter along with the understanding of what Robert was saying and apply them to you and your life. Ask yourself the questions below and discuss them with your study partner. Be honest with yourself and your partner. If you do not like some of the answers you are giving, ask yourself if you are willing to change and accept the challenge to change your thoughts and mindset:

1. Do you agree with rich dad's assessment of Robin Hood, that he was a crook? Why or why not?
2. Have taxes created a bigger problem with government spending?
3. Do you think members of the middle class and the poor realize that the burden of taxes has fallen to them? What effects of that do you see?
4. Do your beliefs fall more under the banner of capitalism or socialism? What are the benefits and downfalls of each way of thinking?
5. Are the rich right to use the advantages of corporations to avoid paying taxes? Do you think more people could follow suit if they understood the system better?
6. What are specific ways that you yourself could benefit from using a corporation for your assets?

Term definitions:

1031: Jargon for Section 1031 of the Internal Revenue Code, which allows a seller to delay paying taxes on a piece of real estate that is sold for a capital gain through an exchange for a more expensive piece of real estate.

CORPORATION: Merely a legal document that creates a legal body without a soul. It's not a big building or a factory or a group of people. Using it, the wealth of the rich is protected.

FINANCIAL IQ: Financial intelligence that comes as a result of financial education. People with high financial IQ learn to use other people's money to become rich.

FINANCIAL LITERACY: The ability to read and understand financial statements, which allows you to identify the strengths and weaknesses of any business.

NOTES

Chapter Five

LESSON 5: THE RICH INVENT MONEY

Often in the real world, it's not the smart who get ahead, but the bold.

Last night, I took a break from writing and watched a TV program on the history of a young man named Alexander Graham Bell. Bell had just patented his telephone and was having growing pains because the demand for his new invention was so strong. Needing a bigger company, he then went to the giant at that time, Western Union, and asked them if they would buy his patent and his tiny company. He wanted $100,000 for the whole package. The president of Western Union scoffed at him and turned him down, saying the price was ridiculous. The rest is history. A multi-billion-dollar industry emerged, and AT&T was born.

The evening news came on right after the story of Alexander Graham Bell. On the news was a story of another downsizing at a local company. The workers were angry and complained that the company ownership was unfair. A terminated manager of about 45 years of age had his wife and two babies at the plant and was begging the guards to let him talk to the owners to ask if they would reconsider his termination. He had just bought a house and was afraid of losing it. The camera focused in on his pleading for all the world to see. Needless to say, it held my attention.

I have been teaching professionally since 1984. It has been a great experience and a rewarding one. It is also a disturbing profession, for I have taught thousands of individuals and I see one thing in common in all of us, myself included. We all have tremendous potential, and we all are blessed with gifts. Yet the one thing that holds all of us back is some degree of self-doubt. It is not so much the lack of technical information that holds us back, but more the lack of self-confidence. Some are more affected than others.

Once we leave school, most of us know that it is not so much a matter of college degrees or good grades that count. In the real world outside of academics, something more than just grades is required. I have heard it called many things; guts, chutzpah, balls, audacity, bravado, cunning, daring, tenacity, and brilliance. This factor, whatever it is labeled, ultimately decides one's future much more than school grades do.

Inside each of us is one of these brave, brilliant, and daring characters. There is also the flip side of that character: people who could get down on their knees and beg if necessary. After a year in Vietnam as a Marine Corps pilot, I got to know both of those characters inside of me intimately. One is not better than the other.

Yet as a teacher, I recognized that it was excessive fear and self-doubt that were the greatest detractors of personal genius. It broke my heart to see students know the answers, yet lack the courage to act on the answer. Often in the real world, it's not the smart who get ahead, but the bold.

In my personal experience, your financial genius requires both technical knowledge as well as courage. If fear is too strong, the genius is suppressed. In my classes, I strongly urge students to learn to take risks, to be bold, and to let their genius convert that fear into power and brilliance. It works for some and just terrifies others. I have come to realize that for most people, when it comes to the subject of money, they would rather play it safe. I have had to field questions such as: "Why take risks?" "Why should I bother developing my financial IQ?" "Why should I become financially literate?" And I answer, "Just to have more options."

There are huge changes ahead. In the coming years, there will be more people just like the young inventor Alexander Graham Bell. There will be a hundred people like Bill Gates and hugely successful companies like Microsoft created every year, all over the world. And there also will be many more bankruptcies, layoffs, and downsizings.

So why bother developing your financial IQ? No one can answer that but you. Yet I can tell you why I myself do it. I do it because it is the most exciting time to be alive. I'd rather be welcoming change than dreading change. I'd rather be excited about making millions than worrying about not getting a raise. This period we are in now is a most exciting time, unprecedented in our world's history. Generations from now, people will look back at this period of time and remark at what an exciting era it must have been. It was the death of the old and birth of the new. It was full of turmoil, and it was exciting.

So why bother developing your financial IQ? Because if you do, you will prosper greatly. And if you don't, this period of time will be a frightening one. It will be a time of watching some people move boldly forward while others cling to worn-out life preservers.

TIMELESS RICH DAD WISDOM

OPPORTUNITY

The list of entrepreneurial success stories continues to grow and names like Jobs, Zuckerberg, Bezos, Musk, Branson, Gates, and Brin are recognized around the world. Hot start-ups like Coinbase are the rage, fueled by technology... in the Land of Opportunity and a global economy.

Land was wealth 300 years ago. So the person who owned the land owned the wealth. Later, wealth was in factories and production, and America rose to dominance. The industrialist owned the wealth. Today, wealth is in information. And the person who has the most timely information owns the wealth. The problem is that information flies around the world at the speed of light. The new wealth cannot be contained by boundaries and borders as land and factories were. The changes will be faster and more dramatic. There will be a dramatic increase in the number of new multimillionaires. There also will be those who are left behind.

I find so many people struggling today, often working harder, simply because they cling to old ideas. They want things to be the way they were, and they resist change. I know people who are losing their jobs or their houses, and they blame technology or the economy or their boss. Sadly, they fail to realize that they might be the problem. Old ideas are their biggest liability. It is a liability simply because they fail to realize that while that idea or way of doing something was an asset yesterday, yesterday is gone.

One afternoon I was teaching how to invest using a board game I had invented, *CASHFLOW*®, as a teaching tool. A friend had brought someone along to attend the class. This friend of a friend was recently divorced, had been badly burned in the divorce settlement, and was now searching for some answers. Her friend thought the class might help.

The game was designed to help people learn how money works. In playing the game, they learn about the interaction of the income statement with the balance sheet. They learn how cash flows between the two and how the road to wealth is through striving to increase your monthly cash flow from the asset column to the point that it exceeds your monthly expenses. Once you accomplish this, you are able to get out of the Rat Race and out onto the Fast Track.

You can play CASHFLOW on the web at www.richdad.com and learn how money works.

As I have said, some people hate the game, some love it, and others miss the point. This woman missed a valuable opportunity to learn something. In the opening round, she drew a "doodad" card with the boat on it. At first she was happy. "Oh, I've got a boat." Then, as her friend tried to explain how the numbers worked on her income statement and balance sheet, she got frustrated because she had never liked math. The rest of her table waited while her friend continued explaining the relationship between the income statement, balance sheet, and monthly cash flow. Suddenly, when she realized how the numbers worked, it dawned on her that her boat was eating her alive. Later on in the game, she was also downsized and had a child. It was a horrible game for her.

After the class, her friend came by and told me that she was upset. She had come to the class to learn about investing and did not like the idea that it took so long to play a silly game.

Her friend attempted to tell her to look within herself to see if the game reflected her in any way. With that suggestion, the woman demanded her money back. She said that the very idea that a game could be a reflection of her was ridiculous. Her money was promptly refunded, and she left.

Since 1984, I have made millions simply by doing what the school system does not do. In school, most teachers lecture. I hated lectures as a student. I was soon bored, and my mind would drift.

In 1984, I began teaching via games and simulations, and I still rely on these tools today. I always encourage adult students to look at games as reflecting back to them what they know and what they need to learn. Most importantly, games reflect behavior. They are instant feedback systems. Instead of the teacher lecturing you, the game is giving you a personalized lecture, one that is custom-made just for you.

The friend of the woman who left later called to give me an update. She said her friend was fine and had calmed down. In her cooling-off period, she could see some slight relationship between the game and her life. Although she and her husband did not own a boat, they did own everything else imaginable. She was angry after their divorce, both because he had run off with a younger woman and because, after 20 years of marriage, they had accumulated little in the way of assets. There was virtually nothing for them to split. Their 20 years of married life had been incredible fun, but all they had accumulated was a ton of doodads.

Games reflect behavior. They are instant feedback systems.

She realized that her anger at doing the numbers — the income statement and balance sheet — came from her embarrassment about not understanding them. She had believed that finances were the man's job. She maintained the house and did the entertaining, and he handled the finances. She was now quite certain, that in the last five years of their marriage, he had hidden money from her. She was angry at herself for not being more aware of where the money was going, as well as for not knowing about the other woman.

Just like a board game, the world is always providing us with instant feedback. We could learn a lot if we tuned in more. One day not long ago, I complained to Kim that the cleaners must have shrunk my pants. Kim gently smiled and poked me in the stomach to inform me that the pants had not shrunk. Something else had expanded — me!

The *CASHFLOW* game was designed to give every player personal feedback. Its purpose is to give you options. If you draw the boat card and it puts you into debt, the question is: "Now what can you do? How many different financial options can you come up with?" That is the purpose of the game: to teach players to think and create new and various financial options. Thousands of people throughout the world have played this game. The players who get out of the Rat Race the quickest are the people who understand numbers and have creative financial minds. They recognize different financial options. Rich people are often creative and take calculated risks. People who take the longest are people who are not familiar with numbers and often do not understand the power of investing.

Some people playing *CASHFLOW* accumulate lots of money in the game, but they don't know what to do with it. Even though they have money, everyone else seems to be getting ahead of them. And that is true in real life. There are a lot of people who have a lot of money and do not get ahead financially.

Play CASHFLOW on the web at www.richdad.com

What did you learn about your true behavior from playing the game?

Limiting your options is the same as hanging on to old ideas. I have a friend from high school who now works at three jobs. Years ago, he was the richest of all my classmates. When the local sugar plantation closed, the company he worked for went down with the plantation. In his mind, he had but one option, and that was the old option: Work hard. The problem was that he couldn't find an equivalent job that recognized his seniority from the old company. As a result, he is overqualified for the jobs he currently has, so his salary is lower. He now works three jobs to earn enough to survive.

I have watched people playing *CASHFLOW* complain that the right opportunity cards are not coming their way. So they sit there. I know people who do that in real life. They wait for the right opportunity.

I have watched people get the right opportunity card and then not have enough money. Then they complain that they would have gotten out of the Rat Race if they had had more money. So they sit there. I know people in real life who do that also. They see all the great deals, but they have no money.

And I have seen people pull a great opportunity card, read it out loud, and have no idea that it is a great opportunity. They have the money, the time is right, they have the card, but they can't see the opportunity staring them in the face. They fail to see how it fits into their financial plan for escaping the Rat Race. And I know more people like that than all the others combined. Most people have an opportunity of a lifetime flash right in front of them, and they fail to see it. A year later, they find out about it, after everyone else got rich.

Financial intelligence is simply having more options. If the opportunities aren't coming your way, what else can you do to improve your financial position? If an opportunity lands in your lap and you have no money and the bank won't talk to you, what else can you do to get the opportunity to work in your favor? If your hunch is wrong, and what you've been counting on doesn't happen, how can you turn a lemon into millions? That is financial intelligence. It is not so much what happens, but how many different financial solutions you can think of to turn a lemon into millions. It is how creative you are in solving financial problems.

Most people only know one solution: Work hard, save, and borrow. So why would you want to increase your financial intelligence? Because you want to be the kind of person who creates your own luck. You take whatever happens and make it better. Few people realize that luck is created, just as money is. And if you want to be luckier and create money instead of working hard, then your financial intelligence is important. If you are the kind of person who is waiting for the right thing to happen, you might wait for a long time. It's like waiting for all the traffic lights to be green for five miles before you'll start your trip.

As young boys, Mike and I were constantly told by my rich dad that "money is not real." Rich dad occasionally reminded us of how close we came to the secret of money on that first day we got together and began "making money" out of plaster of Paris. "The poor and middle class work for money," he would say. "The rich make money. The more real you think money is, the harder you will work for it. If you can grasp the idea that money is not real, you will grow richer faster."

"What is it?" was a question Mike and I often came back with. "What is money if it is not real?"

"What we agree it is," was all rich dad would say.

The single most powerful asset we all have is our mind. If it is trained well, it can create enormous wealth seemingly instantaneously. An untrained mind can also create extreme poverty that can crush a family for generations.

In the Information Age, money is increasing exponentially. A few individuals are getting ridiculously rich from nothing, just ideas and agreements. If you ask many people who trade stocks or other investments for a living, they see it done all the time. Often, millions can be made instantaneously from nothing. And by nothing, I mean no money was exchanged. It is done via agreement: a hand signal in a trading pit, a blip on a trader's screen in Lisbon from a trader's screen in Toronto and

The single most powerful asset we all have is our mind. If it is trained well, it can create enormous wealth.

back to Lisbon, a call to my broker to buy and a moment later to sell. Money did not change hands. Agreements did.

So why develop your financial genius? Only you can answer that. I can tell you why I have been developing this area of my intelligence. I do it because I want to make money fast. Not because I need to, but because I want to. It is a fascinating learning process. I develop my financial IQ because I want to participate in the fastest game and biggest game in the world. And in my own small way, I would like to be part of this unprecedented evolution of humanity, the era where humans work purely with their minds and not with their bodies. Besides, it is where the action is. It is what is happening. It's hip. It's scary. And it's fun.

That is why I invest in my financial intelligence, developing the most powerful asset I have. I want to be with people moving boldly forward. I do not want to be with those left behind.

I will give you a simple example of creating money. In the early 1990s, the economy of Phoenix, Arizona, was horrible. I was watching a TV show when a financial planner came on and began forecasting doom and gloom. His advice was to save money. "Put $100 away every month," he said. "In 40 years you will be a multimillionaire."

Well, putting money away every month is a sound idea. It is one option — the option most people subscribe to. The problem is this: It blinds the person to what is really going on. It causes them to miss major opportunities for much more

25 YEARS LATER...

WHY SAVERS ARE STILL LOSERS

In the 1970s, we could 'save our way to retirement.' Passbook savings accounts earned double-digit interest and savings accounts could actually grow our wealth. Those days are long gone. Enter NIR — negative interest rates or interest rates below zero. Today, many banks are charging "savers" to hold their money... and savers truly are losers.

significant growth of their money. The world is passing them by.

As I said, the economy was terrible at that time. For investors, this is the perfect market condition. A chunk of my money was in the stock market and in apartment houses. I was short of cash. Because people were giving properties away, I was buying. I was not saving money. I was investing. Kim and I had more than a million dollars in cash working in a market that was rising fast. It was the best opportunity to invest. The economy was terrible. I just could not pass up these small deals.

Houses that were once $100,000 were now $75,000. But instead of shopping with local real estate agents, I began shopping at the bankruptcy attorney's office, or the courthouse steps. In these shopping places, a $75,000 house could sometimes be bought for $20,000 or less. For $2,000, which was loaned to me from a friend for 90 days for $200, I gave an attorney a cashier's check as a down payment. While the acquisition was being processed, I ran an ad advertising a $75,000 house for only $60,000 and no money down. The phone rang hard and heavy. Prospective buyers were screened and once the property was legally mine, all the prospective buyers were allowed to look at the house. It was a feeding frenzy. The house sold in a few minutes. I asked for a $2,500 processing fee, which they gladly handed over, and the escrow and title company took over from there. I returned the $2,000 to my friend with an additional $200. He was happy, the home buyer was happy, the attorney was happy, and I was happy. I had sold a house for $60,000 that cost me $20,000. The $40,000 was created from money in my asset column in the form of a promissory note from the buyer. Total working time: five hours.

So now that you are on your way to becoming more financially literate and skilled at reading numbers, I will show you why this is an example of money being invented.

$40,000 is created in the asset column. Money is invented without being taxed. At 10 percent interest, $4,000 a year in cash flow is added to income.

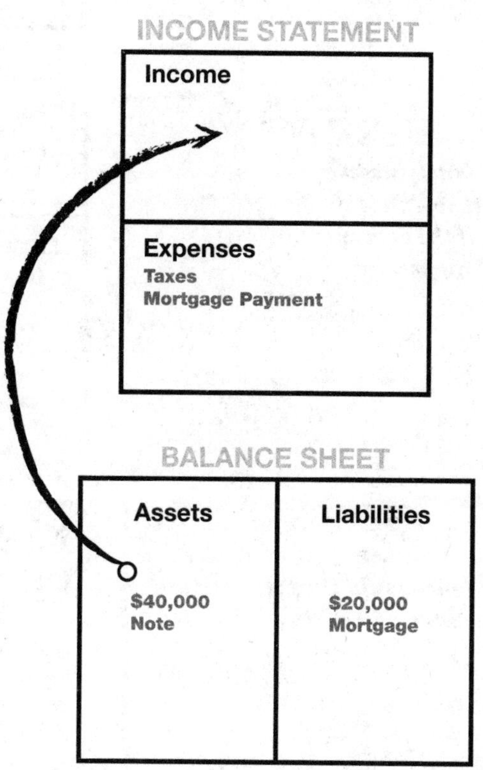

During this depressed market, Kim and I were able to do six of these simple transactions in our spare time. While the bulk of our money was in larger properties and the stock market, we were able to create more than $190,000 in assets (notes at 10 percent interest) in those six "buy, create, and sell" transactions. That comes to approximately $19,000 a year in income, much of it sheltered through our private corporation. Much of that $19,000 a year goes to pay for our company cars, gas, travel, insurance, dinners with clients, and other things. By the time the government gets a chance to tax that income, it's been spent on legally allowed pre-tax expenses.

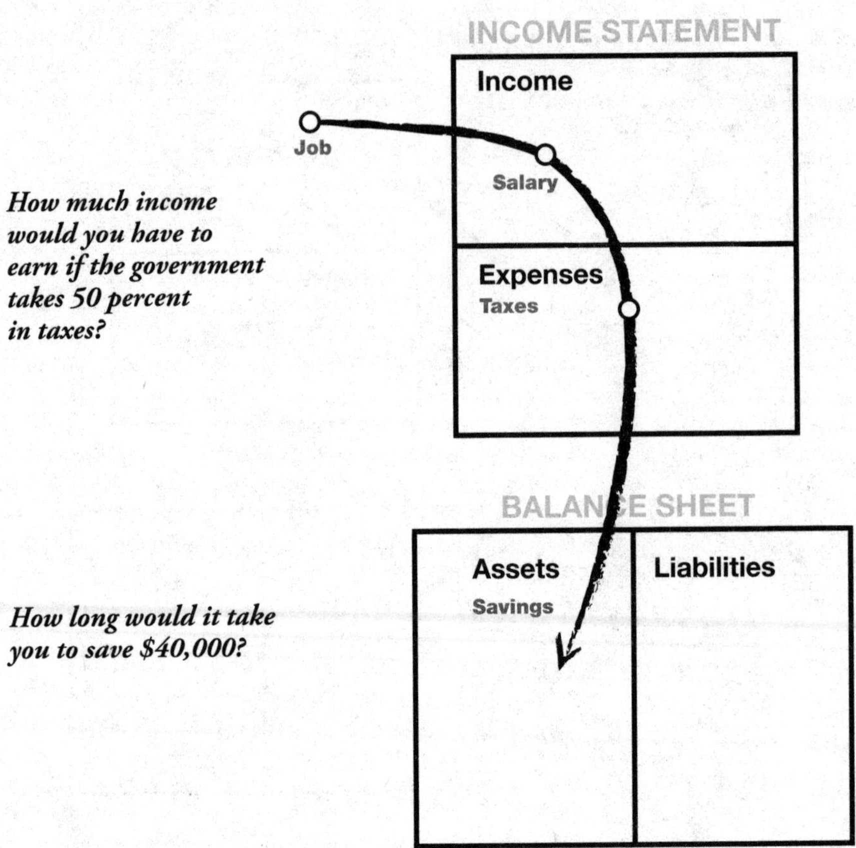
INCOME STATEMENT
Income
Job
Salary
Expenses
Taxes
BALANCE SHEET
Assets
Savings
Liabilities
How much income would you have to earn if the government takes 50 percent in taxes?
How long would it take you to save $40,000?

This was a simple example of how money is invented, created, and protected using financial intelligence.

Ask yourself: How long would it take to save $190,000? Would the bank pay you 10 percent interest on your money? And the promissory note is good for 30 years. I hope they never pay me the $190,000. I have to pay a tax if they pay me the principal, and besides, $19,000 paid over 30 years is a little over $500,000 in income.

I have people ask what happens if the person doesn't pay. That does happen, and it's good news. That $60,000 home could be taken back and re-sold for $70,000, and another $2,500 collected as a loan-processing fee. It would still be a zero-down transaction in the mind of the new buyer. And the process would go on.

The first time I sold the house, I paid back the $2,000, so technically, I have no money in the transaction. My return on investment (ROI) is infinite. It's an example of no money making a lot of money.

In the second transaction, when re-sold, I would have put $2,000 in my pocket and re-extended the loan to 30 years. What would my ROI be if I got paid money to make money? I do not know, but it sure beats saving $100 a month, which actually starts out as $150 because it's after-tax income for 40 years earning low interest. And again, you're taxed on the interest. That is not too intelligent. It may be safe, but it's not smart.

A few years later, as the Phoenix real estate market strengthened, those houses we sold for $60,000 became worth $110,000. Foreclosure opportunities were still available, but became rare. It cost a valuable asset, my time, to go out looking for them. Thousands of buyers were looking for the few available deals. The market had changed. It was time to move on and look for other opportunities to put in the asset column.

Still True Today...

CRASHES

There have been three major crashes in the past 30 years. The first was the crash of 1989-1990 when real estate became cheaper than ever. The second was in 2001-2002 when the dot-com bubble burst, and the third in 2008-2009 when the housing bubble burst. Each of these was an opportunity to invent money.

"You can't do that here." "That is against the law." "You're lying." I hear those comments much more often than "Can you show me how to do that?" The math is simple. You do not need algebra or calculus. And the escrow company handles the legal transaction and the servicing of the payments. I have no roofs to fix or toilets to unplug because the owners do that. It's their house. Occasionally someone does not pay. And that is wonderful because there are late fees, or they move out and the property is sold again. The court system handles that.

And it may not work in your area. The market conditions may be different. But the example illustrates how a simple financial process can create hundreds of thousands of dollars, with little money and low risk. It is an example of money being only an agreement. Anyone with a high school education can do it.

Yet most people won't. Most people listen to the standard advice of "Work hard and save money."

For about 30 hours of work, approximately $190,000 was created in the asset column, and no taxes were paid.

Which one sounds harder to you?

1. **Work hard. Pay 50% in taxes. Save what is left. Your savings then earn 5%, which is also taxed.**

OR

2. **Take the time to develop your financial intelligence Harness the power of your brain and the asset column.**

If you use option number one, be sure to factor in how much time it takes you to save $190,000. Time is one of your greatest assets.

Now you may understand why I silently shake my head when I hear parents say, "My child is doing well in school and receiving a good education." It may be good, but is it adequate?

I know the above investment strategy is a small one. It is used to illustrate how small can grow into big. Again, my success reflects the importance of a strong financial foundation, which starts with a strong financial education.

STILL TRUE TODAY...

THOSE WERE THE DAYS...

Earning 5% on a savings account? Those were the days! A lot has changed over 25 years, and today much of what used to be sound advice has become old, obsolete advice. Like milk that's been around too long, the advice to "save money" is long past its expiration date.

I have said it before, but it's worth repeating. Financial intelligence is made up of these four main technical skills:

1. ***Accounting***
   Accounting is financial literacy, or the ability to read numbers. This is a vital skill if you want to build businesses or investments.
2. ***Investing***
   Investing is the science of money making money.
3. ***Understanding markets***
   Understanding markets is the science of supply and demand. Alexander Graham Bell gave the market what it wanted. So did Bill Gates. A $75,000 house offered for $60,000 that cost $20,000 was also the result of seizing an opportunity created by the market. Somebody was buying, and someone was selling.
4. ***The law***
   The law is the awareness of accounting corporate, state and federal regulations. I recommend playing by the rules.

It is this basic foundation, or the combination of these skills, that is needed to be successful in the pursuit of wealth, whether it be through the buying of small homes, apartment buildings, companies, stocks, bonds, precious metals, baseball cards, or the like.

A few years later, the real estate market rebounded and everyone else was getting in. The stock market was booming, and everyone was getting in. The U.S. economy was getting back on its feet. I began selling and was now traveling to Peru, Norway, Malaysia, and the Philippines. The investment landscape had changed. We were no longer buying real estate. Now I just watch the values climb inside the asset column and will probably begin selling. I suspect that some of those six little house deals will sell and the $40,000 note will be converted to cash. I need to call my accountant to be prepared for cash and seek ways to shelter it.

The point I would like to make is that investments come and go. The market goes up and comes down. Economies improve and crash. The world is always handing you opportunities of a lifetime, every day of your life, but all too often we fail to see them. But they are there. And the more the world changes and the more technology changes, the more opportunities there will be to allow you and your family to be financially secure for generations to come.

So why bother developing your financial intelligence? Again, only you can answer that. I know why I continue to learn and develop. I do it because I know there are changes coming. I'd rather welcome change than cling to the past. I know there will be market booms and market crashes. I want to continually develop my financial intelligence because, at each market change, some people will be on their knees begging for their jobs. Others, meanwhile, will take the lemons that life hands them — and we are all handed lemons occasionally — and turn them into millions. That's financial intelligence.

I am often asked about the lemons I have turned into millions. I hesitate using many more examples of personal investments because I am afraid it comes across as bragging or tooting my own horn. That is not my intention. I use the examples only as numerical and chronological illustrations of actual and simple cases. I use the examples because I want you to know that it is easy. And the more familiar you become with the four pillars of financial intelligence, the easier it becomes.

Personally, I use two main vehicles to achieve financial growth: real estate and small-cap stocks. I use real estate as my foundation. Day in and day out, my properties provide cash flow and occasional spurts of growth in value. The small-cap stocks are used for fast growth.

I do not recommend anything that I do. The examples are just that — examples. If the opportunity is too complex and I do not understand the investment, I don't do it. Simple math and common sense are all you need to do well financially.

There are five reasons for using examples:

1. To inspire people to learn more.
2. To let people know it is easy if the foundation is strong.
3. To show that anyone can achieve great wealth.
4. To show that there are millions of ways to achieve your goals.
5. To show that it's not rocket science.

In 1989, I used to jog through a lovely neighborhood in Portland, Oregon. It was a suburb that had little gingerbread houses. They were small and cute. I almost expected to see Little Red Riding Hood skipping down the sidewalk on her way to Granny's.

There were "For Sale" signs everywhere. The timber market was terrible, the stock market had just crashed, and the economy was depressed. On one street, I noticed a for-sale sign that was up longer than most. It looked old. Jogging past it one day, I ran into the owner, who looked troubled.

"What are you asking for your house?" I asked.

The owner turned and smiled weakly. "Make me an offer," he said. "It's been for sale for over a year. Nobody even comes by anymore to look at it."

"I'll look," I said, and I bought the house a half hour later for $20,000 less than his asking price.

It was a cute little two-bedroom home, with gingerbread trim on all the windows. It was light blue with gray accents and had been built in 1930. Inside there was a beautiful rock fireplace, as well as two tiny bedrooms. It was a perfect rental house.

We gave the owner $5,000 down for a $45,000 house that was really worth $65,000, except that no one wanted to buy it. The owner moved out in a week, happy to be free, and my first tenant moved in, a local college professor. After the mortgage, expenses, and management fees were paid, we put a little less than $40 in my pocket at the end of each month. Hardly exciting.

A year later, the depressed Oregon real estate market had begun to pick up. California investors, flush with money from their still booming real estate market, were moving north and buying up Oregon and Washington. We sold that little house for $95,000 to a young couple from California who thought it was a bargain. Our capital gains of approximately $40,000 were placed into a 1031 tax-deferred exchange, and I went shopping for a place to put my money. In about a month, we found a 12-unit apartment house right next to the Intel plant in Beaverton, Oregon. The owners lived in Germany, had no idea what the place was worth, and again, just wanted to get out of it. I offered $275,000 for a $450,000 building. They agreed to $300,000. I bought it and held it for two years. Utilizing the same 1031-exchange process, we sold the building for $495,000 and bought a 30-unit apartment building in Phoenix, Arizona. Kim and I had moved to Phoenix by then to get out of the rain, and needed to sell anyway. Like the former Oregon market, the real estate market in Phoenix was depressed. The price of the 30-unit apartment building in Phoenix was $875,000, with $225,000 down. The cash flow from the 30 units was a little over $5,000 a month.

The problem with "secure" investments is that they are often sanitized, that is, made so safe that the gains are less.

The Arizona market began moving up and, a few years later, a Colorado investor offered us $1.2 million for the property.

The point of this example is how a small amount can grow into a large amount. Again, it is a matter of understanding financial statements, investment strategies, a sense of the market, and the laws.

If people are not versed in these subjects, then obviously they must follow standard dogma, which is to play it safe, diversify, and only invest in secure investments. The problem with "secure" investments is that they are often sanitized, that is, made so safe that the gains are less.

Most large brokerage houses will not touch speculative transactions in order to protect themselves and their clients. And that is a wise policy. The really hot deals are not offered to people who are novices. Often, the best deals that make the rich even richer are reserved for those who understand the game. It is technically illegal to offer speculative deals to someone who is considered not sophisticated, but of course it happens. The more sophisticated I get, the more opportunities come my way.

Another case for developing your financial intelligence over a lifetime is simply that more opportunities are presented to you. And the greater your financial intelligence, the easier it is to tell whether a deal is good. It's your intelligence that can spot a bad deal, or make a bad deal good. The more we learn — and there is a lot to learn — the more money we make simply because we gain experience and wisdom as the years go on. We have friends who are playing it safe, working hard at their profession, and failing to gain financial wisdom, which does take time to develop.

Our overall philosophy is to plant seeds inside my asset column. That is my formula. We start small and plant seeds. Some grow; some don't. Inside our real estate corporation, we have property worth several million dollars. It is our own REIT, or real estate investment trust.

The point I'm making is that most of those millions started out as little $5,000 to $10,000 investments. All of those down payments were fortunate to catch a fast-rising market and increase tax-free. We traded in and out several times over a number of years.

We also own a stock portfolio, surrounded by a corporation that Kim and I call our "personal mutual fund." We have friends who deal specifically with investors like us who have extra money each month to invest. We buy high-risk, speculative private companies that are just about to go public on a stock exchange in the United States or Canada. An example of how fast gains can be made is 100,000 shares purchased for 25 cents each before the company goes public. Six months later, the company is listed, and the 100,000 shares now are worth $2 each. If the company is well managed, the price keeps going up, and the stock may go to $20 or more per share. There are years when our $25,000 has gone to a million in less than a year.

It is not gambling if you know what you're doing. It is gambling if you're just throwing money into a deal and praying. The idea in anything is to use your technical knowledge, wisdom, and love of the game to cut the odds down, to lower the risk. Of course, there is always risk. It is financial intelligence that improves the odds. Thus, what is risky for one person is less risky to someone else. That is the primary reason I constantly encourage people to invest more in their financial education than in stocks, real estate, or other markets. The smarter you are, the better chance you have of beating the odds.

The stock plays I personally invested in were extremely high-risk for most people and absolutely not recommended. I have been playing that game since 1979 and have paid more than my share in dues. But if you will reread why investments such as these are high-risk for most people, you may be able to set your life up differently, so that the ability to take $25,000 and turn it into $1 million in a year is low-risk for you.

As stated earlier, nothing I have written is a recommendation. It is only used as an example of what is simple and possible. What I do is small potatoes in the grand scheme of things. Yet for the average individual, a passive income of more than $100,000 a year is nice and not hard to achieve. Depending on the market and how smart you are, it could be done in five to 10 years. If you keep your living expenses modest, $100,000 coming in as additional income is pleasant, regardless of whether you work. You can work if you like or take time off if you choose and use the government tax system in your favor, rather than against you.

It is not gambling if you know what you're doing. It is gambling if you're just throwing money into a deal and praying.

My personal basis is real estate. I love real estate because it's stable and slow-moving. I keep the base solid. The cash flow is fairly steady and, if properly managed, has a good chance of increasing in value. The beauty of a solid base of real estate is that it allows me to take greater risks, as I do with speculative stocks.

If I make great profits in the stock market, I pay my capital-gains tax on the gain and then reinvest what's left in real estate, again further securing my asset foundation.

A last word on real estate: I have traveled all over the world and taught investing. In every city, I hear people say you cannot buy real estate cheap. That is not my experience. Even in New York or Tokyo, or just on the outskirts of the city, prime bargains are overlooked by most people. In Singapore,with their high real estate prices, there are still bargains to be found within a short driving distance. So whenever I hear someone say, "You can't do that here," pointing at me, I remind them that maybe the real statement is, "I don't know how to do that here — yet."

Great opportunities are not seen with your eyes. They are seen with your mind. Most people never get wealthy simply because they are not trained financially to recognize opportunities right in front of them.

I am often asked, "How do I start?"

In the final chapter of this book, I offer 10 steps that I followed on the road to my financial freedom. But always remember to have fun. When you learn the rules and the vocabulary of investing and begin to build your asset column, I think you'll find that it's as fun a game as you've ever played. Sometimes you win and sometimes you learn. But have fun. Most people never win because they're more afraid of losing. That is why I found school so silly. In school we learn that mistakes are bad, and we are punished for making them. Yet if you look at the way humans are designed to learn, we learn by making mistakes. We learn to walk by falling down. If we never fell down, we would never walk. The same is true for learning to ride a bike. I still have scars on my knees, but today I can ride a bike without thinking. The same is true for getting rich. Unfortunately, the main reason most people are not rich

Great opportunities are not seen with your eyes. They are seen with your mind.

is because they are terrified of losing. Winners are not afraid of losing. But losers are. Failure is part of the process of success. People who avoid failure also avoid success.

I look at money much like my game of tennis. I play hard, make mistakes, correct, make more mistakes, correct, and get better. If I lose the game, I reach across the net, shake my opponent's hand, smile, and say, "See you next Saturday."

There are two kinds of investors:

1. The first and most common type is a person who buys a packaged investment. They call a retail outlet, such as a real estate company, a stockbroker, or a financial planner, and they buy something. It could be a mutual fund, a REIT, a stock or a bond. It is a clean and simple way of investing. An analogy would be a shopper who goes to a computer store and buys a computer right off the shelf.

2. The second type is an investor who creates investments. This investor usually assembles a deal in the same way a person who buys components builds a computer. I do not know the first thing about putting components of a computer together, but I do know how to put pieces of opportunities together, or know people who know how.

It is this second type of investor who is the more professional investor. Sometimes it may take years for all the pieces to come together. And sometimes they never do. It's this second type of investor that my rich dad encouraged me to be. It is important to learn how to put the pieces together, because that is where the huge wins reside, and sometimes some huge losses if the tide goes against you.

If you want to be the second type of investor, you need to develop three main skills.

1. **Find an opportunity that everyone else missed.**
   You see with your mind what others miss with their eyes. For example, a friend bought this rundown old house. It was spooky to look at. Everyone wondered why he bought it. What he saw that we did not was that the house came with four extra empty lots. He discovered that after going to the title company. After buying the house, he tore the house down and sold the five lots to a builder for three times what he paid for the entire package. He made $75,000 for two months of work. It's not a lot of money, but it sure beats minimum wage. And it's not technically difficult.

2. **Raise money.**
   The average person only goes to the bank. This second type of investor needs to know how to raise capital, and there are many ways that don't require a bank. To get started, I learned how to buy houses without a bank. It was the learned skill of raising money, more than the houses themselves, that was priceless.

   All too often I hear people say, "The bank won't lend me money," or "I don't have the money to buy it." If you want to be a type-two investor, you need to learn how to do that which stops most people. In other words, a majority of people let their lack of money stop them from making a deal. If you can avoid that obstacle, you will be millions ahead of those who don't learn those skills. There have been many times I have bought a house, a stock, or an apartment building without a penny in the bank. I once bought an apartment house for $1.2 million. I did what is called "tying it up," with a written contract between seller and buyer.

   I then raised the $100,000 deposit, which bought me 90 days to raise the rest of the money. Why did I do it? Simply because I knew it was worth $2 million. I never raised the money. Instead,the person who put up the $100,000 gave me $50,000 for finding the deal, took over my position, and I walked away. Total working time: three days. Again, it's what you know more than what you buy. Investing is not buying. It's more a case of knowing.

3. **Organize smart people.**
   Intelligent people are those who work with or hire a person who is more intelligent than they are. When you need advice, make sure you choose your advisor wisely.

There is a lot to learn, but the rewards can be astronomical. If you do not want to learn those skills, then being a type-one investor is highly recommended. It is what you know that is your greatest wealth. It is what you do not know that is your greatest risk.

There is always risk, so learn to manage risk instead of avoiding it.

STUDY SESSION

Chapter Five

LESSON 5: THE RICH INVENT MONEY

Chapter Five

LESSON 5: THE RICH INVENT MONEY

Summary

Robert gives two contrasting examples: First, the story of Alexander Graham Bell being overwhelmed by demand for his product and trying to sell his company to Western Union for $100,000. Western Union didn't see the opportunity and turned him down, and a multi-billion-dollar industry emerged.

The second example is the TV news reporting on the downsizing at a local company, and one terminated manager begging, in front of the cameras, to get his job back. He had just bought a house and was terrified to lose it.

Fear and self-doubt are in all of us. Robert has been teaching professionally since 1984 and has seen it in thousands of individuals, and in himself. We all have tremendous potential, and we all have self-doubt.

Courage can make the difference in leading a successful life. Robert said that as a teacher, it broke his heart to see students who knew the answers but were afraid to act on them.

Financial genius requires technical knowledge as well as courage. Take risks, be bold, let your genius convert that fear into power and brilliance — advice that will terrify some, because so many play it safe when it comes to their money.

There are many changes ahead in our world. And developing your financial IQ allows you to see that future of change through the lens of excitement, not dread. You'll see the opportunities and act on them, as opposed to those who allow their fear to keep them on the sideline, watching others move boldly forward.

Land was wealth 300 years ago. Later, wealth was in factories and production. Today, wealth is in information. But information flies around the world at the speed of light, and changes will be faster and more dramatic. There will be a dramatic increase in the number of new multimillionaires. There also will be those who are left behind.

Some cling to old ideas and, when they struggle, blame technology or the economy. What they fail to see is that old ideas are their biggest liability. An idea or way of doing something that may have been an asset yesterday isn't today.

Robert gives an example of a woman who came to a class he was teaching using a board game he had invented, *CASHFLOW*®. The game teaches people how money works and about the interaction of the income statement with the balance sheet.

Some people love the game, some hate it, and others miss the point. The woman in his example struggled to see that things she would normally think of as an asset — such as a boat — negatively affect her cash flow. She pulled a number of challenging cards and had a terrible game. In the end, she was angry and demanded a refund, refusing to see how the game reflected her.

Games are a powerful way to teach, as they reflect behavior and are instant feedback systems. Later, Robert got an update on the upset woman. She had calmed down and started seeing a slight relationship between the game and her life, a life in which she'd never paid attention to her and her ex-husband's finances and had been burned because of it.

The purpose of the *CASHFLOW*® game is to teach players to think and create new and various financial options. Some do this easily; others struggle. Those who have creative financial minds escape the Rat Race the fastest.

Some playing the game have lots of money but don't know what to do with it. That's true in life as well.

Some playing the game complain that the right cards aren't coming their way and just sit there. Some get a great opportunity card but don't have the money to act on it. And others have the money, get a great card, but don't see it for the opportunity it is. All of these behaviors happen in real life, too.

Financial intelligence is simply having more options, figuring out ways to create opportunities or altering situations to work in your favor.

Luck is created. So go create yours.

Money — which isn't real, by the way, but just what we agree it is — isn't our greatest asset. Our mind is. Train it well. Millions can be made from nothing more than ideas and agreements.

Putting money away each month is a sound idea, but it can blind you to what is really going on and cause you to miss opportunities for much more significant growth.

In the early 1990s, the economy in Phoenix was terrible. Robert and Kim, capitalized on that, investing in real estate. He gave an example of buying a home worth $75,000 for $20,000 using $2,000 as a down payment that a friend had loaned him for $200. While the purchase was being processed, he ran an ad advertising a $75,000 house for only $60,000 and no money down. As soon as the house was legally his, he sold it in minutes. Everyone was happy. And the $40,000 was created from money in Robert's asset column in the form of a promissory note from the buyer. At 10% interest, $4,000 a year in cash flow is added to income. Total working time: five hours.

And if the buyer eventually can't pay, they'll simply take the house back and resell it. The math still beats saving after-tax money each month.

It's legal, the escrow company handles the servicing of the payments, and Robert and Kim don't have to deal with fixing roofs or toilets because the buyer owns the house.

A few years later, the Phoenix market strengthened and it wasn't worth their time to ferret out the deals, so they moved on.

Market conditions may be different where you are, so this strategy may not work for you. But the example illustrates how a simple financial process can create hundreds of thousands of dollars, with little money and low risk. It is an example of money being only an agreement.

Would you rather work hard, pay taxes and save from what's left — with any growth also being taxed — or take the time to develop your financial intelligence?

Markets go up and down, and investments come and go. The world is always handing you opportunities of a lifetime; you simply need to be able to see them.

Robert shares another example of buying a house for $45,000 in a depressed market in Portland, Oregon, and renting it out for very little profit. But a year later, the market picked up and he sold it for $95,000, reinvesting the capital gains into a 12-unit, $300,000 apartment house in Beaverton, Oregon. Two years later, that was sold and the profit put into a 30-unit, $875,000 apartment building in Phoenix. A few years later, an investor offered $1.2 million for the property. It's an example of how a small amount of money can grow into a large amount.

The more you develop your financial intelligence — which takes time — the more opportunities will be offered to you.

Robert's philosophy is to plant seeds in his asset column. Start small and plant seeds. Some grow; some don't. Some grow into millions from little investments.

Robert and Kim also have a stock portfolio where they buy high-risk, speculative private companies that are just about to go public. It's a risk, but the more you develop your financial intelligence, the lower the risk becomes. The smarter you are, the better your chances of beating the odds.

Some may argue that there aren't real estate bargains where they are, but Robert said there are prime opportunities everywhere that are overlooked. Most people aren't trained financially to recognize the opportunities in front of them.

As you develop your financial IQ and begin to put it into practice, remember to have fun. Sometimes you win, sometimes you lose, but always have fun. Don't be afraid of losing, because failure is part of the process of success.

There are two kinds of investors: 1) Those who buy a packaged investment from a retail outlet, such as a financial planner, and 2) Those who create investments; these are also known as professional investors.

If you want to be the second kind of investor, you must develop three main skills. First, find the opportunities that everyone else missed. Second, raise money. And third, organize smart people and hire those with more intelligence than you.

There is always risk, so you must learn to manage it rather than avoid it.

Left-hemisphere moment: Small amounts of money can be turned into large amounts with astute, well-timed investments.

Right-hemisphere moment: Robert always encourages adult students to look at games as reflecting back to them what they know and what they need to learn. Most importantly, games reflect behavior. They are instant feedback systems. Instead of the teacher lecturing you, the game is giving you a personalized lecture, one that is custom-made just for you.

Subconscious moment: We all have tremendous potential, and we all are blessed with gifts. Yet the one thing that holds all of us back is some degree of self-doubt. It is not so much the lack of technical information that holds us back, but more the lack of self-confidence.

What Was Robert Saying

Now it's time to reflect. Ask yourself, "*What* is Robert saying in this quote?" And, "*Why* does he say that?" In this section you do not need to agree or disagree with Robert. The goal is to *understand* what Robert is saying.

Remember, this curriculum is designed to be cooperative and supportive. Two minds are better than one. If you do not understand what Robert is saying, do not shy away from it. Ask for help in understanding. Take the time discuss each quote until you understand it:

> "Often in the real world, it's not the smart who get ahead, but the bold."

"As a teacher, I recognized that it was excessive fear and self-doubt that were the greatest detractors of personal genius. It broke my heart to see students know the answers, yet lack the courage to act on the answer."

"Old ideas are some people's biggest liability. It is a liability simply because they fail to realize that while that idea or way of doing something was an asset yesterday, yesterday is gone."

"Rich people are often creative and take calculated risks."

"Why would you want to increase your financial intelligence? Because you want to be the kind of person who creates your own luck."

"The single most powerful asset we all have is our mind. If it is trained well, it can create enormous wealth seemingly instantaneously. An untrained mind can also create extreme poverty that can crush a family for generations."

"If the opportunity is too complex and I do not understand the investment, I don't do it. Simple math and common sense are all you need to do well financially."

"The problem with 'secure' investments is that they are often sanitized, that is, made so safe that the gains are less."

"It is not gambling if you know what you're doing. It is gambling if you're just throwing money into a deal and praying."

"Great opportunities are not seen with your eyes. They are seen with your mind."

"It is what you know that is your greatest wealth. It is what you do not know that is your greatest risk."

Additional Questions

Now it's time to take the stories in this chapter along with the understanding of what Robert was saying and apply them to you and your life. Ask yourself the questions below and discuss them with your study partner. Be honest with yourself and your partner. If you do not like some of the answers you are giving, ask yourself if you are willing to change and accept the challenge to change your thoughts and mindset:

1. Robert says that it is not so much the lack of technical information that holds us back, but more the lack of self-confidence. What is an example in your life or someone else's where self-doubt got in the way of a great opportunity?
2. Some people have a lot of money but do not get ahead financially. Why is that?
3. As you have developed your own financial intelligence, how has it helped you see more easily whether a deal is good?
4. Robert's philosophy is to plant seed inside his asset column, starting small and seeing what grows. How are you planting seeds in your asset column right now? If you aren't, what could you do to be able to start?
5. Robert lists two kinds of investors: those who buy packaged investments, and those who create investments. Which kind are you? Is that the kind you want to be?
6. How have you seen fear of failure play out in your life, and how did it prevent you from taking advantage of opportunities? What can you do to conquer that fear in the future?

NOTES

Chapter Six

LESSON 6: WORK TO LEARN—DON'T WORK FOR MONEY

Job security meant everything to my educated dad. Learning meant everything to my rich dad.

A few years ago, I granted an interview with a newspaper in Singapore. The young female reporter was on time, and the interview got under way immediately. We sat in the lobby of a luxurious hotel, sipping coffee and discussing the purpose of my visit to Singapore. I was to share the platform with Zig Ziglar. He was speaking on motivation, and I was speaking on "The Secrets of the Rich."

"Someday, I would like to be a best-selling author like you," she said. I had seen some of the articles she had written for the paper, and I was impressed. She had a tough, clear style of writing. Her articles held a reader's interest.

"You have a great style," I said in reply. "What holds you back from achieving your dream?"

"My work does not seem to go anywhere," she said quietly. "Everyone says that my novels are excellent, but nothing happens. So I keep my job with the paper. At least it pays the bills. Do you have any suggestions?"

"Yes, I do," I said brightly. "A friend of mine here in Singapore runs a school that trains people to sell. He runs sales-training courses for many of the top corporations here in Singapore, and I think attending one of his courses would greatly enhance your career."

She stiffened. "Are you saying I should go to school to learn to sell?"

I nodded.

"You aren't serious, are you?"

Again, I nodded. "What is wrong with that?" I was now back-pedaling. She was offended by something, and now I was wishing I had not said anything. In my attempt to be helpful, I found myself defending my suggestion.

The reporter said to me: "I have a master's degree in English Literature. Why would I go to school to learn to be a salesperson? I am a professional. I went to school to be trained in a profession so I would not have to be a salesperson. I hate salespeople. All they want is money. So tell me why I should study sales?" She was packing her briefcase. The interview was over.

On the coffee table sat a copy of an earlier best-selling book I wrote. I picked it up as well as the notes she had jotted down on her legal pad.

"Do you see this?" I said pointing to her notes.

She looked down at her notes. "What?" she said, confused. Again, I pointed deliberately to her notes. On her pad she had written: "Robert Kiyosaki, best-selling author."

"It says best-selling author, not best-writing author," I said quietly. Her eyes widened.

"I am a terrible writer," I said. "You are a great writer. I went to sales school. You have a master's degree. Put them together and you get a 'best-selling author' and a 'best-writing author.'"

Anger flared in her eyes. "I'll never stoop so low as to learn how to sell. People like you have no business writing. I am a professionally trained writer and you are a salesman. It is not fair," she fumed.

She put the rest of her notes away and hurried out through the large glass doors into the humid Singapore morning.

At least she gave me a fair and favorable write-up the next morning. The world is filled with smart, talented, educated, and gifted people. We meet them every day. They are all around us.

A few days ago, my car was not running well. I pulled into a garage, and the young mechanic had it fixed in just a few minutes. He knew what was wrong by simply listening to the engine. I was amazed.

I am constantly shocked at how little talented people earn. I have met brilliant, highly educated people who earn less than $20,000 a year. A business consultant who specializes in the medical trade was telling me how many doctors, dentists, and chiropractors struggle financially. All this time, I thought that when they graduated, the dollars would pour in. It was this business consultant who gave me the phrase: "They are one skill away from great wealth."

What this phrase means is that most people need only to learn and master one more skill and their income would jump exponentially. I have mentioned before that financial intelligence is a synergy of accounting, investing, marketing, and law. Combine those four technical skills and making money with money is easier than most people would believe. When it comes to money, the only skill most people know is to work hard.

The classic example of a synergy of skills was that young writer for the newspaper. If she diligently learned the skills of sales and marketing, her income would jump dramatically. If I were her, I would take some courses in advertising copywriting as well as sales. Then, instead of working at the newspaper, I would seek a job at an advertising agency. Even if it were a cut in pay, she would learn how to communicate in short-cuts that are used in successful advertising. She also would spend time learning public relations, an important skill. She would learn how to get millions in free publicity. Then, at night and on weekends, she could be writing her great novel. When it was finished, she would be better able to sell her book. Then, in a short while, she could be a "best-selling author."

When I came out with my first book, *If You Want To Be Rich and Happy, Don't Go to School,* a publisher suggested I change the title to *The Economics of Education.* I told the publisher that, with a title like that, I would sell two books: one to my family, and one to my best friend. The problem is that they would expect it for free. The obnoxious title, *If You Want To Be Rich and Happy, Don't Go to School,* was chosen because we knew it would get tons of publicity. I am pro-education and believe in education reform. If I were not pro-education, why would I continue to press for changing our antiquated educational system? So I chose a title that would get me on more TV and radio shows, simply because I was willing to be controversial. Many people thought I was a fruitcake, but the book sold and sold.

FAST FORWARD... TO TODAY

WHY EDUCATION IS FAILING

Most teachers lack real-world experience — they have not done what they teach. They haven't actually experienced what they teach, made mistakes, learned from those mistakes, and applied what they've learned as they continue to practice and get better and better.

Schools teach us to read and memorize. I believe that 'studying' is the key to applying what we learn. Kim and I meet with our Advisors several times a year and we choose books to read and study together.

As the Cone of Learning (on page 28) illustrates, discussion and cooperation are great ways to learn.

When I graduated from the U.S. Merchant Marine Academy in 1969, my educated dad was happy. Standard Oil of California had hired me for its oil-tanker fleet as a third mate. The pay was low compared with my classmates, but it was okay for a first real job after college. My starting pay was about $42,000 a year, including overtime, and I only had to work for seven months. I had five months of vacation. If I had wanted to, I could have taken the run to Vietnam with a subsidiary shipping company and easily doubled my pay instead of taking five months of vacation.

"You want to know a little about a lot" was rich dad's suggestion.

I had a great career ahead of me, yet I resigned after six months with the company and joined the Marine Corps to learn how to fly. My educated dad was devastated. Rich dad congratulated me.

In school and in the workplace, the popular opinion is the idea of specialization: that is, in order to make more money or get promoted, you need to specialize. That is why medical doctors immediately begin to seek a specialty such as orthopedics or pediatrics. The same is true for accountants, architects, lawyers, pilots, and others.

My educated dad believed in the same dogma. That is why he was thrilled when he eventually achieved his doctorate. He often admitted that schools reward people who study more and more about less and less.

Rich dad encouraged me to do exactly the opposite. "You want to know a little about a lot" was his suggestion. That is why for years I worked in different areas of his companies. For a while, I worked in his accounting department. Although I would probably never have been an accountant, he wanted me to learn via osmosis. Rich dad knew I would pick up jargon and a sense of what is important and what is not. I also worked as a bus boy and construction worker as well as in sales, reservations, and marketing. He was grooming Mike and me. That is why he insisted we sit in on the meetings with his bankers, lawyers, accountants, and brokers. He wanted us to know a little about every aspect of his empire.

When I quit my high-paying job with Standard Oil, my educated dad had a heart-to-heart talk with me. He was bewildered. He could not understand my decision to resign from a career that offered high pay, great benefits, lots of time off, and opportunity for promotion. When he asked me one evening, "Why did you quit?" I could not explain it to him, though I tried hard to. My logic did not fit his logic. The big problem was that my logic was my rich dad's logic.

Job security meant everything to my educated dad. Learning meant everything to my rich dad.

Educated dad thought I went to school to learn to be a ship's officer. Rich dad knew that I went to school to study international trade. So as a student, I made cargo runs, navigating large freighters, oil tankers, and passenger ships to the Far East and the South Pacific. Rich dad emphasized that I should stay in the Pacific instead of taking ships to Europe because he knew that the emerging nations were in Asia, not

Europe. While most of my classmates, including Mike, were partying at their fraternity houses, I was studying trade, people, business styles, and cultures in Japan, Taiwan, Thailand, Singapore, Hong Kong, Vietnam, Korea, Tahiti, Samoa, and the Philippines. I was partying also, but it was not in any frat house. I grew up rapidly.

Educated dad just could not understand why I decided to quit and join the Marine Corps. I told him I wanted to learn to fly, but really I wanted to learn to lead troops. Rich dad explained to me that the hardest part of running a company is managing people. He had spent three years in the Army; my educated dad was draft-exempt. Rich dad valued learning to lead men into dangerous situations. "Leadership is what you need to learn next," he said. "If you're not a good leader, you'll get shot in the back, just like they do in business."

Returning from Vietnam in 1973, I resigned my commission, even though I loved flying. I found a job with Xerox Corp. I joined it for one reason, and it was not for the benefits. I was a shy person, and the thought of selling was the most frightening subject in the world. Xerox has one of the best sales-training programs in America.

Rich dad was proud of me. My educated dad was ashamed. Being an intellectual, he thought that salespeople were below him. I worked with Xerox for four years until I overcame my fear of knocking on doors and being rejected. Once I could consistently be in the top five in sales, I again resigned and moved on, leaving behind another great career with an excellent company.

In 1977, I formed my first company. Rich dad had groomed Mike and me to take over companies. So I now had to learn to form them and put them together. My first product, the nylon-and-Velcro wallet, was manufactured in the Far East and shipped to a warehouse in New York, near where I had gone to school. My formal education was complete, and it was time to test my wings. If I failed, I would go broke. Rich dad thought it best to go broke before 30. "You still have time to recover" was his advice. On the eve of my 30th birthday, my first shipment left Korea for New York.

JOB is an acronym for "Just Over Broke."

Today, I still do business internationally. And as my rich dad encouraged me to do, I keep seeking the emerging nations. Today my investment company invests in South American countries and Asian countries, as well as in Norway and Russia.

There is an old cliché that goes: "Job is an acronym for 'Just Over Broke.'" Unfortunately, I would say that applies to millions of people. Because school does not think financial intelligence is an intelligence, most workers live within their means. They work and they pay the bills.

There is another horrible management theory that goes, "Workers work hard enough to not be fired, and owners pay just enough so that workers won't quit." And if you look at the pay scales of most companies, again I would say there is a degree of truth to that statement.

The net result is that most workers never get ahead. They do what they've been taught to do: Get a secure job. Most workers focus on working for pay and benefits that reward them in the short term, but are often disastrous in the long run.

Instead, I recommend to young people to seek work for what they will learn, more than what they will earn. Look down the road at what skills they want to acquire before choosing a specific profession and before getting trapped in the Rat Race.

TIMELESS RICH DAD WISDOM

WHO ARE YOUR TEACHERS?

One lesson from rich dad that has become crystal clear over the past 25 years is the importance of choosing teachers who have actually DONE what you want to do.

Once people are trapped in the lifelong process of bill-paying, they become like those little hamsters running around in those metal wheels. Their little furry legs are spinning furiously, the wheel is turning furiously, but come tomorrow morning, they'll still be in the same cage. Great job.

In the movie *Jerry Maguire* starring Tom Cruise, there are many great one-liners. Probably the most memorable is: "Show me the money." But there is one line I thought most truthful. It comes from the scene where Tom Cruise is leaving the firm. He has just been fired, and he is asking the entire company, "Who wants to come with me?" And the whole place is silent and frozen. Only one woman speaks up and says, "I'd like to, but I'm due for a promotion in three months."

That statement is probably the most truthful statement in the whole movie. It is the type of statement that people use to keep themselves busy, working away to pay bills. I know my educated dad looked forward to his pay raise every year, and every year he was disappointed. So he would go back to school to earn more qualifications so he could get another raise. Then, once again, there would be another disappointment.

The question I often ask people is, "Where is this daily activity taking you?" Just like the little hamster, I wonder if people look at where their hard work is taking them. What does the future hold?

In his book *The Retirement Myth,* Craig S. Karpel writes: "I visited the headquarters of a major national pension consulting firm and met with a managing director who specializes in designing lush retirement plans for top management. When I asked her what people who don't have corner offices will be able to expect in the way of pension income, she said with a confident smile, 'The Silver Bullet.'

"What, I asked, is 'The Silver Bullet?'"

"She shrugged and said, 'If baby boomers discover they don't have enough money to live on when they're older, they can always blow their brains out.'"

Karpel goes on to explain the difference between the old defined-benefit retirement plans and the new 401(k) plans that are riskier. It is not a pretty picture for most people working today. And that is just for retirement. Add medical fees and long-term nursing-home care and the picture is frightening.

STILL TRUE TODAY...

THE #1 FEAR

This merits repeating: The #1 fear among aging Americans is outliving their money. As many pension plans changed — to a 'defined contribution' versus a 'defined benefit' plan with a cap on total dollars available — it changed the rules for how people plan for retirement and continues to stress government assistance programs and entitlements.

Already, many hospitals in countries with socialized medicine need to make tough decisions such as, "Who will live, and who will die?" They make those decisions purely on how much money they have and how old the patients are. If the patient is old, they often will give the medical care to someone younger. The older poor patient gets put to the back of the line. Just as the rich can afford better education, the rich will be able to keep themselves alive, while those who have little wealth will die.

So I wonder: Are workers looking into the future or just until their next paycheck, never questioning where they are headed?

When I speak to adults who want to earn more money, I always recommend the same thing. I suggest taking a long view of their life. Instead of simply working for the money and security, which I admit are important, I suggest they take a second job that will teach them a second skill. Often I recommend joining a network-marketing company, also called multilevel marketing, if they want to learn sales skills. Some of these companies have excellent training programs that help people get over their fear of failure and rejection, which are the main reasons people are unsuccessful. Education is more valuable than money, in the long run.

FAST FORWARD... TO TODAY

MEDICAL COSTS SOAR

People are living longer and the cost of care is getting more and more expensive. Drug manufacturers are charging more and insurance companies are paying less. Nearly everyone is feeling the pinch.

While the specifics and stats vary, most research points to the fact that a majority of bankruptcies in the U.S. are a result of out-of-control medical costs.

When I offer this suggestion, I often hear in response, "Oh that is too much hassle," or "I only want to do what I am interested in."

If they say, "It's too much of a hassle," I ask, "So you would rather work all your life giving 50 percent of what you earn to the government?" If they tell me, "I only do what I am interested in,"

I say, "I'm not interested in going to the gym, but I go because I want to feel better and live longer."

Unfortunately, there is some truth to the old statement, "You can't teach an old dog new tricks." Unless a person is used to changing, it's hard to change.

But for those of you who might be on the fence when it comes to the idea of working to learn something new, I offer this word of encouragement: Life is much like going to the gym. The most painful part is deciding to go. Once you get past that, it's easy. There have been many days I have dreaded going to the gym, but once I am there and in motion, it is a pleasure. After the workout is over, I am always glad I talked myself into going.

If you are unwilling to work to learn something new and instead insist on becoming highly specialized within your field, make sure the company you work for is unionized. Labor unions are designed to protect specialists. My educated dad, after falling from grace with the governor, became the head of the teachers union in Hawaii. He told me that it was the hardest job he ever held. My rich dad, on the other hand, spent his life doing his best to keep his companies from becoming unionized. He was successful. Although the unions came close, rich dad was always able to fight them off.

Personally, I take no sides because I can see the need for and the benefits of both sides. If you do as school recommends, become highly specialized. Then seek union protection. For example, had I continued with my flying career, I would have sought a company that had a strong pilots union. Why? Because my life would be dedicated to learning a skill that was valuable in only one industry. If I were pushed out of that industry, my life's skills would not be as valuable to another industry. A displaced senior pilot — with 100,000 hours of heavy airline transport time, earning $150,000 a year — would have a hard time finding an equivalent high-paying job teaching in school. Skills do not necessarily transfer from industry to industry. Skills the pilots are paid for in the airline industry are not as important in, say, the school system.

The same is true even for doctors today. With all the changes in medicine, many medical specialists are needing to conform to medical organizations such as HMOs. Schoolteachers definitely need to be union members. Today in America, the teachers union is the largest and the richest labor union of all. The NEA, the National Education Association, has tremendous political clout. Teachers need the protection of their union because their skills are also of limited value to an industry outside of education. So the rule of thumb is: "Highly specialized; then unionize." It's the smart thing to do.

When I ask the classes I teach, "How many of you can cook a better hamburger than McDonald's?" almost all the students raise their hands. I then ask, "So if most of you can cook a better hamburger, how come McDonald's makes more money than you?"

The answer is obvious: McDonald's is excellent at business systems. The reason so many talented people are poor is because they focus on building a better hamburger and know little to nothing about business systems.

STILL TRUE TODAY...

SYSTEMS = IT

In today's world, Systems are IT... your Internet Technology. How well are you using all of today's tools?

This is another example of choosing your team, your advisors, and your teachers wisely. Today at The Rich Dad Company we are always looking for new ways to use technology and how we can improve our systems, processes, and communications. Sometimes it's easier to resist change than to embrace it — but technology offers us ways to better serve our global community and its needs..

A friend of mine in Hawaii is a great artist. He makes a sizable amount of money. One day his mother's attorney called to tell him that she had left him $35,000. That is what was left of her estate after the attorney and the government took their shares. Immediately, he saw an opportunity to increase his business by using some of this money to advertise. Two months later, his first four-color, full-page ad appeared in an expensive magazine that targeted the very rich. The ad ran for three months. He received no replies from the ad, and all of his inheritance is now gone. He now wants to sue the magazine for misrepresentation.

This is a common case of someone who can build a beautiful hamburger, but knows little about business. When I asked him what he learned, his only reply was, "Advertising salespeople are crooks." I then asked him if he would be willing to take a course in sales and a course in direct marketing. His reply, "I don't have the time, and I don't want to waste my money."

The world is filled with talented poor people. All too often, they're poor or struggle financially or earn less than they are capable of, not because of what they know, but because of what they do not know. They focus on perfecting their skills at building a better hamburger rather than the skills of selling and delivering the hamburger. Maybe McDonald's does not make the best hamburger, but they are the best at selling and delivering a basic average burger.

Poor dad wanted me to specialize. That was his view on how to be paid more. Even after being told by the governor of Hawaii that he could no longer work in state government, my educated dad continued to encourage me to get specialized. Educated dad then took up the cause of the teachers' union, campaigning for further protection and benefits for these highly skilled and educated professionals. We argued often, but I know he never agreed that overspecialization is what caused the need for union protection. He never understood that the more specialized you become, the more you are trapped and dependent on that specialty.

Rich dad advised that Mike and I groom ourselves. Many corporations do the same thing. They find a young bright student just out of business school and begin grooming that person to someday take over the company. So these bright young employees do not specialize in one department. They are moved from department to department to learn all the aspects of business systems. The rich often groom their children or the children of others. By doing so, their children gain an overall knowledge of the operations of the business and how the various departments interrelate.

For the World War II generation, it was considered bad to skip from company to company. Today, it is considered smart. Since people will skip from company to company rather than seek greater specialization in skills, why not seek to learn more than to earn? In the short term, it may earn you less, but it will pay dividends in the long term.

The main management skills needed for success are:

1. Management of cash flow
2. Management of systems
3. Management of people

The most important specialized skills are sales and marketing. The ability to sell — to communicate to another human being, be it a customer, employee, boss, spouse, or child — is the base skill of personal success. Communication skills such as writing, speaking, and negotiating are crucial to a life of success. These are skills I work on constantly, attending courses or buying educational resources to expand my knowledge.

STILL TRUE TODAY...

SALES = INCOME

Rich Dad Advisor and great friend Blair Singer — our team specialist on Sales — has been beating this into my head for 30 years: Sales = Income. Your ability to sell — to communicate and position your strengths — directly impacts your success.

As I have mentioned, my educated dad worked harder and harder the more competent he became. He also became more trapped the more specialized he got. Although his salary went up, his choices diminished. Soon after he was locked out of government work, he found out how vulnerable he really was professionally. It is like professional athletes who suddenly are injured or are too old to play. Their once high-paying position is gone, and they have limited skills to fall back on. I think that is why my educated dad sided so much with the unions after that. He realized how much a union would have benefited him.

Rich dad encouraged Mike and me to know a little about a lot. He encouraged us to work with people smarter than we were and to bring smart people together to work as a team. Today it would be called a synergy of professional specialities.

Today, I meet ex-schoolteachers earning hundreds of thousands of dollars a year. They earn that much because they have specialized skills in their field as well as other skills. They can teach, as well as sell and market. I know of no other skills to be more important than selling and marketing. The skills of selling and marketing are difficult for most people, primarily due to their fear of rejection. The better you are at communicating, negotiating, and handling your fear of rejection, the easier life is. Just as I advised that newspaper writer who wanted to become a best-selling author, I advise anyone else today.

Being technically specialized has its strengths as well as its weaknesses. I have friends who are geniuses, but they cannot communicate effectively with other human beings and, as a result, their earnings are pitiful. I advise them to just spend a year learning to sell. Even if they earn nothing, their communication skills will improve. And that is priceless.

In addition to being good learners, sellers, and marketers, we need to be good teachers as well as good students. To be truly rich, we need to be able to give as well as to receive. In cases of financial or professional struggle, there is often a lack of giving and receiving. I know many people who are poor because they are neither good students nor good teachers.

Both of my dads were generous men. Both made it a practice to give first. Teaching was one of their ways of giving. The more they gave, the more they received. One glaring difference was in the giving of money. My rich dad gave lots of money away. He gave to his church, to charities, and to his foundation. He knew that to receive money, you had to give money. Giving money is the secret to most great wealthy families. That is why there are organizations like the Rockefeller Foundation and the Ford Foundation. These are organizations designed to take their wealth and increase it, as well as give it away in perpetuity.

My educated dad always said, "When I have some extra money, I'll give it." The problem was that there was never any extra. So he worked harder to draw more money in, rather than focus on the most important law of money: "Give, and you shall receive." Instead, he believed in: "Receive, and then you give."

In conclusion, I became both dads. One part of me is a hard-core capitalist who loves the game of money making money. The other part is a socially responsible teacher who is deeply concerned with this ever-widening gap between the haves and have-nots. I personally hold the archaic educational system primarily responsible for this growing gap.

25 YEARS LATER...

WINDS OF CHANGE

The winds of change — related to education and educational systems — continue to blow... with new blood in Washington, new momentum related to school choice, and students gravitating to (and even demanding) teachers with real-world experience. I've always believed that for things to change, first I must change. Today, many people are choosing to change and advocate for change... in an antiquated, obsolete system. Advocacy among parents is rising. The real winners will be the kids — who may finally learn about money in school.

STUDY SESSION

Chapter Six

LESSON 6: WORK TO LEARN—DON'T WORK FOR MONEY

Chapter Six

LESSON 6: WORK TO LEARN—DON'T WORK FOR MONEY

Summary

Robert was interviewed a few years ago in Singapore by a journalist who, over the course of their conversation, revealed that she wanted to become a best-selling author like him. But her novels, which everyone said were excellent, never went anywhere.

Robert suggested that she take a course in sales training. That offended the reporter, who said she had a master's in English literature and didn't see how learning to sell would help her. In fact, she hated salespeople. When Robert pointed out that he's a best-selling author, not a best-writing author, she replied she would never stoop so low as to learn to sell, and left the interview.

There are talented people all around us who struggle financially, just like that reporter. In the words of one business consultant, "They are one skill away from greatness."

What that means is that too many of us specialize. If we would learn and master just one more skill, our income would jump exponentially. When it comes to money, the only skill most people know is to work hard.

If that reporter took some courses in ad copywriting as well as sales, then got a job at an advertising agency, she would learn how to get millions in free publicity — a skill she could put to use turning her next novel into a best-seller.

When Robert came out with his first book, *If You Want To Be Rich and Happy, Don't Go to School,* a publisher suggested he change the title to *The Economics of Education*. But Robert knew that title wouldn't sell. Even though he is pro-education, he chose a title that was controversial because he knew it would get him on more TV and radio shows. And it worked.

When he graduated from the U.S. Merchant Marine Academy in 1969, he was hired as a third-mate on a Standard Oil tanker fleet. The pay was OK, but it came with five months of vacation a year. It could've been a good career, but after six months Robert quit to join the Marine Corps and learn how to fly.

Rather than specialize — as so many do, including poor dad — Robert sought out new skills. Rich dad encouraged that, telling him to learn a little about a lot. That's why Robert and his friend, Mike, had worked so many jobs growing up, to gain a variety of experiences.

Poor dad didn't understand the decision to leave the Standard Oil job. He thought Robert had gone to school to become a ship's officer. But what rich dad knew was that Robert went to school to learn about international trade. And he joined the Marine Corps to learn how to lead troops. That leadership skill would serve him well in whatever business lay ahead.

In 1973, Robert resigned his commission and took a job at Xerox in sales, even though he was a shy person. In fact, it was *because* he was a shy person that he took the job. Xerox had one of the best sales-training programs in the country, and there Robert overcame his fear of knocking on doors and being rejected. When he became one of the consistently highest-producing salespeople there, he left.

Robert launched his first company in 1977, selling wallets manufactured in the Far East and shipped to a New York warehouse. It was time to test his wings. Today, he still does business internationally.

Most people work hard to get a secure job, focusing on pay and benefits in the short term.

What they should do is seek work that will teach them the skills they'll need.

Are people looking to where they're headed or just until their next paycheck? In his book *The Retirement Myth,* Craig S. Karpel writes of the many challenges awaiting most people in retirement, and the frightening picture of what most people's reality will be.

Robert recommends a long view: Instead of simply working for money and security, take a second job to learn a second skill. Many will resist this, because they aren't ready for change. But it's like going to the gym. You might have to talk yourself into starting, but you'll be so glad you did when the workout is over.

If you are unwilling to work to learn something new and instead insist on becoming highly specialized within your field, make sure the company you work for is unionized. Your specialized skills may be useless outside your field, otherwise.

Robert asks his students how many of them can make a better hamburger than McDonald's. Most raise their hands. But the reason McDonald's is making millions and they aren't is because McDonald's is excellent at business systems.

The world is full of talented poor people. They must take the time to learn more skills, like McDonald's business systems, to succeed.

Poor dad wanted Robert to become specialized, even though that didn't work out well in his own life. He never understood that the more specialized you become, the more you are trapped and dependent on that specialty.

Rich dad, on the other hand, encouraged Mike and Robert to groom themselves and learn about a lot of different areas of business.

For the World War II generation, it was considered bad to skip from company to company. Today, it is considered smart. It enables you to learn more and will pay dividends in the long runs.

The main management skills needed for success are:
1) Management of cash flow, 2) Management of systems, and
3) Management of people. And the most important specialized skills are sales and marketing. Communication skills such as writing, speaking, and negotiating are crucial to a life of success. These are skills Robert works on constantly, attending courses or buying educational resources to expand his knowledge.

The skills of selling and marketing are difficult for most people, primarily due to their fear of rejection. The better you are at communicating, negotiating, and handling your fear of rejection, the easier life is.

Being technically specialized has its strengths and weaknesses. People in this category must expand their communication skills.

We all must learn to be good teachers as well as good students. To be truly rich, we must be able to give as well as receive.

Teaching was one of the ways both rich dad and poor dad gave to others. But rich dad also gave money to his church, to charities, and to his foundation. He knew that to receive money, he also had to give it. Poor dad always said he'd give money if he had extra — but he never had that extra. Rather than, "Give, and you shall receive," he believed in, "Receive, and then you give."

Robert became both dads, both a hard-core capitalist who loves the game of making money, and a socially responsible teacher who is deeply concerned with this ever-widening gap between the haves and have-nots. He holds the archaic educational system primarily responsible for this growing gap.

Left-hemisphere moment: It may not make immediate mathematical sense to leave a promising job for another, but the skills you will gain will lead to greater numbers in the long run.

Right-hemisphere moment: Learning skills outside what you think of as your profession will benefit you.

Subconscious moment: The situation you fear most is the skill that you need to learn and conquer. And you may have to force yourself to do it, though — like going to the gym — you'll be glad you did.

What Was Robert Saying

Now it's time to reflect. Ask yourself, "*What* is Robert saying in this quote?" And, "*Why* does he say that?" In this section you do not need to agree or disagree with Robert. The goal is to *understand* what Robert is saying.

Remember, this curriculum is designed to be cooperative and supportive. Two minds are better than one. If you do not understand what Robert is saying, do not shy away from it. Ask for help in understanding. Take the time discuss each quote until you understand it:

"Job security meant everything to my educated dad. Learning meant everything to my rich dad."

"I am constantly shocked at how little talented people earn."

"There is an old cliché that goes: 'Job is an acronym for "Just Over Broke."' Unfortunately, that applies to millions of people."

"I recommend to young people to seek work for what they will learn, more than what they will earn."

"Life is much like going to the gym. The most painful part is deciding to go. Once you get past that, it's easy."

"The world is filled with talented poor people. All too often, they're poor or struggle financially or earn less than they are capable of, not because of what they know, but because of what they do not know."

"Being technically specialized has its strengths as well as its weaknesses."

"Giving money is the secret to most great wealthy families."

Additional Questions

Now it's time to take the stories in this chapter along with the understanding of what Robert was saying and apply them to you and your life. Ask yourself the questions below and discuss them with your study partner. Be honest with yourself and your partner. If you do not like some of the answers you are giving, ask yourself if you are willing to change and accept the challenge to change your thoughts and mindset:

1. Do you know extremely talented people who make very little money? What could they be doing differently?
2. How have you sought additional skills beyond your specialty? What was the result?
3. Was there a time you stayed in a secure job rather than strike out into a new position that might've gained you more in the long run? What was the basis of your decision?

4. If someone were to ask you advice on what the most important skills are for them to learn in their working life, what would you tell them?
5. What role does giving play in your life? Do you see it as an important part of your success?
6. What are different ways you could give that you aren't currently?

NOTES

Chapter Seven

OVERCOMING OBSTACLES

The primary difference between a rich person and a poor person is how they manage fear.

Once people have studied and become financially literate, they may still face roadblocks to becoming financially independent. There are five main reasons why financially literate people may still not develop abundant asset columns that could produce a large cash flow. The five reasons are:

1. Fear
2. Cynicism
3. Laziness
4. Bad habits
5. Arrogance

Overcoming Fear

I have never met anyone who really likes losing money. And in all my years, I have never met a rich person who has never lost money. But I have met a lot of poor people who have never lost a dime — investing, that is.

The fear of losing money is real. Everyone has it. Even the rich. But it's not having fear that is the problem. It's how you handle fear. It's how you handle losing. It's how you handle failure that makes the difference in one's life. The primary difference between a rich person and a poor person is how they manage that fear.

It's okay to be fearful. It's okay to be a coward when it comes to money. You can still be rich. We're all heroes at something, and cowards at something else. My friend's wife is an emergency-room nurse. When she sees blood, she flies into action. When I mention investing, she runs away. When I see blood, I don't run. I pass out.

My rich dad understood phobias about money. "Some people are terrified of snakes. Some people are terrified about losing money. Both are phobias," he would say. So his solution to the phobia of losing money was this little rhyme: "If you hate risk and worry, start early."

If you start young, it's easier to be rich. I won't go into it here, but there is a staggering difference between a person who starts investing at age 20 versus age 30. The purchase of Manhattan Island is said to be one of the greatest bargains of all time. New York was purchased for $24 in trinkets and beads. Yet if that $24 had been invested at 8 percent annually, that $24 would have been worth more than $28 trillion by 1995. Manhattan could be repurchased with money left over to buy much of Los Angeles.

But what if you don't have much time left or would like to retire early? How do you handle the fear of losing money?

My poor dad did nothing. He simply avoided the issue, refusing to discuss the subject.

My rich dad, on the other hand, recommended that I think like a Texan. "I like Texas and Texans," he used to say. "In Texas, everything is bigger. When Texans win, they win big. And when they lose, it's spectacular."

"They like losing?" I asked.

"That's not what I'm saying. Nobody likes losing. Show me a happy loser, and I'll show you a loser," said rich dad. "It's a Texan's attitude toward risk, reward, and failure I'm talking about. It's how they handle life. They live it big. Not like most of the people around here, living like roaches when it comes to money, terrified that someone will shine a light on them, and whimpering when the grocery clerk shortchanges them a quarter."

Rich dad went on. "What I like best is the Texas attitude. They're proud when they win, and they brag when they lose. Texans have a saying, 'If you're going to go broke, go big.' You don't want to admit you went broke over a duplex."

He constantly told Mike and me that the greatest reason for lack of financial success was because most people played it too safe. "People are so afraid of losing that they lose" were his words.

Fran Tarkenton, a one-time great NFL quarterback, says it still another way: "Winning means being unafraid to lose."

In my own life, I've noticed that winning usually follows losing. Before I finally learned to ride a bike, I first fell down many times. I've never met a golfer who has never lost a golf ball. I've never met people who have fallen in love who have never had their heart broken. And I've never met someone rich who has never lost money.

STILL TRUE TODAY...

THE ART OF WINNING

The concept of winning and our desire to win in all areas of our lives have long been mainstays among athletes and in the sports world. It's a mindset, a goal to which we can all aspire, and one that motivates us to embrace our mistakes, learn from them, and keep our sights focused on winning.

So for most people, the reason they don't win financially is because the pain of losing money is far greater than the joy of being rich.

For most people, the reason they don't win financially is because the pain of losing money is far greater than the joy of being rich.

Another saying in Texas is, "Everyone wants to go to heaven, but no one wants to die." Most people dream of being rich, but are terrified of losing money. So they never get to heaven.

Rich dad used to tell Mike and me stories about his trips to Texas. "If you really want to learn the attitude of how to handle risk, losing, and failure, go to San Antonio and visit the Alamo. The Alamo is a great story of brave people who chose to fight, knowing there was no hope of success. They chose to die instead of surrendering. It's an inspiring story worthy of study. Nonetheless, it's still a tragic military defeat. They got their butts kicked. So how do Texans handle failure? They still shout, 'Remember the Alamo!'"

Mike and I heard this story a lot. He always told us this story when he was about to go into a big deal, and he was nervous. After he had done all his due diligence and it was time to put up or shut up, he told us this story. Every time he was afraid of making a mistake or losing money, he told us this story. It gave him strength, for it reminded him that he could always turn a financial loss into a financial win. Rich dad knew that failure would only make him stronger and smarter. It's not that he wanted to lose. He just knew who he was and how he would take a loss. He would take a loss and make it a win. That's what made him a winner and others losers. It gave him the courage to cross the line when others backed out. "That's why I like Texans so much," he would say. "They took a great failure and turned it into inspiration… as well a tourist destination that makes them millions."

Failure inspires winners. Failure defeats losers.

But probably his words that mean the most to me today are these: "Texans don't bury their failures. They get inspired by them. They take their failures and turn them into rallying cries. Failure inspires Texans to become winners. But that formula is not just the formula for Texans. It is the formula for all winners."

I've said that falling off my bike was part of learning to ride. I remember falling off only made me more determined to learn to ride, not less. I also said that I have never met a golfer who has never lost a ball. For top professional golfers, losing a ball or a tournament provides the inspiration to be better, to practice harder, to study more. That's what makes them better. For winners, losing inspires them. For losers, losing defeats them.

I like to quote John D. Rockefeller, who said, "I always tried to turn every disaster into an opportunity."

And being Japanese-American, I can say this. Many people say that Pearl Harbor was an American mistake. I say it was a Japanese mistake. From the movie, *Tora, Tora, Tora*, a somber Japanese admiral says to his cheering subordinates, "I am afraid we have awakened a sleeping giant." "Remember Pearl Harbor" became a rallying cry. It turned one of America's greatest losses into the reason to win. This great defeat gave America strength, and America soon emerged as a world power.

Failure inspires winners. And failure defeats losers. It is the biggest secret of winners. It's the secret that losers do not know. The greatest secret of winners is that failure inspires winning; thus, they're not afraid of losing. Repeating Fran Tarkenton's quote, "Winning means being unafraid to lose." People like Fran Tarkenton are not afraid of losing, because they know who they are. They hate losing, so they know that losing will only inspire them to become better. There is a big difference between hating losing and being afraid to lose. Most people are so afraid of losing money that they lose. They go broke over a duplex. Financially, they play life too safe and too small. They buy big houses and big cars, but not big investments. The main reason that over 90 percent of the American public struggles financially is because they play not to lose. They don't play to win.

They go to their financial planners or accountants or stockbrokers and buy a balanced portfolio. Most have lots of cash in CDs, low-yield bonds, mutual funds that can be traded within a mutual-fund family, and a few individual stocks. It is a safe and sensible portfolio. But it is not a winning portfolio. It is a portfolio of someone playing not to lose.

Don't get me wrong. It's probably a better portfolio than more than 70 percent of the population has, and that's frightening. It's a great portfolio for someone who loves safety. But playing it safe and balanced on your investment portfolio is not the way successful investors play the game. If you have little money and you want to be rich, you must first be focused, not balanced. If you look at any successful person, at the start they were not balanced. Balanced people go nowhere. They stay in one spot. To make progress, you must first go unbalanced. Just look at how you make progress walking.

Thomas Edison was not balanced. He was focused. Bill Gates was not balanced. He was focused. Donald Trump is focused. George Soros is focused. George Patton did not take his tanks wide. He focused them and blew through the weak spots in the German line. The French went wide with the Maginot Line, and you know what happened to them.

If you have any desire to be rich, you must focus. Do not do what poor and middle-class people do: put their few eggs in many baskets. Put a lot of your eggs in a few baskets and FOCUS: Follow One Course Until Successful.

If you hate losing, play it safe. If losing makes you weak, play it safe. Go with balanced investments. If you're over 25 years old and are terrified of taking risks, don't change. Play it safe, but start early. Start accumulating your nest egg early because it will take time.

But if you have dreams of freedom — of getting out of the Rat Race — the first question to ask yourself is, "How do I respond to failure?" If failure inspires you to win, maybe you should go for it — but only maybe. If failure makes you weak or causes you to throw temper tantrums — like spoiled brats who call attorneys to file lawsuits every time something doesn't go their way — then play it safe. Keep your daytime job. Or buy bonds or mutual funds. But remember, there is risk in those financial instruments also, even though they may appear safe.

I say all this, mentioning Texas and Fran Tarkenton, because stacking the asset column is easy. It's really a low-aptitude game. It doesn't take much education. Fifth-grade math will do. But building your asset column is a game in which attitude plays a major role. It takes guts, patience, and a great attitude toward failure. Losers avoid failing. And failure turns losers into winners. Just remember the Alamo.

Overcoming Cynicism

"The sky is falling! The sky is falling!" Most of us know the story of Chicken Little who ran around warning the barnyard of impending doom. We all know people who are that way. There's a Chicken Little inside each of us.

As I stated earlier, the cynic is really a little chicken. We all get a little chicken when fear and doubt cloud our thoughts.

All of us have doubts: "I'm not smart." "I'm not good enough." "So-and-so is better than me." Our doubts often paralyze us. We play the "What if?" game. "What if the economy crashes right after I invest?" "What if I lose control and I can't pay the money back?" "What if things don't go as I planned?" Or we have friends or loved ones who will remind us of our shortcomings. They often say, "What makes you think you can do that?" "If it's such a good idea, how come someone else hasn't done it?" "That will never work. You don't know what you're talking about." These words of doubt often get so loud that we fail to act. A horrible feeling builds in our stomach. Sometimes we can't sleep. We fail to move forward. So we stay with what is safe, and opportunities pass us by. We watch life passing by as we sit immobilized with a cold knot in our body. We have all felt this at one time in our lives, some more than others.

TIMELESS RICH DAD WISDOM

MISTAKES ARE OPPORTUNITIES TO LEARN

School has conditioned us to avoid mistakes — and punishes students for making them. In the real world, I've learned that mistakes — if acknowledged and evaluated and used as a tool to make better decisions in the future — are invaluable. A little fear can be a healthy thing, but we shouldn't live in fear of making mistakes. Mistakes are good things, if we find the lesson in every failure.

Peter Lynch of Fidelity Magellan mutual-fund fame refers to warnings about the sky falling as "noise," and we all hear it.

Noise is either created inside our heads or comes from outside, often from friends, family, co-workers, and the media. Lynch recalls the time during the 1950s when the threat of nuclear war was so prevalent in the news that people began building fallout shelters and storing food and water. If they had invested that money wisely in the market, instead of building a fallout shelter, they'd probably be financially independent today.

When violence breaks out in a city, gun sales go up all over the country. A person dies from rare hamburger meat in the state of Washington, and the Arizona Health Department orders restaurants to have all beef cooked well-done. A drug company runs a TV commercial in February showing people catching the flu. Colds go up as well as sales of cold medicine.

Most people are poor because, when it comes to investing, the world is filled with Chicken Littles running around yelling, "The sky is falling! The sky is falling!" And Chicken Littles are effective, because every one of us is a little chicken. It often takes great courage to not let rumors and talk of doom and gloom affect your doubts and fears. But a savvy investor knows that the seemingly worst of times is actually the best of times to make money. When everyone else is too afraid to act, they pull the trigger and are rewarded.

Some time ago, a friend named Richard came from Boston to visit Kim and me in Phoenix. He was impressed with what we had done through stocks and real estate. The Phoenix real estate prices were depressed. We spent two days showing him what we thought were excellent opportunities for cash flow and capital appreciation.

Kim and I are not real estate agents. We are strictly investors. After identifying a unit in a resort community, we called an agent who sold it to him that afternoon. The price was a mere $42,000 for a two-bedroom townhome. Similar units were going for $65,000. He had found a bargain. Excited, he bought it and returned to Boston.

Two weeks later, the agent called to say that our friend had backed out. I called immediately to find out why. All he said was that he talked to his neighbor, and his neighbor told him it was a bad deal. He was paying too much. I asked Richard if his neighbor was an investor. Richard said he was not. When I asked why he listened to him, Richard got defensive and simply said he wanted to keep looking.

The real estate market in Phoenix turned, and a few years later, that little unit was renting for $1,000 a month — $2,500 in the peak winter months. The unit was worth $95,000. All Richard had to put down was $5,000 and he would have had a start at getting out of the Rat Race. Today, he still has done nothing.

Richard's backing out did not surprise me. It's called buyer's remorse, and it affects all of us. The little chicken won, and a chance at freedom was lost.

In another example, I hold a small portion of my assets in tax-lien certificates instead of CDs. I earn 16 percent per year on my money, which certainly beats the interest rates banks offer on CDs. The certificates are secured by real estate and enforced by state law, which is also better than most banks. The formula they're bought on makes them safe. They just lack liquidity. So I look at them as 2- to 7-year CDs. Almost every time I tell someone that I hold my money this way, especially if they have money in CDs, they will tell me it's risky. They tell me why I should not do it. When I ask them where they get their information, they say from a friend or an investment magazine. They've never done it, and they're telling someone who's doing it why they shouldn't. The lowest yield I look for is 16 percent, but people who are filled with doubt are willing to accept a far lower return. Doubt is expensive.

My point is that it's those doubts and cynicism that keep most people poor and playing it safe. The real world is simply waiting for you to get rich. Only a person's doubts keep them poor. As I said, getting out of the Rat Race is technically easy. It doesn't take much education, but those doubts are cripplers for most people.

"Cynics never win," said rich dad. "Unchecked doubt and fear creates a cynic." "Cynics criticize, and winners analyze" was another of his favorite sayings. Rich dad explained that criticism blinded while analysis opened eyes. Analysis allowed winners to see that critics were blind, and to see opportunities that everyone else missed. And finding what people miss is key to any success.

Real estate is a powerful investment tool for anyone seeking financial independence or freedom. It is a unique investment tool. Yet every time I mention real estate as a vehicle, I often hear, "I don't want to fix toilets." That's what Peter Lynch calls noise. That's what my rich dad would say is the cynic talking, someone who criticizes and does not analyze, someone who lets their doubts and fears close their mind instead of open their eyes.

TIMELESS RICH DAD WISDOM

USING DEBT AND TAX LAWS

There are many people offering financial advice today. Some tell people to cut up their credit cards; others advocate becoming debt free. Today, Kim and I continue to follow the lessons of rich dad in using debt and taxes to grow our wealth. Financial education, understanding the difference between good debt and bad debt, and using the tax laws that the rich do are all part of our formula.

So when someone says, "I don't want to fix toilets," I want to fire back, "What makes you think I want to?" They're saying a toilet is more important than what they want. I talk about freedom from the Rat Race, and they focus on toilets. That is the thought pattern that keeps most people poor. They criticize instead of analyze.

"I-don't-wants hold the key to your success," rich dad would say. Because I, too, do not want to fix toilets, I shop hard for a property manager who does fix toilets. And by finding a great property manager who runs houses or apartments, well, my cash flow goes up. But, more importantly, a great property manager allows me to buy a lot more real estate since I don't have to fix toilets. A great property manager is key to success in real estate. Finding a good manager is more important to me than the real estate. A great property manager often hears of great deals before real estate agents do, which makes them even more valuable.

That is what rich dad meant by "I-don't-wants hold the key to your success." Because I do not want to fix toilets either, I figured out how to buy more real estate and expedite my getting out of the Rat Race. The people who continue to say "I don't want to fix toilets" often deny themselves the use of this powerful investment vehicle. Toilets are more important than their freedom.

In the stock market, I often hear people say, "I don't want to lose money." Well, what makes them think I or anyone else likes losing money? They don't make money because they choose to not lose money. Instead of analyzing, they close their minds to another powerful investment vehicle, the stock market.

I was riding with a friend past our neighborhood gas station. He looked up and saw that the price of gas was going up and thus the price of oil. My friend is a worry wart or a Chicken Little. To him, the sky is always going to fall, and it usually does, on him.

When we got home, he showed me all the stats as to why the price of oil was going to go up over the next few years, statistics I had never seen before, even though I already owned substantial shares of an existing oil company. With that information, I immediately began looking for and found a new, undervalued oil company that was about to find some oil deposits. My broker was excited about this new company, and I bought 15,000 shares for 65 cents per share.

Three months later, this same friend and I drove by the same gas station, and sure enough, the price per gallon had gone up nearly 15 percent. Again, the Chicken Little worried and complained. I smiled because, a month earlier, that little oil company hit oil and those 15,000 shares went up to more than $3 per share since he had first given me the tip. And the price of gas will continue to go up if what my friend says is true.

If most people understood how a "stop" worked in stock-market investing, there would be more people investing to win instead of investing not to lose. A stop is simply a computer command that sells your stock automatically if the price begins to drop, helping to minimize your losses and maximize some gains. It's a great tool for those who are terrified of losing.

So whenever I hear people focusing on their I-don't-wants, rather than what they do want, I know the noise in their head must be loud. Chicken Little has taken over their brain and is yelling, "The sky is falling, and toilets are breaking!" So they avoid their don't-wants, but they pay a huge price. They may never get what they want in life. Instead of analyzing, their inner Chicken Little closes their mind.

Rich dad gave me a way of looking at Chicken Little. "Just do what Colonel Sanders did." At the age of 66, he lost his business and began to live on his Social Security check. It wasn't enough. He went around the country selling his recipe for fried chicken. He was turned down 1,009 times before someone said yes. And he went on to become a multimillionaire at an age when most people are quitting. "He was a brave and tenacious man," rich dad said of Harlan Sanders.

So when you're in doubt and feeling a little afraid, just do what Colonel Sanders did to his little chicken. He fried it.

Overcoming Laziness

Busy people are often the most lazy. We have all heard stories of a businessman who works hard to earn money. He works hard to be a good provider for his wife and children. He spends long hours at the office and brings work home on weekends. One day he comes home to an empty house. His wife has left with the kids. He knew he and his wife had problems, but rather than work to make the relationship strong, he stayed busy at work. Dismayed, his performance at work slips and he loses his job.

Today, I often meet people who are too busy to take care of their wealth. And there are people too busy to take care of their health. The cause is the same. They're busy, and they stay busy as a way of avoiding something they do not want to face. Nobody has to tell them. Deep down they know. In fact, if you remind them, they often respond with anger or irritation.

If they aren't busy at work or with the kids, they're often busy watching TV, fishing, playing golf, or shopping. Yet deep down they know they are avoiding something important. That's the most common form of laziness: laziness by staying busy.

So what is the cure for laziness? The answer is — a little greed.

For many of us, we were raised thinking of greed or desire as bad. "Greedy people are bad people," my mom used to say. Yet we all have inside of us this yearning to have nice, new, or exciting things.

So to keep that emotion of desire under control, often parents find ways of suppressing that desire with guilt. "You only think about yourself. Don't you know you have brothers and sisters?" was one of my mom's favorites. "You want me to buy you what?" was a favorite of my dad. "Do you think we're made of money? Do you think money grows on trees? We're not rich people, you know."

It wasn't so much the words, but the angry guilt trip that went with the words that got to me.

Or the reverse guilt trip was the "I'm sacrificing my life to buy this for you. I'm buying this for you because I never had this advantage when I was a kid." I have a neighbor who is stone-broke but can't park his car in his garage. The garage is filled with toys for his kids. Those spoiled brats get everything they ask for. "I don't want them to know the feeling of want" are his everyday words. He has nothing set aside for their college or his retirement, but his kids have every toy ever made. He recently got a new credit card in the mail and took his kids to visit Las Vegas. "I'm doing it for the kids," he said with great sacrifice.

Rich dad believed that the words "I can't afford it" shut down your brain. "How can I afford it?" opens up possibilities, excitement, and dreams.

Rich dad forbade the words, "I can't afford it." In my real home, that's all I heard. Instead, rich dad required his children to say, "How can I afford it?" He believed that the words "I can't afford it" shut down your brain. It didn't have to think anymore. "How can I afford it?" opened up the brain and forced it to think and search for answers.

But most importantly, he felt the words, "I can't afford it," were a lie. And the human spirit knows it. "The human spirit is very, very powerful," he would say. "It knows it can do anything." By having a lazy mind that says, "I can't afford it," a war breaks out inside you. Your spirit is angry, and your lazy mind must defend its lie. The spirit is screaming, "Come on. Let's go to the gym and work out." And the lazy mind says, "But I'm tired. I worked really hard today." Or the human spirit says, "I'm sick and tired of being poor. Let's get out there and get rich." To which the lazy mind says, "Rich people are greedy. Besides it's too much bother. It's not safe. I might lose money. I'm working hard enough as it is. I've got too much to do at work anyway. Look at what I have to do tonight. My boss wants it finished by morning."

"I can't afford it" also causes sadness, a helplessness that leads to despondency and often depression. "How can I afford it?" opens up possibilities, excitement, and dreams. So rich dad was not so concerned about what we wanted to buy as long as we understood that "How can I afford it?" creates a stronger mind and a dynamic spirit.

Thus he rarely gave Mike or me anything. He would instead ask, "How can you afford it?" and that included college, which we paid for ourselves. It was not the goal, but the process of attaining the goal that he wanted us to learn.

The problem I see today is that there are millions of people who feel guilty about their desire or their "greed." It's old conditioning from their childhood. While they desire to have the finer things that life offers, most have been conditioned subconsciously to say, "I can't have that," or "I'll never be able to afford that."

When I decided to exit the Rat Race, it was simply a question of "How can I afford to never work again?" And my mind began to kick out answers and solutions. The hardest part was fighting my real parents' dogma: "We can't afford that." "Stop thinking only about yourself." "Why don't you think about others?" and other similar sentiments designed to instill guilt to suppress my "greed."

So how do you beat laziness? Once again, the answer is a little greed. It's that radio station WII-FM, which stands for "What's In It For Me?" A person needs to sit down and ask, "What would my life be like if I never had to work again?" "What would I do if I had all the money I needed?" Without that little greed, the desire to have something better, progress is not made. Our world progresses because we all desire a better life. New inventions are made because we desire something better. We go to school and study hard because we want something better. So whenever you find yourself avoiding something you know you should be doing, then the only thing to ask yourself is, "What's in it for me?" Be a little greedy. It's the best cure for laziness.

Too much greed, however, as anything in excess can be, is not good. But just remember what Michael Douglas said in the movie *Wall Street*: "Greed is good." Rich dad said it differently: "Guilt is worse than greed, for guilt robs the body of its soul." I think Eleanor Roosevelt said it best: "Do what you feel in your heart to be right — for you'll be criticized anyway. You'll be damned if you do, and damned if you don't."

Overcoming Bad Habits

Our lives are a reflection of our habits more than our education. After seeing the movie *Conan the Barbarian,* starring Arnold Schwarzenegger, a friend said, "I'd love to have a body like Schwarzenegger." Most of the guys nodded in agreement.

"I even heard he was really puny and skinny at one time," another friend added.

"Yeah, I heard that too," another one said. "I heard he has a habit of working out almost every day in the gym."

"Yeah, I'll bet he has to."

"Nah," said the group cynic. "I'll bet he was born that way. Besides, let's stop talking about Arnold and get some beers."

This is an example of habits controlling behavior. I remember asking my rich dad about the habits of the rich. Instead of answering me outright, he wanted me to learn through example, as usual.

"When does your dad pay his bills?" rich dad asked.

"The first of the month," I said.

"Does he have anything left over?" he asked.

"Very little," I said.

"That's the main reason he struggles," said rich dad. "He has bad habits. Your dad pays everyone else first. He pays himself last, but only if he has anything left over."

"Which he usually doesn't," I said. "But he has to pay his bills, doesn't he? You're saying he shouldn't pay his bills?"

"Of course not," said rich dad. "I firmly believe in paying my bills on time. I just pay myself first. Before I pay even the government."

"But what happens if you don't have enough money?" I asked. "What do you do then?"

"The same," said rich dad. "I still pay myself first. Even if I'm short of money. My asset column is far more important to me than the government."

"But," I said. "Don't they come after you?"

"Yes, if you don't pay," said rich dad. "Look, I did not say not to pay. I just said I pay myself first, even if I'm short of money."

"But," I replied. "How do you do that?"

"It's not how. The question is 'Why?'" rich dad said.

"Okay, why?"

"Motivation," said rich dad. "Who do you think will complain louder if I don't pay them — me, or my creditors?"

"Your creditors will definitely scream louder than you," I said, responding to the obvious. "You wouldn't say anything if you didn't pay yourself."

"So you see, after paying myself, the pressure to pay my taxes and the other creditors is so great that it forces me to seek other forms of income. The pressure to pay becomes my motivation. I've worked extra jobs, started other companies, traded in the stock market, anything just to make sure those guys don't start yelling at me. That pressure made me work harder, forced me to think, and all in all, made me smarter and more active when it comes to money. If I had paid myself last, I would have felt no pressure, but I'd be broke."

"So it is the fear of the government or other people you owe money to that motivates you?"

"That's right," said rich dad. "You see, government bill collectors are big bullies. So are bill collectors in general. Most people give into these bullies. They pay them and never pay themselves. You know the story of the 98-pound weakling who gets sand kicked in his face?"

If I pay myself first, I get financially stronger, mentally and fiscally.

I nodded. "I see that ad for weightlifting and bodybuilding lessons in the comic books all the time."

"Well, most people let the bullies kick sand in their faces. I decided to use the fear of the bully to make me stronger.

Others get weaker. Forcing myself to think about how to make extra money is like going to the gym and working out with weights. The more I work my mental money muscles out, the stronger I get. Now I'm not afraid of those bullies."

I liked what rich dad was saying. "So if I pay myself first, I get financially stronger, mentally and fiscally."

Rich dad nodded.

"And if I pay myself last, or not at all, I get weaker. So people like bosses, managers, tax collectors, bill collectors, and landlords push me around all my life — just because I don't have good money habits."

Rich dad nodded. "Just like the 98-pound weakling."

Overcoming Arrogance

"What I know makes me money. What I don't know loses me money. Every time I have been arrogant, I have lost money. Because when I'm arrogant, I truly believe that what I don't know is not important," rich dad would often tell me.

I have found that many people use arrogance to try to hide their own ignorance. It often happens when I am discussing financial statements with accountants or even other investors.

They try to bluster their way through the discussion. It is clear to me that they don't know what they're talking about. They're not lying, but they are not telling the truth.

There are many people in the world of money, finances, and investments who have absolutely no idea what they're talking about. Most people in the money industry are just spouting off sales pitches like used-car salesmen. When you know you are ignorant in a subject, start educating yourself by finding an expert in the field or a book on the subject.

STUDY SESSION

Chapter Seven

LESSON 7: OVERCOMING OBSTACLES

Chapter Seven

LESSON 7: OVERCOMING OBSTACLES

Summary

The five main reasons financially literate people may still not develop abundant cash flow are: 1) fear, 2) cynicism, 3) laziness, 4) bad habits, and 5) arrogance. Let's look at each of those in detail.

Overcoming fear

No one likes to lose money. The only people who have never lost money investing are those who haven't done it.

Everyone has the fear of losing money; the difference is how you handle fear and losing. The primary difference between a rich person and a poor person is how they manage that fear.

It's OK to be fearful. One way to overcome that is to start early and allow the power of compound interest work for you. There is a staggering difference between a person who starts saving at age 20 versus age 30. But what if you don't have much time left to invest or want to retire early?

Rich dad recommends thinking like a Texan. Win big, lose big — it's your attitude toward that loss that matters. Texans are proud when they win and brag when they lose.

In Robert's life, winning has often followed losing. He has never met a rich person who hasn't lost money. But they don't let the fear of that take them out of the game.

The fall of the Alamo was a tragic military defeat, but Texans have turned that into a rallying cry — "Remember the Alamo!" — to spur them on to great victories.

Just like the Texans, don't bury your losses. Be inspired by them.

For winners, losing inspires them. For losers, losing defeats them. John D. Rockefeller, once said, "I always tried to turn every disaster into an opportunity."

Even Pearl Harbor was turned from one of America's greatest losses to what propelled the nation into becoming a world power.

Winners know that failure inspires winning — so why be afraid of failure, when it can lead to greatness? Understand that not being afraid of failure doesn't mean you can't still hate failing.

Most people play not to lose, when they need to be playing to win. And that's why so many people struggle financially. They might have a safe, sensible and balanced portfolio, but it's not a winning portfolio. They're playing not to lose.

A balanced portfolio isn't a bad thing. But it's not going to help you win big. It's not how successful investors play the game. You must be a little unbalanced in the beginning — but you must be focused. Put your eggs in a few baskets and focus.

Building your asset column doesn't take hard math, but it does take courage and the right attitude toward failure.

Overcoming cynicism

Whether it's our own self-doubt or the doubts of other people in our lives, often we allow that doubt to keep us from acting. We play it safe, and opportunities pass us by.

It often takes great courage to not let rumors and talk of doom and gloom affect your doubts and fears. But a savvy investor knows that the seemingly worst of times is actually the best of times to make money. When everyone else is too afraid to act, they pull the trigger and are rewarded.

Robert shared the example of a friend who was about to buy an investment condo for a great price but backed out at the last minute when a neighbor — who wasn't an investor — told him it was a bad deal. Had he stayed in it, he would've doubled his investment and started to get out of the Rat Race.

Robert holds a small portion of his assets in tax-lien certificates instead of CDs. Others tell him he shouldn't do this, but they're coming from a place of doubt. They've never done it, and they're telling someone who's doing it why they shouldn't. The lowest yield Robert looks for is 16 percent, but people who are filled with doubt are willing to accept a far lower return. Doubt is expensive.

Doubts and cynicism keep most people poor. Rich dad liked to say, "Cynics criticize, and winners analyze." Winners keep their eyes open and see opportunities everyone else missed.

Real estate is a powerful investment tool for anyone seeking financial independence or freedom. It is a unique investment tool. Yet every time Robert mentions real estate as a vehicle, he often hears, "I don't want to fix toilets." They focus on toilets, and it keeps them poor.

Many people stay out of the stock market because they don't want to lose money. But they're keeping themselves from making money by closing their minds to that investment vehicle.

Overcoming laziness

One of the most common forms of laziness is staying busy. Too busy to take care of your wealth, or your health, or your relationships.

What's the cure? A little greed. That can be hard to hear because so many of us were raised to see greed or desire as a bad thing.

Rather than saying, "I can't afford it," change your mindset to, "How can I afford it?" That opens the brain and forces it to think of solutions.

"I can't afford it" is a lie. The human spirit knows it can do anything. By saying you can't do something, you're creating a conflict between your spirit and your lazy mind. "How can I afford it?" creates a stronger mind and a dynamic spirit.

When Robert decided to exit the Rat Race, he asked, "How can I afford to never work again?" His mind started kicking out solutions, but the hardest part was fighting against the old dogma that tried to instill guilt to suppress such "greed."

Without that little greed, the desire to have something better, progress is not made. Our world progresses because we all desire a better life. New inventions are made because we desire something better. We go to school and study hard because we want something better.

Too much greed is bad, but a little can help spur you on.

Overcoming bad habits

To be successful, you must develop successful habits. Poor dad always paid everyone else first and himself last, but he rarely had any left over. Rich dad always paid himself first, even if he was short of money.

He knew that creditors and the government would make a big enough flap if he didn't pay them that it would motivate him to seek other forms of income to pay them. If he paid himself last, he wouldn't feel that kind of productive pressure. Forcing himself to think about how to come up with the extra income to pay the creditors made him fiscally stronger.

Overcoming arrogance

Rich dad said every time he had been arrogant, he had lost money because he thought that what he didn't know wasn't important.

Many people use arrogance to hide their own ignorance. Robert has found in discussions with accountants and other investors that they will try to bluster their way through the discussion, and it becomes clear they don't know what they're talking about.

Ignorance isn't a bad thing, if you react to your own ignorance by educating yourself by finding an expert in the field.

Left-hemisphere moment: Choose to analyze instead of criticize. Cynics criticize, but winners analyze and spot overlooked opportunities that others have missed.

Right-hemisphere moment: Overcome bad habits by putting new ones in place, such as paying yourself first instead of last.

Subconscious moment: Fear of failure keeps too many people out of the game. Instead, use failure as inspiration to succeed, as Texans do with the memory of the Alamo.

What Was Robert Saying

Now it's time to reflect. Ask yourself, "*What* is Robert saying in this quote?" And, "*Why* does he say that?" In this section you do not need to agree or disagree with Robert. The goal is to *understand* what Robert is saying.

Remember, this curriculum is designed to be cooperative and supportive. Two minds are better than one. If you do not understand what Robert is saying, do not shy away from it. Ask for help in understanding. Take the time discuss each quote until you understand it:

"The primary difference between a rich person and a poor person is how they manage fear."

"I've never met a golfer who has never lost a golf ball. I've never met people who have fallen in love who have never had their heart broken. And I've never met someone rich who has never lost money."

"For most people, the reason they don't win financially is because the pain of losing money is far greater than the joy of being rich."

"Rich dad knew that failure would only make him stronger and smarter. It's not that he wanted to lose. He just knew who he was and how he would take a loss. He would take a loss and make it a win."

"Texans don't bury their failures. They get inspired by them. They take their failures and turn them into rallying cries."

"We all get a little chicken when fear and doubt cloud our thoughts."

"Getting out of the Rat Race is technically easy. It doesn't take much education, but those doubts are cripplers for most people."

"'I can't afford it' causes sadness, a helplessness that leads to despondency and often depression. 'How can I afford it?' opens up possibilities, excitement, and dreams."

"If I pay myself first, I get financially stronger, both mentally and fiscally."

"There are many people in the world of money, finances, and investments who have absolutely no idea what they're talking about."

Additional Questions

Now it's time to take the stories in this chapter along with the understanding of what Robert was saying and apply them to you and your life. Ask yourself the questions below and discuss them with your study partner. Be honest with yourself and your partner. If you do not like some of the answers you are giving, ask yourself if you are willing to change and accept the challenge to change your thoughts and mindset:

1. How have you experienced the fear of failure in your life? Were you able to conquer that fear? How?
2. Rich dad recommended we have the attitude of Texans: Win big, but if you lose big, shout about it and use it as a rallying cry. What's the biggest challenge for you in taking on that attitude? Does it excite you or frighten you?
3. How do you handle the cynics in your life who try to discourage you from taking risks that you believe have a good chance of winning?
4. Have you avoided certain investment vehicles because of "I-don't-want-to" (such as, I don't invest in real estate because I don't want to fix toilets)? How might you react differently next time?
5. Do you agree with the statement that a little greed is the answer to curing laziness? Why or why not?
6. How has greed or desire driven you in your life?
7. Do you pay yourself first, or your bills? If you pay yourself last, what are steps you can take to change that?
8. Has arrogance ever cost you an opportunity? What did you learn from that?

9. What's an area of financial knowledge that you are ignorant in? What are some resources you could seek out to educate yourself on that topic?

Term definition:

STOP: A stop is simply a computer command that sells your stock automatically if the price begins to drop, helping to minimize your losses and maximize some gains.

NOTES

Chapter Eight

GETTING STARTED

There is gold everywhere.
Most people are not trained to see it.

I wish I could say acquiring wealth was easy for me, but it wasn't.

So in response to the question "How do I start?" I offer the thought process I go through on a day-to-day basis. It really is easy to find great deals. I promise you that. It's just like riding a bike. After a little wobbling, it's a piece of cake. But when it comes to money, it takes determination to get through the wobbling. That's a personal thing.

To find million-dollar "deals of a lifetime" requires us to call on our financial genius. I believe that each of us has a financial genius within us. The problem is that our financial genius lies asleep, waiting to be called upon. It lies asleep because our culture has educated us into believing that the love of money is the root of all evil. It has encouraged us to learn a profession so we can work for money, but failed to teach us how to have money work for us. It taught us not to worry about our financial future because our company or the government would take care of us when our working days are over. However, it is our children, educated in the same school system, who will end up paying for this absence of financial education. The message is still to work hard, earn money, and spend it, and when we run short, we can always borrow more.

Unfortunately, 90 percent of the Western world subscribes to the above dogma, simply because it's easier to find a job and work for money. If you are not one of the masses, I offer you the following 10 steps to awaken your financial genius. I simply offer you the steps

I have personally followed. If you want to follow some of them, great. If you don't, make up your own. Your financial genius is smart enough to develop its own list.

While in Peru, I asked a gold miner of 45 years how he was so confident about finding a gold mine. He replied, "There is gold everywhere. Most people are not trained to see it."

And I would say that is true. In real estate, I can go out and in a day come up with four or five great potential deals, while the average person will go out and find nothing, even looking in the same neighborhood. The reason is that they have not taken the time to develop their financial genius.

I offer you the following 10 steps as a process to develop your God-given powers, powers over which only you have control.

1. Find a reason greater than reality: the power of spirit

If you ask most people if they would like to be rich or financially free, they would say yes. But then reality sets in. The road seems too long with too many hills to climb. It's easier to just work for money and hand the excess over to your broker.

I once met a young woman who had dreams of swimming for the U.S. Olympic team. The reality was that she had to get up every morning at four o'clock to swim for three hours before going to school. She did not party with her friends on Saturday night. She had to study and keep her grades up, just like everyone else.

When I asked her what fueled her super-human ambition and sacrifice, she simply said, "I do it for myself and the people I love. It's love that gets me over the hurdles and sacrifices."

A reason or a purpose is a combination of "wants" and "don't wants." When people ask me what my reason for wanting to be rich is, I tell them that it is a combination of deep emotional "wants" and "don't wants."

I will list a few: first, the "don't wants," for they create the "wants." I don't want to work all my life. I don't want what my parents aspired for, which was job security and a house in the suburbs. I don't like being an employee. I hated that my dad always missed my football games because he was so busy working on his career. I hated it when my dad worked hard all his life and the government took most of what he worked for at his death. He could not even pass on what he worked so hard for when he died. The rich don't do that. They work hard and pass it on to their children.

Now the "wants." I want to be free to travel the world and live in the lifestyle I love. I want to be young when I do this. I want to simply be free. I want control over my time and my life. I want money to work for me.

Those are my deep-seated emotional reasons. What are yours? If they are not strong enough, then the reality of the road ahead may be greater than your reasons. I have lost money and been set back many times, but it was the deep emotional reasons that kept me standing up and going forward. I wanted to be free by age 40, but it took me until I was 47, with many learning experiences along the way.

As I said, I wish I could say it was easy. It wasn't. But it wasn't that hard either. I've learned that, without a strong reason or purpose, anything in life is hard.

IF YOU DO NOT HAVE A STRONG REASON, THERE IS NO SENSE READING FURTHER. IT WILL SOUND LIKE TOO MUCH WORK.

2. Make daily choices: the power of choice

Choice is the main reason people want to live in a free country. We want the power to choose.

Financially, with every dollar we get in our hands, we hold the power to choose our future: to be rich, poor, or middle class. Our spending habits reflect who we are. Poor people simply have poor spending habits. The benefit I had as a boy was that I loved playing Monopoly constantly. Nobody told me Monopoly was only for kids, so I just kept playing the game as an adult. I also had a rich dad who pointed out to me the difference between an asset and a liability. So a long time ago, as a little boy, I chose to be rich, and I knew that all I had to do was learn to acquire assets, real assets. My best friend, Mike, had an asset column handed to him, but he still had to choose to learn to keep it. Many rich families lose their assets in the next generation simply because there was no one trained to be a good steward over their assets.

Most people choose not to be rich. For 90 percent of the population, being rich is too much of a hassle. So they invent sayings that go: "I'm not interested in money." "I'll never be rich." "I don't have to worry. I'm still young." "When I make some money, then I'll think about my future." "My husband/wife handles the finances." The problem with those statements is that they rob the person who chooses to think such thoughts of two things: One is time, which is your most precious asset. The second is learning. Having no money should not be an excuse to not learn. But that is a choice we all make daily: the choice of what we do with our time, our money, and what we put in our heads. That is the power of choice. All of us have choice. I just choose to be rich, and I make that choice every day.

Invest first in education. In reality, the only real asset you have is your mind, the most powerful tool we have dominion over. Each of us has the choice of what we put in our brain once we're old enough. You can watch TV, read golf magazines, or go to ceramics class or a class on financial planning. You choose. Most people simply buy investments rather than first investing in learning about investing.

A friend of mine recently had her apartment burglarized. The thieves took her electronics and left all the books. And we all have that same choice. 90 percent of the population buys TV sets, and only about 10 percent buy business books.

So what do I do? I go to seminars. I like it when they are at least two days long because I like to immerse myself in a subject. In 1973, I was watching this guy on TV who was advertising a three-day seminar on how to buy real estate for nothing down. I spent $385 and that course has made me at least $2 million, if not more. But more importantly, it bought me life. I don't have to work for the rest of my life because of that one course. I go to at least two such courses every year.

I love CDs and audio books. The reason: I can easily review what I just heard. I was listening to an investor say something I completely disagreed with. Instead of becoming arrogant and critical, I simply listened to that five-minute stretch at least 20 times, maybe more. But suddenly, by keeping my mind open, I understood why he said what he said. It was like magic. I felt like I had a window into the mind of one of the greatest investors of our time. I gained tremendous insight into the vast resources of his education and experience.

The net result: I still have the old way I used to think, and I now have a new way of looking at the same problem or situation. I have two ways to analyze a problem or trend, and that is priceless. Today, I often say, "How would Donald Trump do this, or Warren Buffett or George Soros?" The only way I can access their vast mental power is to be humble enough to read or listen to what they have to say. Arrogant or critical people are often people with low self-esteem who are afraid of taking risks. That's because, if you learn something new, you are then required to make mistakes in order to fully understand what you have learned.

If you have read this far, arrogance is not one of your problems. Arrogant people rarely read or listen to experts. Why should they? They are the center of the universe.

There are so many "intelligent" people who argue or defend when a new idea clashes with the way they think. In this case, their so-called intelligence combined with arrogance equals ignorance. Each of us knows people who are highly educated, or believe they are smart, but their balance sheet paints a different picture. A truly intelligent person welcomes new ideas, for new ideas can add to the synergy of other accumulated ideas. Listening is more important than talking. If that were not true, God would not have given us two ears and only one mouth. Too many people think with their mouth instead of listening in order to absorb new ideas and possibilities. They argue instead of asking questions.

I take a long view on my wealth. I do not subscribe to the get-rich-quick mentality most lottery players or casino gamblers have. I may go in and out of stocks, but I am long on education. If you want to fly an airplane, I advise taking lessons first. I am always shocked at people who buy stocks or real estate, but never invest in their greatest asset, their mind. Just because you bought a house or two does not make you an expert at real estate.

3. Choose friends carefully: the power of association

First of all, I do not choose my friends by their financial statements. I have friends who have actually taken a vow of poverty as well as friends who earn millions every year. The point is that I learn from all of them.

Now, I will admit that there are people I have actually sought out because they had money. But I was not after their money; I was seeking their knowledge. In some cases, these people who had money have become dear friends. I've noticed that my friends with money talk about money. They don't do it to brag. They're interested in the subject. So I learn from them, and they learn from me. My friends who are in dire financial straits do not like talking about money, business, or investing. They often think it rude or unintellectual. So I also learn from my friends who struggle financially. I find out what not to do.

I have several friends who have generated over a billion dollars in their short lifetimes. The three of them report the same phenomenon: Their friends who have no money have never come to them to ask them how they did it. But they do come asking for one of two things, or both: a loan, or a job.

WARNING: Don't listen to poor or frightened people. I have such friends, and while I love them dearly, they are the Chicken Littles of life. To them, when it comes to money, especially investments, it's always, "The sky is falling! The sky is falling!" They can always tell you why something won't work. The problem is that people listen to them. But people who blindly accept doom-and-gloom information are also Chicken Littles. As that old saying goes, "Birds of a feather flock together."

If you watch business channels on TV, they often have a panel of so-called experts. One expert will say the market is going to crash, and the other will say it's going to boom. If you're smart, you listen to both. Keep your mind open, because both have valid points. Unfortunately, most poor people listen to Chicken Little.

I have had many close friends try to talk me out of a deal or an investment. Not long ago, a friend told me he was excited because he found a 6 percent certificate of deposit. I told him I earn 16 percent from the state government. The next day he sent me an article about why my investment was dangerous. I have received 16 percent for years now, and he still receives 6 percent.

I would say that one of the hardest things about wealth-building is to be true to yourself and to be willing to not go along with the crowd. This is because, in the market, it is usually the crowd that shows up late that is slaughtered. If a great deal is on the front page, it's too late in most instances. Look for a new deal. As we used to say as surfers: "There is always another wave." People who hurry and catch a wave late usually are the ones who wipe out.

Smart investors don't time the markets. If they miss a wave, they search for the next one and get themselves in position. This is hard for most investors because buying what is not popular is frightening. Timid investors are like sheep going along with the crowd. Or their greed gets them in when wise investors have already taken their profits and moved on. Wise investors buy an investment when it's not popular. They know their profits are made when they buy, not when they sell. They wait patiently. As I said, they do not time the market. Just like a surfer, they get in position for the next big swell.

It's all "insider trading." There are forms of insider trading that are illegal, and there are forms of insider trading that are legal. But either way, it's insider trading. The only distinction is: How far away from the inside are you? The reason you want to have rich friends is because that is where the money is made. It's made on information. You want to hear about the next boom, get in, and get out before the next bust. I'm not saying do it illegally, but the sooner you know, the better your chances are for profits with minimal risk. That is what friends are for. And that is financial intelligence.

4. **Master a formula and then learn a new one: the power of learning quickly**

In order to make bread, every baker follows a recipe, even if it's only held in their head. The same is true for making money.

Most of us have heard the saying, "You are what you eat." I have a different slant. I say, "You become what you study." In other words, be careful what you learn, because your mind is so powerful that you become what you put in your head. For example, if you study cooking, you then tend to cook. If you don't want to be a cook anymore, then you need to study something else.

When it comes to money, the masses generally have one basic formula they learned in school and it's this: Work for money. The predominant formula I see in the world is that every day millions of people get up, go to work, earn money, pay bills, balance checkbooks, buy some mutual funds, and go back to work. That is the basic formula, or recipe.

If you're tired of what you're doing, or you're not making enough, it's simply a case of changing the formula via which you make money.

Years ago, when I was 26, I took a weekend class called "How to Buy Real Estate Foreclosures." I learned a formula. The next trick was to have the discipline to actually put into action what I had learned. That is where most people stop. For three years, while working for Xerox, I spent my spare time learning to master the art of buying foreclosures. I've made several million dollars using that formula.

So after I mastered that formula, I went in search of other formulas. For many of the classes, I did not directly use the information I learned, but I always learned something new.

I have attended classes designed for derivative traders, commodity option traders, and chaologists. I was way out of my league, being in a room full of people with doctorates in nuclear physics and space science. Yet, I learned a lot that made my stock and real estate investing more meaningful and lucrative.

Most junior colleges and community colleges have classes on financial planning and buying traditional investments. They are good places to start, but I always search for a faster formula. That is why, on a fairly regular basis, I make more in a day than many people will make in their lifetime.

Another side note: In today's fast-changing world, it's not so much what you know anymore that counts, because often what you know is old. It is how fast you learn. That skill is priceless. It's priceless in finding faster formulas — recipes, if you will — for making dough. Working hard for money is an old formula born in the day of cavemen.

5. Pay yourself first: the power of self-discipline

If you cannot get control of yourself, do not try to get rich. It makes no sense to invest, make money, and blow it. It is the lack of self-discipline that causes most lottery winners to go broke soon after winning millions. It is the lack of self-discipline that causes people who get a raise to immediately go out and buy a new car or take a cruise.

It is difficult to say which of the 10 steps is the most important. But of all the steps, this step is probably the most difficult to master if it is not already a part of your makeup. I would venture to say that personal self-discipline is the number-one delineating factor between the rich, the poor, and the middle class.

Simply put, people who have low self-esteem and low tolerance for financial pressure can never be rich. As I have said, a lesson learned from my rich dad was that the world will push you around. The world pushes people around, not because other people are bullies, but because the individual lacks internal control and discipline. People who lack internal fortitude often become victims of those who have self-discipline.

In the entrepreneur classes I teach, I constantly remind people to not focus on their product, service, or widget, but to focus on developing management skills. The three most important management skills necessary to start your own business are management of:

1. Cash flow
2. People
3. Personal time

I would say the skills to manage these three apply to anything, not just entrepreneurs. The three matter in the way you live your life as an individual, or as part of a family, a business, a charitable organization, a city, or a nation.

Each of these skills is enhanced by the mastery of self-discipline. I do not take the saying, "Pay yourself first," lightly.

The statement, "Pay yourself first," comes from George Clason's book, *The Richest Man in Babylon.* Millions of copies have been sold. But while millions of people freely repeat that powerful statement, few follow the advice. As I said, financial literacy allows one to read numbers, and numbers tell the story. By looking at a person's income statement and balance sheet, I can readily see if people who spout the words, "Pay yourself first," actually practice what they preach.

A picture is worth a thousand words. So let's review the financial statements of people who pay themselves first against someone who doesn't.

Study the diagrams and see if you can pick up some distinctions. Again, it has to do with understanding cash flow, which tells the story. Most people look at the numbers and miss the story.

People Who Pay Themselves First

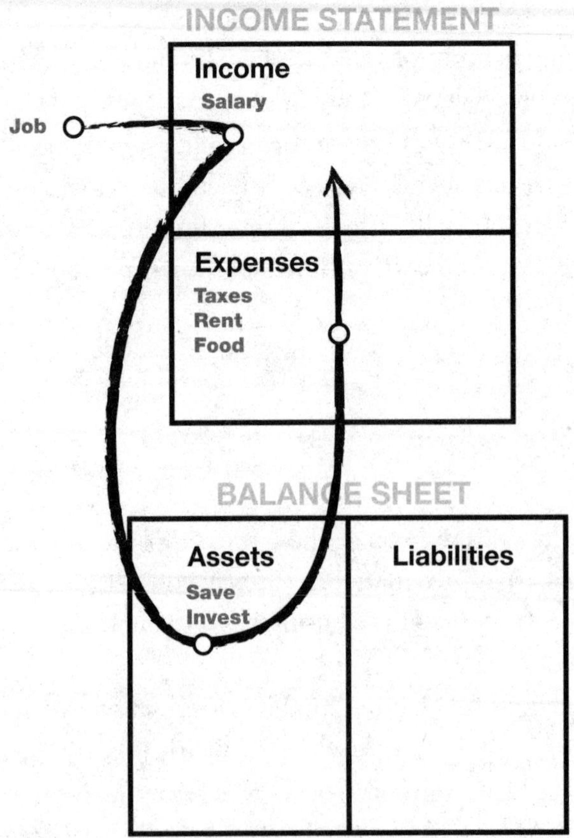

Do you see it? The diagram reflects the actions of individuals who choose to pay themselves first. Each month, they allocate money to their asset column before they pay their monthly expenses. Although millions of people have read Clason's book and understand the words, "Pay yourself first," in reality they pay themselves last.

Now I can hear the howls from those of you who sincerely believe in paying your bills first. And I can hear all the responsible people who pay their bills on time. I am not saying be irresponsible and not pay your bills. All I am saying is do what the book says, which is: Pay yourself first. And the previous diagram is the correct accounting picture of that action.

People Who Pay Everyone Else First

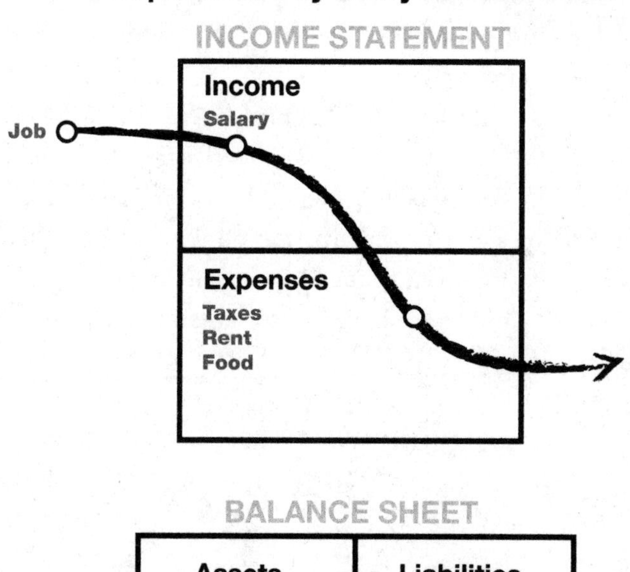

If you can truly begin to understand the power of cash flow, you will soon realize what is wrong with the previous diagram, or why 90 percent of people work hard all their lives and need government support like Social Security when they are no longer able to work.

Kim and I have had many bookkeepers, accountants, and bankers who have had a major problem with this way of looking at, "Pay yourself first." The reason is that these financial professionals actually do what the masses do: They pay themselves last.

There have been times in my life when, for whatever reason, cash flow was far less than my bills. I still paid myself first. My accountant and bookkeeper screamed in panic, "They're going to come after you. The IRS is going to put you in jail." "You're going to ruin your credit rating." "They'll cut off the electricity." I still paid myself first.

"Why?" you ask. Because that's what the story, *The Richest Man In Babylon,* was all about: the power of self-discipline and the power of internal fortitude. As my rich dad taught me the first month I worked for him, most people allow the world to push them around. A bill collector calls and you "pay or else." A sales clerk says, "Oh, just put it on your charge card." Your real estate agent tells you, "Go ahead. The government allows you a tax deduction on your home." That is what the book is really about — having the guts to go against the tide and get rich. You may not be weak, but when it comes to money, many people get wimpy.

I am not saying be irresponsible. The reason I don't have high credit-card debt, and doodad debt, is because I pay myself first. The reason I minimize my income is because I don't want to pay it to the government. That is why my income comes from my asset column, through a Nevada corporation. If I work for money, the government takes it.

Although I pay my bills last, I am financially astute enough to not get into a tough financial situation. I don't like consumer debt. I actually have liabilities that are higher than 99 percent of the population, but I don't pay for them. Other people pay for my liabilities. They're called tenants. So rule number one in paying yourself first is: Don't get into consumer debt in the first place. Although I pay my bills last, I set it up to have only small unimportant bills that are due.

When I occasionally come up short, I still pay myself first. I let the creditors and even the government scream. I like it when they get tough. Why? Because those guys do me a favor. They inspire me to go out and create more money. So I pay myself first, invest the money, and let the creditors yell. I generally pay them right away anyway. Kim and I have excellent credit. We just don't cave in to pressure and spend our savings or liquidate stocks to pay for consumer debt. That is not too financially intelligent.

To successfully pay yourself first, keep the following in mind:

1. Don't get into large debt positions that you have to pay for. Keep your expenses low. Build up assets first. Then buy the big house or nice car. Being stuck in the Rat Race is not intelligent.
2. When you come up short, let the pressure build and don't dip into your savings or investments. Use the pressure to inspire your financial genius to come up with new ways of making more money, and then pay your bills. You will have increased your ability to make more money as well as your financial intelligence.

So many times I have gotten into financial hot water and used my brain to create more income while staunchly defending the assets in my asset column. My bookkeeper has screamed and dived for cover, but I was like a good soldier defending the fort — Fort Assets.

Poor people have poor habits. A common bad habit is innocently called "dipping into savings." The rich know that savings are only used to create more money, not to pay bills.

I know that sounds tough, but as I said, if you're not tough inside, the world will always push you around anyway.

If you do not like financial pressure, then find a formula that works for you. A good one is to cut expenses, put your money in the bank, pay more than your fair share of income tax, buy safe mutual funds, and take the vow of the average. But this violates the pay-yourself-first rule.

This rule does not encourage self-sacrifice or financial abstinence. It doesn't mean pay yourself first and starve. Life was meant to be enjoyed.

If you call on your financial genius, you can have all the goodies of life, get rich, and pay bills. And that is financial intelligence.

6. Pay your brokers well: the power of good advice

Sometimes I see people posting a sign in front of their house that says, "For Sale by Owner." Or I see people on TV claiming to be "Discount Brokers."

My rich dad taught me to take the opposite approach. He believed in paying professionals well, and I have adopted that policy also. Today, I have expensive attorneys, accountants, real estate brokers, and stockbrokers. Why? Because if, and I do mean if, the people are professionals, their services should make you money. And the more money they make, the more money I make.

We live in the Information Age. Information is priceless. A good broker should provide you with information, as well as take the time to educate you. I have several brokers who do that for me. Some taught me when I had little or no money, and I am still with them today.

What I pay a broker is tiny in comparison with what kind of money I can make because of the information they provide. I love it when my real estate broker or stockbroker makes a lot of money because that usually means I made a lot of money.

A good broker saves me time, in addition to making me money — like when I bought the vacant land for $9,000 and sold it immediately for over $25,000 so I could buy my Porsche quicker.

A broker is my eyes and ears in the market. They're there every day so I do not have to be. I'd rather play golf.

People who sell their house on their own must not value their time much. Why would I want to save a few bucks when I could use that time to make more money or spend it with those I love? What I find funny is that so many poor and middle-class people insist on tipping restaurant help 15 to 20 percent, even for bad service, but complain about paying a broker three to seven percent. They enjoy tipping people in the expense column and stiffing people in the asset column. That is not financially intelligent.

Keep in mind that not all brokers are created equal. Unfortunately, most brokers are only salespeople. They sell, but they themselves own little or no real estate. There is a tremendous difference between a broker who sells houses and a broker who sells investments. The same is true for stock, bond, mutual fund, and insurance, brokers who call themselves financial planners.

When I interview any paid professional, I first find out how much property or stocks they personally own and what percentage they pay in taxes. And that applies to my tax attorney as well as my accountant. I have an accountant who minds his own business. His profession is accounting, but his business is real estate. I used to have an accountant who was a small-business accountant, but he had no real estate. I switched because we did not love the same business.

Find a broker who has your best interests at heart. Many brokers will spend the time educating you, and they could be the best asset you find. Just be fair, and most of them will be fair to you. If all you can think about is cutting their commissions, then why should they want to help you? It's just simple logic.

As I said earlier, one of the management skills is the management of people. Many people only manage people they feel smarter than and they have power over. Many middle managers remain middle managers, failing to get promoted, because they know how to work with people below them, but not with people above them. The real skill is to manage and reward the people who are smarter than you in some technical area. That is why companies have a board of directors. You should have one too. That is financial intelligence.

7. Be an Indian giver: the power of getting something for nothing

When the first European settlers came to America, they were taken aback by a cultural practice some American Indians had. For example, if a settler was cold, the Indian would give the person a blanket. Mistaking it for a gift, the settler was often offended when the Indian asked for it back.

The Indians also got upset when they realized the settlers did not want to give it back. That is where the term "Indian giver" came from, a simple cultural misunderstanding.

In the world of the asset column, being an Indian giver is vital to wealth. The sophisticated investor's first question is: "How fast do I get my money back?" They also want to know what they get for free, also called a "piece of the action." That is why the ROI, or return on investment, is so important.

For example, I found a small condominium that was in foreclosure a few blocks from where I lived. The bank wanted $60,000, and I submitted a bid for $50,000, which they took, simply because, along with my bid, was a cashier's check for $50,000. They realized I was serious. Most investors would say, "Aren't you tying up a lot of cash? Would it not be better to get a loan on it?" The answer is, "Not in this case." My investment company uses this condominium as a vacation rental in the winter months when the "snowbirds" come to Arizona. It rents for $2,500 a month for four months out of the year. For rental during the off-season, it rents for only $1,000 a month. I had my money back in about three years. Now I own this asset, which pumps money out for me, month in and month out.

The sophisticated investor's first question is: "How fast do I get my money back?"

The same is done with stocks. Frequently, my broker calls and recommends I move a sizable amount of money into the stock of a company that he feels is just about to make a move that will add value to the stock, like announcing a new product. I will move my money in for a week to a month while the stock moves up. Then I pull my initial dollar amount out, and stop worrying about the fluctuations of the market, because my initial money is back and ready to work on another asset. So my money goes in, and then it comes out, and I own an asset that was technically free.

True, I have lost money on many occasions, but I only play with money I can afford to lose. I would say, on an average 10 investments, I hit home runs on two or three, while five or six do nothing, and I lose on two or three. But I limit my losses to only the money I have in at that time.

People who hate risk put their money in the bank. In the long run, safe savings are better than no savings. But it takes a long time to get your money back and, in most instances, you don't get anything for free with it.

On every one of my investments, there must be an upside, something for free — like a condominium, a mini-storage, a piece of free land, a house, stock shares, or an office building. And there must be limited risk, or a low-risk idea. There are books devoted entirely to this subject, so I will not talk about it here. Ray Kroc, of McDonald's fame, sold hamburger franchises, not because he loved hamburgers, but because he wanted the real estate under the franchise for free.

So wise investors must look at more than ROI. They look at the assets they get for free once they get their money back. That is financial intelligence.

8. Use assets to buy luxuries: the power of focus

A friend's child has been developing a nasty habit of burning a hole in his pocket. Just 16, he wanted his own car. The excuse: "All his friends' parents gave their kids cars." The child wanted to go into his savings and use it for a down payment. That was when his father called me and then came to see me.

"Do you think I should let him do it, or should I just buy him a car?"

I answered, "It might relieve the pressure in the short term, but what have you taught him in the long term? Can you use this desire to own a car and inspire your son to learn something?" Suddenly the lights went on, and he hurried home.

Two months later I ran into my friend again. "Does your son have his new car?" I asked.

"No, he doesn't. But I gave him $3,000 for the car. I told him to use my money instead of his college money."

"Well, that's generous of you," I said.

"Not really. The money came with a hitch."

"So what was the hitch?" I asked.

"Well, first we played your *CASHFLOW* game. We then had a long discussion about the wise use of money. After that, I gave him a subscription to the *Wall Street Journal* and a few books on the stock market."

"Then what?" I asked. "What was the catch?"

"I told him the $3,000 was his, but he could not directly buy a car with it. He could use it to find a stockbroker and buy and sell stocks. Once he had made $6,000 with the $3,000, the money would be his for the car, and the $3,000 would go into his college fund."

"And what are the results?" I asked.

"Well, he got lucky early in his trading, but lost everything a few days later. Then he really got interested. Today, I would say he is down $2,000, but his interest is up. He has read all the books I bought him, and he's gone to the library to get more. He reads the *Wall Street Journal* voraciously, watching for indicators. He's got only $1,000 left, but his interest and learning are sky-high. He knows that if he loses that money, he walks for two more years. But he does not seem to care. He even seems uninterested in getting a car, because he's found a game that is more fun."

"What happens if he loses all the money?" I asked.

"We'll cross that bridge when we get to it. I'd rather have him lose everything now than wait till he's our age to risk losing everything. And besides, that is the best $3,000 I've ever spent on his education. What he is learning will serve him for life, and he seems to have gained a new respect for the power of money."

As I said earlier, if a person cannot master the power of self-discipline, it is best not to try to get rich. I say this because, although the process of developing cash flow from an asset column is easy in theory, what's hard is the mental fortitude to direct money to the correct use. Due to external temptations, it is much easier in today's consumer world to simply blow money out the expense column. With weak mental fortitude, that money flows into the paths of least resistance. That is the cause of poverty and financial struggle.

The following example illustrates the financial intelligence needed to direct money to make more money.

If we give 100 people $10,000 at the start of the year, I believe that at the end of the year:

- 80 would have nothing left. In fact, many would have created greater debt by making a down payment on a new car, refrigerator, electronics, or a holiday.
- 16 would have increased that $10,000 by 5-10 percent.
- Four would have increased it to $20,000 or into the millions.

We go to school to learn a profession so we can work for money. It is my opinion that it's just as important to learn how to have money work for you.

I love my luxuries as much as anyone else. The difference is I don't buy them on credit. It's the keep-up-with-the-Joneses trap. When I wanted to buy a Porsche, the easy road would have been to call my banker and get a loan. Instead of choosing to focus in the liability column, I chose to focus in the asset column.

As a habit, I use my desire to consume to inspire and motivate my financial genius to invest.

Too often today, we focus on borrowing money to get the things we want instead of focusing on creating money. One is easier in the short term, but harder in the long term. It's a bad habit that we as individuals, and as a nation, have gotten into. Remember, the easy road often becomes hard, and the hard road often becomes easy.

The earlier you can train yourself and those you love to be masters of money, the better. Money is a powerful force. Unfortunately, people use the power of money against themselves. If your financial intelligence is low, money will run all over you. It will be smarter than you. If money is smarter than you, you will work for it all your life.

To be the master of money, you need to be smarter than it. Then money will do as it is told. It will obey you. Instead of being a slave to it, you will be the master of it. That is financial intelligence.

9. Choose heroes: the power of myth

When I was a kid, I greatly admired Willie Mays, Hank Aaron, and Yogi Berra. They were my heroes, and I wanted to be just like them. I treasured their baseball cards, I knew their stats, the RBIs, the ERAs, their batting averages, how much they got paid, and how they came up from the minor leagues.

As a nine-year-old kid, when I stepped up to bat or played first base or catcher, I wasn't me. I pretended I was a famous baseball player. It's one of the most powerful ways we learn, and we often lose that as adults. We lose our heroes.

Today, I watch young kids playing basketball near my home. On the court they're not little Johnny. They're pretending to be their favorite basketball hero. Copying or emulating heroes is true power learning.

I have new heroes as I grow older. I have golf heroes and I copy their swings and do my best to read everything I can about them. I also have heroes such as Donald Trump, Warren Buffett, Peter Lynch, George Soros, and Jim Rogers. I know their stats just like I knew the ERAs and RBIs of my childhood baseball heroes. I follow what Warren Buffett invests in, and I read anything I can about his point of view on the market and how he chooses stocks. And I read about Donald Trump, trying to find out how he negotiates and puts deals together.

STILL TRUE TODAY...

NEW HEROES

At the top of my list of heroes today are David Stockman, Jim Rickards, George Gammon, and Thomas Sowell.

Just as I was not me when I was up to bat, when I'm in the market or I'm negotiating a deal, I am subconsciously acting with the bravado and confidence of Trump. Or when analyzing a trend, I look at it as though Warren Buffett were doing it. By having heroes, we tap into a tremendous source of raw genius.

But heroes do more than simply inspire us. Heroes make things look easy. Making it look easy convinces us to want to be just like them.

"If they can do it, so can I."

When it comes to investing, too many people make it sound hard. Instead, find heroes who make it look easy.

10. Teach and you shall receive: the power of giving

Both of my dads were teachers. My rich dad taught me a lesson I have carried all my life: the necessity of being charitable or giving. My educated dad gave a lot of his time and knowledge, but almost never gave away money.

He usually said that he would give when he had some extra money, but of course there was rarely any extra.

My rich dad gave money as well as education. He believed firmly in tithing. "If you want something, you first need to give," he would always say. When he was short of money, he gave money to his church or to his favorite charity.

If I could leave one single idea with you, it is that idea. Whenever you feel short or in need of something, give what you want first and it will come back in buckets. That is true for money, a smile, love, or friendship. I know it is often the last thing a person may want to do, but it has always worked for me. I trust that the principle of reciprocity is true, and I give what I want. I want money, so I give money, and it comes back in multiples. I want sales, so I help someone else sell something, and sales come to me. I want contacts, and I help someone else get contacts. Like magic, contacts come to me. I heard a saying years ago that went: "God does not need to receive, but humans need to give."

My rich dad would often say, "Poor people are more greedy than rich people." He would explain that if a person was rich, that person was providing something that other people wanted. In my life, whenever I have felt needy or short of money or short of help, I simply went out or found in my heart what I wanted, and decided to give it first. And when I gave, it always came back.

It reminds me of the story of the guy sitting with firewood in his arms on a cold, freezing night. He is yelling at the pot-bellied stove, "When you give me some heat, then I'll put some wood in you!" And when it comes to money, love, happiness, sales, and contacts, all one needs to remember is to give first.

Often just the process of thinking of what I want, and how I could give that to someone else, breaks free a torrent of bounty. Whenever I feel that people aren't smiling at me, I simply begin smiling and saying hello. Like magic, the next thing I know I'm surrounded by smiling people. It is true that your world is only a mirror of you.

So that's why I say, "Teach, and you shall receive." I have found that the more I teach those who want to learn, the more I learn. If you want to learn about money, teach it to someone else. A torrent of new ideas and finer distinctions will come in.

There are times when I have given and nothing has come back, or what I have received is not what I wanted. But upon closer inspection and soul searching, I was often giving to receive in those instances, instead of giving for the joy that giving itself brings.

My dad taught teachers, and he became a master teacher. My rich dad always taught young people his way of doing business. In retrospect, it was their generosity with what they knew that made them smarter. There are powers in this world that are much smarter than we are. You can get there on your own, but it's easier with the help of the powers that be. You only need to be generous with what you have.

STUDY SESSION

Chapter Eight

LESSON 8: GETTING STARTED

Chapter Eight

LESSON 8: **GETTING STARTED**

Summary

It is easy to find great deals. It's just like riding a bike. After a little wobbling, it's a piece of cake. But when it comes to money, it takes determination to get through the wobbling.

You must awaken the financial genius sleeping within in order to find these great deals. Our culture has told us that the love of money is the root of all evil, that we just need to find a profession and work hard and the government will take care of us when we're old. The message is still to work hard, earn money, and spend it, and when we run short, we can always borrow more — and that is why, for so many of us, our financial genius within is asleep.

But we must awaken that financial genius in order to find million-dollar deals of a lifetime. It's far easier to simply find a job and work for money, but that is not the path to wealth. If you want to go against the masses, Robert offers the thought process he goes through every day: 10 steps that you can use to awaken your financial genius. Follow the ones you want, or make up your own — your financial genius is up to the task.

1. Find a reason greater than reality: the power of spirit

Many want to be rich or financially free, but they turn away because the road seems too difficult to get there. Like a future Olympic swimmer who sacrifices time and social engagements in order to put in hours at the pool and studying hard, people need a strong, clear goal or reason in order to push through the obstacles.

A reason or a purpose is a combination of "wants" and "don't wants" — just like Robert's reason for wanting to be rich.

First, his "don't wants," as those create the wants. He didn't want to work his whole life. He didn't want job security and a house in the suburbs, unlike his parents. He didn't like being an employee and didn't want to stay busy working on his career — to the detriment of time with loved ones — only to have the government take most of what he worked when he dies, as happened with his father.

What does he want? Robert wants to be free to travel the world while young and live the lifestyle he loves. He wants to be free and have control over his time. He wants his money to work for him.

Like Robert, you must have strong enough emotional reasons behind wanting to be rich to sustain you through setbacks. Robert has lost money many times, but he kept going because his reason was strong enough. He wanted to be free by 40, but it took until he was 47.

Becoming rich wasn't easy, but it wasn't that hard, either. But if Robert hadn't had a strong reason behind it, it would've been incredibly difficult.

If you don't have a strong enough reason, Robert urges you to not read further as it will sound like too much work.

2. Make daily choices: the power of choice

You have the choice every day whether to be rich, poor or middle class. Your spending habits reflect who you are. The poor have poor spending habits.

Long ago, Robert chose to be rich. His friend Mike, after inheriting a healthy asset column, chose to learn how to keep it — which is not the default situation when rich families pass on their assets to the next generation.

Most people choose not to be rich. They tell themselves they're not interested in money, or that they're young and don't need to worry about it yet, or myriad other excuses.

But those excuses rob them of time (their most precious asset) and learning. We all have the choice every single day what we do with our time and money, and what we put in our heads.

Robert chooses to be rich and makes that choice every day.

He urges people to invest first in education, as our mind is our most powerful tool. Once we are old enough, we all have the choice of what to put in our brains. But instead of choosing to invest in learning, most people simply buy investments.

To continue his own learning, Robert goes to at least two seminars each year. In 1973, he went to a three-day seminar on buying real estate with nothing down. He spent $385 on the seminar, and it made him at least $2 million and enabled him not to have to work for the rest of his life.

Robert also likes CDs and audio books so he can review what he just heard. One time, he was listening to an investor he disagreed with, but after listening to the talk 20 times, he finally understood why the man said what he said.

He was able to grasp that because he kept his mind open, even though he originally disagreed with the investor. And now he has two ways of analyzing problems, which is priceless. Robert has chosen to read or listen to what a number of people think, from Donald Trump to George Soros, and that gives him access to their mental power.

When you learn something new, you often must make mistakes to fully understand it. Arrogant or critical people are afraid of taking risks, so they often won't listen to experts.

It is not a question of intelligence. Intelligent people can be ignorant if they combine their smarts with arrogance. A truly intelligent person, on the other hand, welcomes new ideas. New ideas can combine with already accumulated ones and result in something great.

Listen. Learn. Take a long view of wealth, not a get-rich-quick mentality. Invest in your greatest asset — your mind — before investing in stocks or real estate.

3. Choose friends carefully: the power of association

Robert learns from all of his friends, both those who have money — seeking their knowledge — and those who struggle financially. The latter group teaches him what not to do.

He says several of his friends who have generated more than a billion dollars all report the same phenomenon: Their friends who have no money never ask them how they did it. They just ask for a job or a loan, or both.

Robert warns us not to listen to poor or frightened people. To them, when it comes to investments, the sky is always falling. They can always tell you why something won't work.

Any panel of experts will have one who says the market is going to crash and another who says it is going to boom. Listen to both, because both have valid points.

Be true to yourself and don't go along with the crowd. This can be one of the hardest parts of wealth-building. The crowd usually shows up too late to a great deal. Instead, look for a new deal — a prospect that can be frightening.

Don't try to time the market. Get in position for the next wave. Wise investors buy an investment when it's not popular. They know their profits are made when they buy, not when they sell.

It's all about "insider trading" (the legal forms of it): being close to the inside, having rich friends who have information on where the money is being made. You want to hear about the next boom, get in, and then get out before the next bust. That's what friends are for, and that's what financial intelligence is.

4. Master a formula and then learn a new one: the power of learning quickly

Be careful what you learn, because you become what you put in your head.

The masses have one basic formula: Go to work, earn money, pay bills, balance checkbooks, buy some mutual funds, and go back to work.

If you're not making enough, you need to change the formula.

Years ago, Robert took a weekend class called "How to Buy Real Estate Foreclosures." He learned a formula and put it into action, making several million dollars in the process.

So he went in search of new formulas. He didn't always directly use the new information, but he was always learning.

Many colleges have classes on financial planning and buying traditional investments. It's a good place to start, but Robert is always searching for a faster formula. He says that's why he can make more in a day than many will make in their lifetime.

And it's not just about faster formulas, but learning new formulas faster.

5. Pay yourself first: the power of self-discipline

Of all the steps, self-discipline may be the most difficult to master if it's not part of your makeup. But personal self-discipline is the No. 1 delineating factor between the rich, the poor, and the middle class.

The world pushes you around and puts pressure on you. And if you don't have the tolerance for financial pressure, you'll never become rich.

Robert teaches students in his entrepreneurship classes that the three most important management skills to starting a business are management of cash flow, people, and personal time. These apply to everyone, not just entrepreneurs, and each of these skills is enhanced by the mastery of self-discipline.

Though many repeat the statement, "Pay yourself first," few have the discipline to put it into practice. Compare these two diagrams.

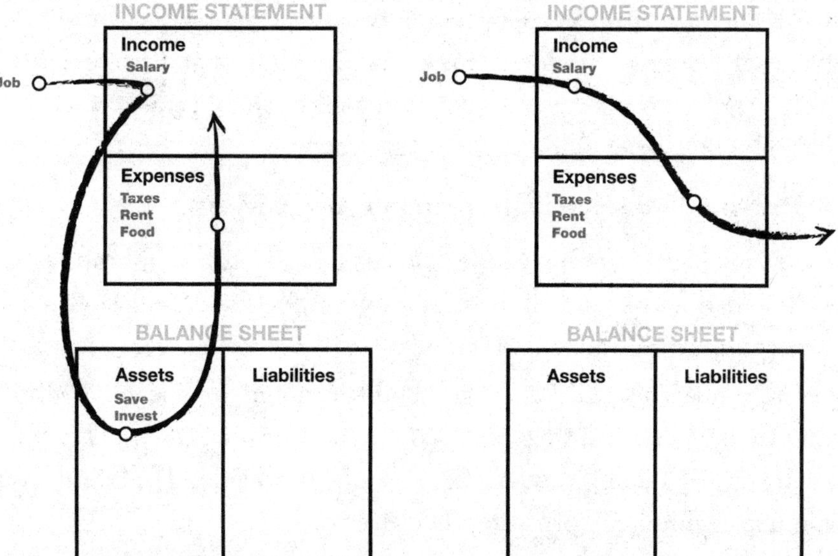

Follow the flow of money and see how these individuals pays themselves first (via investing in the asset column) before paying bills. This doesn't mean you don't pay your bills responsibly; it just means to pay yourself first.

You can see how paying someone else first leaves little or nothing left to invest in the assets column.

It has happened to Robert and to others that there were times when the cash flow wasn't enough to cover paying themselves first and the bills. They paid themselves first anyway. It takes internal fortitude when bill collectors are screaming, but it makes investing in assets a priority and leads to becoming rich.

To successfully pay yourself first:

1. Don't get into large debt positions that you have to pay for. Keep your expenses low. Build up assets first. Then buy the big house or nice car.
2. When you come up short, let the pressure build and don't dip into your savings or investments. Use the pressure to inspire your financial genius to come up with new ways of making more money, and then pay your bills. You will have increased your ability to make more money as well as your financial intelligence.

Remember that this rule does not encourage self-sacrifice or financial abstinence. It doesn't mean pay yourself first and starve. Life was meant to be enjoyed. If you call on your financial genius, you can have all the goodies of life, get rich, and pay bills.

6. Pay your brokers well: the power of good advice

Many people try to save a few dollars by using discount brokers or selling their house on their own. But not only do good professionals save you time, they make you money.

Information is priceless. A good broker should provide you with information, as well as making you money. Learn from them. In truth, what you pay them is tiny in comparison with what kind of money you can make with the information they give you.

Not all brokers are created equal. Interview them and find out how much property or investments they own. Find one who has your best interests at heart, and treat him or her fairly.

Companies have a board of directors because they know the value in having people smarter than they are around. You should have a board of directors, too.

7. Be an Indian giver: the power of getting something for nothing

The term "Indian giver" arose out of a cultural misunderstanding when the first European settlers came to the New World. If a settler was cold, an Indian would give the person a blanket. The settler mistook it for a gift and was offended when the Indian asked for it back. The Indian got upset when the settler did not want to give it back. It was a misunderstanding of what the transaction was.

In terms of investing and the asset column, it's key to be an Indian giver; that is, getting your initial investment back, and quickly.

One example is a condo Robert bought with cash for $50,000. It rented in the high season for $2,500 and for $1,000 the rest of the year. Within about three years, it paid for itself. In essence, Robert's original $50,000 was back in his pocket. And the asset continues to make him money, month in and month out.

Some don't like the risk and prefer to keep their money in a savings account, but there it's not making anything. And they also don't get anything for free with it.

For each of his investments, Robert says there must be an upside, something for free — like a mini storage, a piece of free land, stock shares, a house. And there must be limited risk.

8. Use assets to buy luxuries: the power of focus

Robert loves luxuries as much as the next person. But he won't borrow money for them, instead focusing on the asset column to create the money to buy those luxuries.

He shares the example of a friend whose teenage son wanted a car. Rather than buy it himself or have the son use his savings for it, the father gave him $3,000 and some information on the stock market and told him he couldn't use that $3,000 directly to buy a car. He had to invest it, and when he'd made $6,000, he could use that for a car and the original $3,000 would go into his college fund.

Although the son had yet to realize that profit, his interest and learning grew sky-high. He was learning a lesson that would serve him well in life: growing assets in order to pay for the things he wanted.

Developing cash flow from an asset column is easy in theory — what's hard is the mental fortitude to direct money to the correct use. Borrowing money is easy in the short term but harder in the long run.

9. Choose heroes: the power of myth

One of the most powerful ways we learn as children is pretending to be our heroes.

Robert continues that as an adult, though his heroes have changed. Instead of pretending to be Willie Mays at bat, he channels the bravado of Trump while negotiating a deal or the analytical skill of Warren Buffett when looking at trends.

By having heroes, we tap into their genius, and because they make it look easy, the inspire us to try.

10. Teach and you shall receive: the power of giving

Robert learned from rich dad to give money as well as education. He would say, "If you want something, you first need to give." When he was short of money, he gave to his church or to his favorite charity.

Whenever you feel in need of something — whether that's money, a smile, love or friendship — give it first and it will come back in buckets.

This is also true in teaching. The more you teach, the more you learn. Both of Robert's dads proved that.

Be generous with what you have, and make sure you are giving for the joy that giving itself brings, not giving simply to receive.

Left-hemisphere moment: Use self-discipline to pay yourself first, in order to protect the priority of growing your asset column.

Right-hemisphere moment: Keep your mind open to new ideas and new ways of doing things. These can add to the synergy of other accumulated ideas.

Subconscious moment: Harness the deep-seated emotional reasons you want to become rich. Make them strong. They will help you weather the obstacles along the road to wealth.

What Was Robert Saying

Now it's time to reflect. Ask yourself, "*What* is Robert saying in this quote?" And, "*Why* does he say that?" In this section you do not need to agree or disagree with Robert. The goal is to *understand* what Robert is saying.

Remember, this curriculum is designed to be cooperative and supportive. Two minds are better than one. If you do not understand what Robert is saying, do not shy away from it. Ask for help in understanding. Take the time discuss each quote until you understand it:

"There is gold everywhere. Most people are not trained to see it."

"Without a strong reason or purpose, anything in life is hard."

"Financially, with every dollar we get in our hands, we hold the power to choose our future: to be rich, poor, or middle class."

"Ninety percent of the population buys TV sets, and only about 10 percent buy business books."

"Each of us knows people who are highly educated, or believe they are smart, but their balance sheet paints a different picture."

"I've noticed that my friends with money talk about money. They don't do it to brag. They're interested in the subject. So I learn from them, and they learn from me."

"If you're tired of what you're doing, or you're not making enough, it's simply a case of changing the formula via which you make money."

"People who lack internal fortitude often become victims of those who have self-discipline."

"I have lost money on many occasions, but I only play with money I can afford to lose."

"The easy road often becomes hard, and the hard road often becomes easy."

Additional Questions

Now it's time to take the stories in this chapter along with the understanding of what Robert was saying and apply them to you and your life. Ask yourself the questions below and discuss them with your study partner. Be honest with yourself and your partner. If you do not like some of the answers you are giving, ask yourself if you are willing to change and accept the challenge to change your thoughts and mindset:

1. What are the reasons you want to become rich, your "wants" and "don't wants"? Would Robert think they are strong enough?
2. Are your spending habits reflecting the life you want? If not, what can you change?
3. What are you choosing to put in your head every day? When was the last time you took a seminar or read a business book (other than this one)?
4. What have you learned from your friends about finances, good or bad?
5. Would you say your self-discipline muscle is in shape or needs a good workout?
6. Do you have a board of directors — brokers and other professionals you pay well for their excellent information and ability to make you money — in your life?
7. Did you understand the concept put forth in step 7? If not, discuss it with your study partner.
8. The last time you purchased a luxury, how did you pay for it?
9. Who is your financial hero? How do you emulate this person in your actions?

Term definition:

ROI: Return on investment

NOTES

NOTES

Chapter Nine

STILL WANT MORE? HERE ARE SOME TO DOS

Many people may not be satisfied with my 10 steps. They see them more as philosophies than actions. I think understanding the philosophy is just as important as the action. There are many people who want to do instead of think, and then there are people who think but do not do. I would say that I am both. I love new ideas, and I love action.

So for those who want a to-do list on how to get started, I will share with you some of the things I do, in abbreviated form.

- *Stop doing what you're doing.* In other words, take a break and assess what is working and what is not working. The definition of insanity is doing the same thing over and over and expecting a different result. Stop doing what is not working, and look for something new.

- *Look for new ideas.* For new investing ideas, I go to bookstores and search for books on different and unique subjects. I call them formulas. I buy how-to books on formulas I know nothing about.

  For example, in the bookstore I found the book *The 16 Percent Solution* by Joel Moskowitz. I bought the book and read it and the next Thursday, I did exactly as the book said. Most people do not take action, or they let someone talk them out of whatever new formula they are studying. My neighbor told me why 16 percent would not work. I did not listen to him because he's never done it.

- *Find someone who has done what you want to do.* Take them to lunch and ask them for tips and tricks of the trade. As for 16 percent tax-lien certificates, I went to the county tax office and found the government employee who worked in that office. I found out that she, too, invested in the tax liens. Immediately, I invited her to lunch. She was thrilled to tell me everything she knew and how to do it. After lunch, she spent all afternoon showing me everything. By the next day, I found two great properties with her help that have been accruing interest at 16 percent ever since. It took a day to read the book, a day to take action, an hour for lunch, and a day to acquire two great deals.

- *Take classes, read, and attend seminars.* I search newspapers and the Internet for new and interesting classes, many of which are free or inexpensive. I also attend and pay for expensive seminars on what I want to learn. I am wealthy and free from needing a job simply because of the courses I took. I have friends who did not take those classes who told me I was wasting my money, and yet they're still at the same job.

- *Make lots of offers.* When I want a piece of real estate, I look at many properties and generally write an offer. If you don't know what the right offer is, neither do I. That is the job of the real estate agent. They make the offers. I do as little work as possible.

A friend wanted me to show her how to buy apartment houses. So one Saturday she, her agent, and I went and looked at six apartment houses. Four were dogs, but two were good. I said to write offers on all six, offering half of what the owners asked for. She and the agent nearly had heart attacks. They thought it was rude, and would offend the sellers, but I really don't think the agent wanted to work that hard. So they did nothing and went on looking for a better deal.

No offers were ever made, and that person is still looking for the right deal at the right price. Well, you don't know what the right price is until you have a second party who wants to deal. Most sellers ask too much. It is rare that a seller asks a price that is less than something is worth.

Moral of the story: Make offers. People who are not investors have no idea what it feels like to try to sell something. I have had a piece of real estate that I wanted to sell for months. I would have welcomed any offer. They could have offered me 10 pigs, and I would have been happy — not at the offer, but just because someone was interested. I would have countered, maybe for a pig farm in exchange. But that's how the game works. The game of buying and selling is fun. Keep that in mind. It's fun and only a game. Make offers. Someone might say yes.

I always make offers with escape clauses. In real estate, I make an offer with language that details "subject-to" contingencies, such as the approval of a business partner. Never specify who the business partner is. Most people don't know that my partner is my cat. If they accept the offer, and I don't want the deal, I call home and speak to my cat. I make this ridiculous statement to illustrate how absurdly easy and simple the game is. So many people make things too difficult and take it too seriously.

Finding a good deal, the right business, the right people, the right investors, or whatever is just like dating. You must go to the market and talk to a lot of people, make a lot of offers, counteroffers, negotiate, reject, and accept. I know single people who sit at home and wait for the phone to ring, but it's better to go to the market, even if it's only the supermarket. Search, offer, reject, negotiate, and accept are all parts of the process of almost everything in life.

- *Jog, walk, or drive a certain area once a month for 10 minutes.* I have found some of my best real estate investments doing this. I will jog a certain neighborhood for a year and look for change. For there to be profit in a deal, there must be two elements: a bargain and change. There are lots of bargains, but it's change that turns a bargain into a profitable opportunity. So when I jog, I jog a neighborhood I might like to invest in. It is the repetition that causes me to notice slight differences. I notice real estate signs that are up for a long time. That means the seller might be more agreeable to deal. I watch for moving trucks going in or out. I stop and talk to the drivers. I talk to the postal carriers. It's amazing how much information they acquire about an area. I find a bad area, especially an area that the news has scared everyone away from. I drive it for sometimes a year waiting for signs of some thing changing for the better. I talk to retailers, especially new ones, and find out why they're moving in. It takes only a few minutes a month, and I do it while doing something else, like exercising, or going to and from the store.

- *Shop for bargains in all markets.* Consumers will always be poor. When the supermarket has a sale, say on toilet paper, the consumer runs in and stocks up. But when the housing or stock market has a sale, most often called a crash or correction, the same consumer often runs away from it. When the supermarket raises its prices, the consumer shops somewhere else. But when housing or the stock market raise their prices, the same consumer often rushes in and starts buying. Always remember: Profits are made in the buying, not in the selling.

- *Look in the right places.* A neighbor bought a condominium for $100,000. I bought the identical condo next door for $50,000. He told me he's waiting for the price to go up. I told him that profit is made when you buy, not when you sell. He shopped with a real estate broker who owns no property of her own. I shopped at the foreclosure auction. I paid $500 for a class on how to do this.

  My neighbor thought that the $500 for a real estate investment class was too expensive. He said he could not afford the money, or the time. So he waits for the price to go up.

- *Look for people who want to buy first. Then look for someone who wants to sell.* A friend was looking for a certain piece of land. He had the money but did not have the time. I found a large piece of land, larger than what my friend wanted to buy, tied it up with an option, called my friend, and he said he wanted a piece of it. So I sold the piece to him and then bought the land. I kept the remaining land as mine for free. Moral of the story:

Buy the pie, and cut it in pieces. Most people look for what they can afford, so they look too small. They buy only a piece of the pie, so they end up paying more for less. Small thinkers don't get the big breaks. If you want to get richer, think big.

- *Think big.* Retailers love giving volume discounts, simply because most business people love big spenders. So even if you're small, you can always think big. When my company was in the market for computers, I called several friends and asked them if they were ready to buy also. We then went to different dealers and negotiated a great deal because we wanted to buy so many. I have done the same with stocks. Small people remain small because they think small, act alone, or don't act all.

- *Learn from history.* All the big companies on the stock exchange started out as small companies. Colonel Sanders did not get rich until after he lost everything in his 60s. Bill Gates was one of the richest men in the world before he was thirty.

- *Action always beats inaction.*

These are just a few of the things I have done and continue to do to recognize opportunities. The important words are "have done" and "do." As repeated many times throughout the book, you must take action before you can receive the financial rewards. Act now!

STUDY SESSION

Chapter Nine

STILL WANT MORE? HERE ARE SOME TO DOS

Chapter Nine

STILL WANT MORE?

HERE ARE SOME TO DOS

Summary

For those who want a to-do list of actions to tackle, here are some of the things Robert does, in abbreviated form.

- *Stop doing what you're doing.* Take a break and assess what is working and what is not working.
- *Look for new ideas.* Go to bookstores and search for books on different and unique subjects. The book *The 16 Percent Solution* by Joel Moskowitz taught Robert something new and spurred him to action.
- *Find someone who has done what you want to do.* Take them to lunch and ask them for tips and tricks of the trade.
- *Take classes, read, and attend seminars.* Robert searches newspapers and the Internet for new and interesting classes.
- *Make lots of offers.* You don't know what the right price is until you have a second party who wants to deal. Most sellers ask too much. It is rare that a seller asks a price that is less than something is worth. It's fun and only a game. Make offers. Someone might say yes. (And make offers with escape clauses.)
- *Jog, walk, or drive a certain area once a month for 10 minutes.* Robert has found some of his best real estate investments doing this. He will jog a certain neighborhood for a year and look for change. For there to be profit in a deal, there must be two elements: a bargain and change. There are lots of bargains, but it's change that turns a bargain into a profitable opportunity. It takes only a few minutes a month, and he does it while doing something else, like exercising, or going to and from the store.
- *Shop for bargains in all markets.* Consumers will always be poor. When the supermarket has a sale, say on toilet paper, the consumer runs in and stocks up. But when the housing or stock

market has a sale, most often called a crash or correction, the same consumer often runs away from it. Remember: Profits are made in the buying, not in the selling.

- *Look in the right places.* A neighbor bought a condominium for $100,000. Robert bought the identical condo next door for $50,000. He told Robert he was waiting for the price to go up. Robert told him that profit is made when you buy, not when you sell. He shopped with a real estate broker who owns no property of her own. Robert shopped at the foreclosure auction, having paid $500 for a class on how to do this.

His neighbor thought that the $500 for a real estate investment class was too expensive. He said he could not afford the money, or the time. So he waits for the price to go up.

- *Look for people who want to buy first. Then look for someone who wants to sell.* Buy the pie, and cut it in pieces. Most people look for what they can afford, so they look too small. They buy only a piece of the pie, so they end up paying more for less. Small thinkers don't get the big breaks. If you want to get richer, think big.
- *Think big.* Retailers love giving volume discounts, simply because most business people love big spenders. Even if you're small, you can band together with others to negotiate for a great deal because you want to buy so many of a certain object. Small people remain small because they think small, act alone, or don't act all.
- *Learn from history.* All the big companies on the stock exchange started out as small companies. Colonel Sanders did not get rich until after he lost everything in his 60s. Bill Gates was one of the richest men in the world before he was 30.
- *Action always beats inaction.* You must take action before you can receive the financial rewards. Act now!

Additional Questions

Now it's time to take the stories in this chapter along with the understanding of what Robert was saying and apply them to you and your life. Ask yourself the questions below and discuss them with your study partner. Be honest with yourself and your partner. If you do not like some of the answers you are giving, ask yourself if you are willing to change and accept the challenge to change your thoughts and mindset:

1. Does this to-do list inspire you or intimidate you?
2. What actions are you already taking from the above list?
3. After reading the list, which item jumps out at you as something you hadn't considered or fully utilized? What steps can you take to put it into action in your life?

NOTES

FINAL THOUGHTS

I would like to share some final thoughts with you.

The main reason I wrote this book, and the reason it has remained a bestseller since 2000, was to share insights into how increased financial intelligence can be used to solve many of life's common problems. Without financial training, we all too often use the standard formulas to get through life: Work hard, save, borrow, and pay excessive taxes. Today, more than ever, we need better information.

I use the following story as an example of a financial problem that confronts many young families today. How do you afford a good education for your children and provide for your own retirement? It requires using financial intelligence instead of hard work.

A friend of mine was griping one day about how hard it was to save money for his four children's college educations. He was putting $300 away in a college fund each month and had so far accumulated only about $12,000. He had about 12 more years to save for college since his oldest child was then six years old.

At the time, the real estate market in Phoenix was terrible. People were giving houses away. I suggested to my friend that he buy a house with some of the money in his college fund. The idea intrigued him, and we began to discuss the possibility. His primary concern was that he did not have credit with the bank to buy another house since he was so over-extended. I assured him that there were other ways to finance a property rather than through the bank.

We looked for a house for two weeks, a house that would fit all our criteria. There were plenty to choose from so shopping was fun. Finally, we found a three-bedroom, two-bath home in a prime neighborhood. The owner had been downsized and needed to sell that day because he and his family were moving to California where another job waited. The owner wanted $102,000, but we offered only $79,000. He took it immediately and agreed to carry back the loan with a 10 percent down payment. All my friend had to come up with was $7,900. As soon as the owner moved, my friend put the house up for rent. After all expenses were paid, including the mortgage, he put about $125 in his pocket each month.

His plan was to keep the house for 12 years and let the mortgage get paid down faster by applying the extra $125 to the principal each month. We figured that in 12 years, a large portion of the mortgage would be paid off and he could possibly be clearing $800 a month by the time his first child went to college. He could also sell the house if it had appreciated in value.

Three years later, the real estate market greatly improved in Phoenix and he was offered $156,000 for the same house by the tenant who lived in it. Again, he asked me what I thought. I advised that he sell it, using a 1031 tax-deferred exchange.

Suddenly, he had nearly $80,000 to operate with. I called another friend in Austin, Texas, who then moved this tax-deferred capital gain into a mini-storage facility. Within three months, he began receiving checks for a little less than a $1,000 a month which he then poured back into the college fund.

A couple of years later, the mini-warehouse sold, and he received a check for nearly $330,000 as proceeds from the sale. He rolled those funds into a new project that would now generate over $3,000 a month in income, again, going into the college fund. He is now very confident that his goal will be met easily.

It only took $7,900 to start and a little financial intelligence. His children will be able to afford the education they want, and he will then use the underlying asset, wrapped in his legal entity, to pay for his retirement. As a result of this successful investment strategy, he will be able to retire early.

Thank you for reading this book. I hope it has provided some insights into utilizing the power of money to work for you. Today, we need greater financial intelligence to simply survive. The idea that "it takes money to make money" is the thinking of financially unsophisticated people. It does not mean that they're not intelligent. They have simply not learned the science of money making money.

Money is only an idea. If you want more money, simply change your thinking. Every self-made person started small with an idea, and then turned it into something big. The same applies to investing. It takes only a few dollars to start and grow it into something big. I meet so many people who spend their lives chasing the big deal, or trying to amass a lot of money to get into a big deal, but to me that is foolish. Too often I have seen unsophisticated investors put their large nest egg into one deal and lose most of it rapidly. They may have been good workers, but they were not good investors.

Education and wisdom about money are important. Start early. Buy a book. Go to a seminar. Practice. Start small. I turned $5,000 cash into a one-million-dollar asset producing $5,000 a month cash flow in less than six years. But I started learning as a kid. I encourage you to learn, because it's not that hard. In fact, it's pretty easy once you get the hang of it.

I think I have made my message clear. It's what is in your head that determines what is in your hands. Money is only an idea. There is a great book called *Think and Grow Rich.* The title is not *Work Hard and Grow Rich.* Learn to have money work hard for you, and your life will be easier and happier. Today, don't play it safe. Play it smart.

The Three Incomes

In the world of accounting, there are three different types of income:

1. Ordinary earned
2. Portfolio
3. Passive

When my poor dad said to me, “Go to school, get good grades, and find a safe secure job,” he was recommending I work for earned income. When my rich dad said, “The rich don’t work for money. They have their money work for them,” he was talking about passive income and portfolio income. Passive income, in most cases, is income derived from real estate investments. Portfolio income is income derived from paper assets such as stocks and bonds. Portfolio income is the income that makes Bill Gates the richest man in the world, not earned income.

Rich dad used to say, “The key to becoming wealthy is the ability to convert earned income into passive income or portfolio income as quickly as possible.” He would say, “Taxes are highest on earned income. The least-taxed income is passive income. That is another reason why you want your money working hard for you. The government taxes the income you work hard for more than the income your money works hard for.”

In my second book, *Rich Dad’s CASHFLOW Quadrant,* I explain the four different types of people who make up the world of business. They are E (Employee), S (Self-employed), B (Business Owner), and I (Investor). Most people go to school to learn to be an E or an S. The *CASHFLOW Quadrant* is written about the core differences of these four types and how people can change their quadrant. In fact, most of our products are created for people in the B and I quadrants.

In *Rich Dad’s Guide to Investing,* book number three in the Rich Dad series, I go into more detail on the importance of converting earned income into passive and portfolio income. Rich dad used to say, “All a real investor does is convert earned income into passive and portfolio income.

FAST FORWARD... TO TODAY

MISSION: FINANCIAL EDUCATION

New books in the Rich Dad series that you may enjoy:

FAKE

Second Chance

Why the Rich Are Getting Richer

More Important Than Money

If you know what you're doing, investing is not risky. It's just common sense."

The Key to Financial Freedom

The key to financial freedom and great wealth is a person's ability to convert earned income into passive and/or portfolio income. My rich dad spent a lot of time teaching Mike and me this skill. Having this ability is the reason Kim and I are financially free, never needing to work again. We continue to work because we choose to. Today we own a real estate investment company for passive income and participate in private placements and initial public offerings of stock for portfolio income.

We also went back to work to build a financial-education company so that we can continue to create and publish books and games. All of our educational products are created to teach the same skills my rich dad taught me, the skills of converting earned income into passive and portfolio income.

The games we create are important because they teach what books cannot teach. For example, you could never learn to ride a bicycle by only reading a book. Our *CASHFLOW* games for adults and *CASHFLOW for Kids* game are designed to teach players the basic investment skills of converting earned income into passive and portfolio income. They also teach the principles of accounting and financial literacy. These games are the only educational products in the world that teach people all of these skills simultaneously.

You can play CASHFLOW on the web at www.richdad.com and learn to convert earned income into passive and/or portfolio income

CASHFLOW 202 is the advanced version of *CASHFLOW 101* and requires the game board from 101, as well as a full understanding of 101, before it can be played. *CASHFLOW 101* and *CASHFLOW for Kids* teach the principles of fundamental investing. *CASHFLOW 202* teaches the principles of technical investing. Technical investing involves advanced trading techniques such as short selling, call options, put options, and straddles. A person who understands these advanced techniques is able to make money when the market goes up, as well as when the market comes down. As my rich dad would say, "A real investor makes money in an up market and a down market. That is why they make so much money." One of the reasons they make more money is simply because they have more self-confidence. Rich dad would say, "They have more self-confidence because they are less afraid of losing." In other words, the average investor does not make as much money because they are so afraid of losing money. The average investor does not know how to protect themselves from losses, and that is what *CASHFLOW 202* teaches.

Average investors think investing is risky because they have not been formally trained to be professional investors. As Warren Buffett, America's richest investor says, "Risk comes from not knowing what you're doing." My board games teach the simple basics of fundamental investing and technical investing while people are having fun.

I occasionally hear someone say, "Your educational games are expensive," which poses the question of ROI, the return on investment, or the value returned for the price paid. I nod my head and reply, "Yes, they may be expensive, especially when compared to entertainment board games. But my games are not as expensive as a college education, working hard all your life for earned income, paying excessive taxes, and then living in terror of losing all of your money in the investment markets."

When someone walks away mumbling about the price, I can hear my rich dad saying, "If you want to be rich, you must know what kind of income to work hard for, how to keep it, and how to protect it from loss. That is the key to great wealth." Rich dad would also say, "If you do not understand the differences in those three incomes and do not learn the skills on how to acquire and protect those incomes, you will probably spend your life earning less than you could and working harder than you should."

My poor dad thought a good education, a good job, and years of hard work were all you needed to be successful. My rich dad also thought a good education was important. But to him it was also important that

Mike and I know the differences in the three incomes and what kind of income to work hard for. To him, that was basic financial education. Knowing the differences in the three incomes and learning the investment skills of how to acquire the different incomes is basic education for anyone who strives to acquire great wealth and achieve financial freedom — a special kind of freedom that only a few will ever know. As rich dad states in lesson number one, "The rich do not work for money. They know how to have money work hard for them."

Rich dad said, "Ordinary earned income is money you work for, and passive and portfolio income is money working for you." Knowing that little difference has been significant in my life. Or, as Robert Frost ends his poem, "And that has made all the difference."

Take Action!

All of you were given two great gifts: your mind and your time. It is up to you to do what you please with both. With each dollar bill that enters your hand, you, and only you, have the power to determine your destiny. Spend it foolishly, and you choose to be poor. Spend it on liabilities, and you join the middle class. Invest it in your mind and learn how to acquire assets, and you will be choosing wealth as your goal and your future. The choice is yours, and only yours. Every day with every dollar, you decide to be rich, poor, or middle class.

Choose to share this knowledge with your children, and you choose to prepare them for the world that awaits. No one else will.

You and your children's future will be determined by choices you make today, not tomorrow.

I wish you great wealth and much happiness with this fabulous gift called life.

– Robert Kiyosaki

STUDY SESSION

FINAL THOUGHTS

Summary

The main reason Robert wrote this book was to share insights into how increased financial intelligence can be used to solve many of life's common problems.

He shares an example of how a friend, worried about being able to save enough money for his children's college education, was able to turn an initial $7,900 down payment in a house in Phoenix into a project a few years later that generates $3,000 a month in income. It took just a little money to start, and financial intelligence.

Education and wisdom about money are important. Start early. Buy a book. Go to a seminar. Practice. Start small. It's what is in your head that determines what is in your hands. Money is only an idea.

In the world of accounting, there are three kinds of income: ordinary earned, portfolio, and passive. Passive income, in most cases, is income derived from real estate investments. Portfolio income is income derived from paper assets such as stocks and bonds.

Taxes are highest on earned income and lowest on passive. As rich dad would say, "The government taxes the income you work hard for more than the income your money works hard for."

In Robert's second book, *Rich Dad's CASHFLOW Quadrant®*, he explains the four different types of people who make up the world of business — E (Employee), S (Self-employed), B (Business Owner), and I (Investor) — and how people can change their quadrant.

In *Rich Dad's Guide to Investing,* book No. 3 in the Rich Dad series, Robert goes into more detail on the importance of converting earned income into passive and portfolio income.

Robert and Kim's board games continue this education, as well, teaching what books cannot. The *CASHFLOW®* games for adults and *CASHFLOW for Kids* game are designed to teach players the basic investment skills of converting earned income into passive and portfolio income. They also teach the principles of accounting and financial literacy.

Knowing the differences in the three incomes and learning the investment skills of how to acquire the different incomes is basic education for anyone who strives to acquire great wealth and achieve financial freedom — a special kind of freedom that only a few will ever know.

All of you were given two great gifts: your mind and your time. It is up to you to do what you please with both. With each dollar bill that enters your hand, you, and only you, have the power to determine your destiny. Every day with every dollar, you decide to be rich, poor, or middle class. Choose to share this knowledge with your children, and you choose to prepare them for the world that awaits.

Additional Questions

1. What's the first thing you're going to do when you finish this study guide?
2. What are you waiting for?

NOTES

Acknowledgments

How does a person say "thank you" when there are so many people to thank? Obviously this book is a thank you to my two fathers, who were powerful role models, and to my mom, who taught me love and kindness.

The person most responsible for this book becoming a reality is Kim. She has been a strong and steady force on this journey... a treasured partner in business and in life.

About The Author
Robert Kiyosaki

Best known as the author of *Rich Dad Poor Dad* — the #1 personal finance book of all time — Robert Kiyosaki has challenged and changed the way tens of millions of people around the world think about money. He is an entrepreneur, educator, and investor who believes the world needs more entrepreneurs who will create jobs.

With perspectives on money and investing that often contradict conventional wisdom, Robert has earned an international reputation for straight talk, irreverence, and courage and has become a passionate and outspoken advocate for financial education.

Robert and Kim Kiyosaki are founders of The Rich Dad Company, a financial education company, and creators of the *CASHFLOW*® games.

Robert has been heralded as a visionary who has a gift for simplifying complex concepts — ideas related to money, investing, finance, and economics — and has shared his personal journey to financial freedom in ways that resonate with audiences of all ages and backgrounds. His core principles and messages — like "your house is not an asset" and "invest for cash flow" and "savers are losers" — ignited a firestorm of criticism and ridicule. Over the past two decades, his teachings and philosophies have played out on the world economic stage in ways that have been both unsettling and prophetic.

His point of view is that "old" advice — go to college, get a good job, save money, get out of debt, invest for the long term, and diversify — has become obsolete advice in today's fast-paced Information Age. His Rich Dad philosophies and messages challenge the status quo. His teachings encourage people to become financially educated and to take an active role in investing for their future.

The author of 25 books, including the international blockbuster *Rich Dad Poor Dad*, Robert has been a featured guest with media outlets in every corner of the world — from CNN, the BBC, Fox News, Al Jazeera, GBTV and PBS, to *Larry King Live*, *Oprah*, *People*, *Investors Business Daily*, *Sydney Morning Herald*, *The Doctors*, *Straits Times*, *Bloomberg*, *NPR*, *USA TODAY*, and hundreds of others — and his books have topped international bestsellers lists for two decades. He continues to teach and inspire audiences around the world.

His most recent books include *Unfair Advantage: The Power of Financial Education*, *Midas Touch*, the second book he has co-authored with Donald Trump, *Why "A" Students Work for "C" Students*, *8 Lessons in Military Leadership for Entrepreneurs*, *Second Chance*, *More Important Than Money*, *Why the Rich Are Getting Richer*, and *FAKE*.

To learn more, visit RichDad.com

Bonus

Book Excerpt

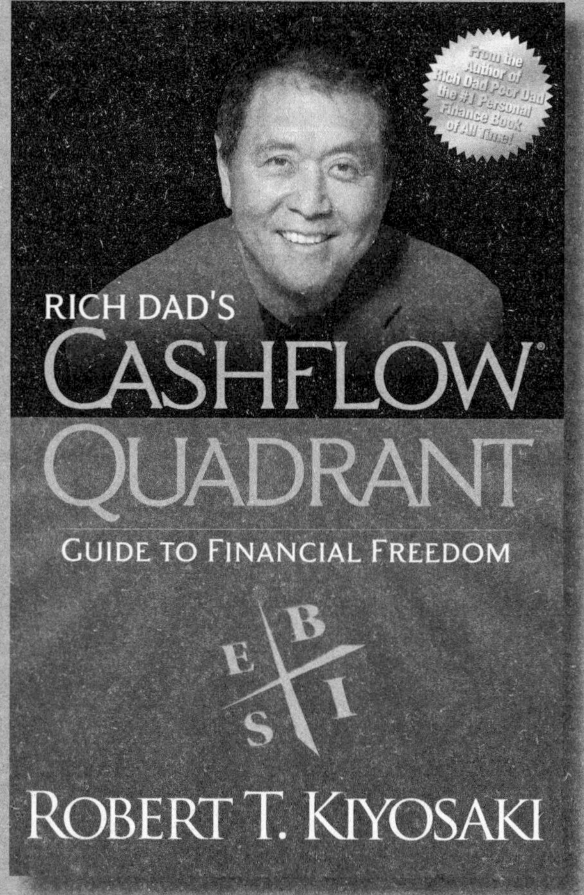

Editor's Note

The Times They Are A-Changin'

There have been many changes in our economy and the investing landscape since *Rich Dad Poor Dad* was first published in 1997. Two decades ago, Robert Kiyosaki challenged conventional wisdom with his bold statement that "your house is not an asset." His contrarian views on money and investing were met with skepticism, criticism, and outrage.

In 2002, Robert's book, *Rich Dad's Prophecy,* advised that we prepare for an upcoming financial market crash. In 2006, Robert joined forces with Donald Trump to write *Why We Want You To Be Rich,* a book inspired by their concern for the shrinking middle class in America.

Robert continues to be a passionate advocate for the importance and power of financial education. Today, in the wake of the subprime fiasco, record home foreclosures, and a global economic meltdown that is still raging, his words seem not only prophetic, but enlightened. Many skeptics have become believers.

In reviewing *Rich Dad's CASHFLOW Quadrant,* Robert realized two things: that his message and teachings have withstood the test of time, and that the investment landscape, the world in which investors operate, has changed dramatically. These changes have affected, and will continue to affect, those in the I (Investor) quadrant and have fueled Robert's decision to update an important section in this book — Chapter Five: The Five Levels of Investors.

CONTENTS

Preface

WHAT IS YOUR LIFE'S GOAL?

"What do you want to be when you grow up?" That is a question most of us have been asked.

I had many interests as a kid, and it was easy to choose. If it sounded exciting and glamorous, I wanted to do it. I wanted to be a marine biologist, an astronaut, a Marine, a ship's officer, a pilot, and a professional football player.

I was fortunate enough to achieve three of those goals: a Marine Corps officer, a ship's officer, and a pilot.

I knew I did not want to become a teacher, a writer, or an accountant. I did not want to be a teacher because I did not like school. I did not want to be a writer because I failed English twice. And I dropped out of my MBA program because I could not stand accounting.

Ironically, now that I have grown up, I have become everything I never wanted to become. Although I disliked school, today I own an education company. I personally teach around the world because I love teaching. Although I failed English twice because I could not write, today I am best known as an author. My book, *Rich Dad Poor Dad,* was on the *New York Times* best-sellers list for over seven years and is one of the top three best-selling books in the United States. The only books ahead of it are *The Joy of Sex* and *The Road Less Traveled.* Adding one more irony, *Rich Dad Poor Dad* and my *CASHFLOW®* board game are a book and a game about accounting, another subject I struggled with.

So what does this have to do with the question: "What is your goal in life?"

The answer is found in the simple, yet profound, statement by a Vietnamese monk, Thich Naht Hahn: "The path is the goal." In other words, finding your path in life is your goal in life. Your path is not your profession, how much money you make, your title, or your successes and failures.

Finding your path means finding out what you were put here on this earth to do. What is your life's purpose? Why were you given this gift called life? And what is the gift you give back to life?

Looking back, I know going to school was not about finding my life's path. I spent four years in military school, studying and training to be a ship's officer. If I had made a career sailing for Standard Oil on their oil tankers, I would never have found my life's path. If I had stayed in the Marines or had gone to fly for the airlines, I would never have found my life's path.

Had I continued on as a ship's officer or become an airline pilot, I would never have become an international best-selling author, been a guest on the *Oprah* show, written a book with Donald Trump, or started an international education company that teaches entrepreneurship and investing throughout the world.

Finding Your Path

This *CASHFLOW Quadrant* book is important because it is about finding your path in life. As you know, most people are programmed early in life to "Go to school and get a job." School is about finding a job in the E or S quadrant. It is not about finding your life's path.

I realize there are people who know exactly what they are going to do early in life. They grow up knowing they are going to be a doctor, lawyer, musician, golfer or actor. We have all heard about child prodigies, kids with exceptional talents. Yet you may notice, these are professions, not necessarily a life's path.

So How Does One Find Their Path in Life?

My answer is: I wish I knew. If I could wave my magic wand and your life's path would magically appear, I would.

Since I do not have a magic wand nor can I tell you what to do, the best thing I can do is tell you what I did. And what I did was trust my intuition, my heart, and my guts. For example, in 1973, returning from the war, when my poor dad suggested I go back to school, get my higher degrees, and work for the government, my brain went numb, my heart went heavy and my gut said, "No way."

When he suggested I get my old job back with Standard Oil or fly for the airlines, again my mind, heart, and gut said no. I knew I was through sailing and flying, although they were great professions and the pay was pretty good.

In 1973 at the age of 26, I was growing up. I had followed my parent's advice and gone to school, received my college degree, and had two professions: a license to be a ship's officer and a license to fly. The problem was, they were professions and the dreams of a child.

At the age of 26, I was old enough to know that education is a process. For example, when I wanted to be a ship's officer, I went to a school that turned out ships' officers. And when I wanted to learn to fly, I went to Navy flight school, a two-year process that turns non-pilots into pilots. I was cautious about my next educational process. I wanted to know what I was going to become before I started my next educational process.

Traditional schools had been good to me. I had achieved my childhood professions. Reaching adulthood was confusing because there were no signs saying, "This is the way." I knew what I *didn't* want to do, but I did not know what I *wanted* to do.

It would have been simple if all I wanted was a new profession. If I had wanted to be a medical doctor, I would have gone to medical school. If I had wanted to be a lawyer, I would have gone to law school. But I knew there was more to life than just going to school to gain another professional credential.

I did not realize it at the time, but at 26 years of age, I was now looking for my path in life, not my next profession.

A Different Education

In 1973, in my last year of active duty flying for the Marine Corps when I was stationed near home in Hawaii, I knew I wanted to follow in my rich dad's footsteps. While in the Marines, I signed up for real estate courses and business courses on the weekends, preparing to become an entrepreneur in the B and I quadrants.

At the same time, upon a friend's recommendation of a friend, I signed up for a personal-development course, hoping to find out who I really was. A personal-development course is non-traditional education because I was not taking it for credits or grades. I did not know what I was going to learn, as I did when I signed up for real estate courses. All I knew was that it was time to take courses to find out about me.

In my first weekend course, the instructor drew this simple diagram on the flip chart:

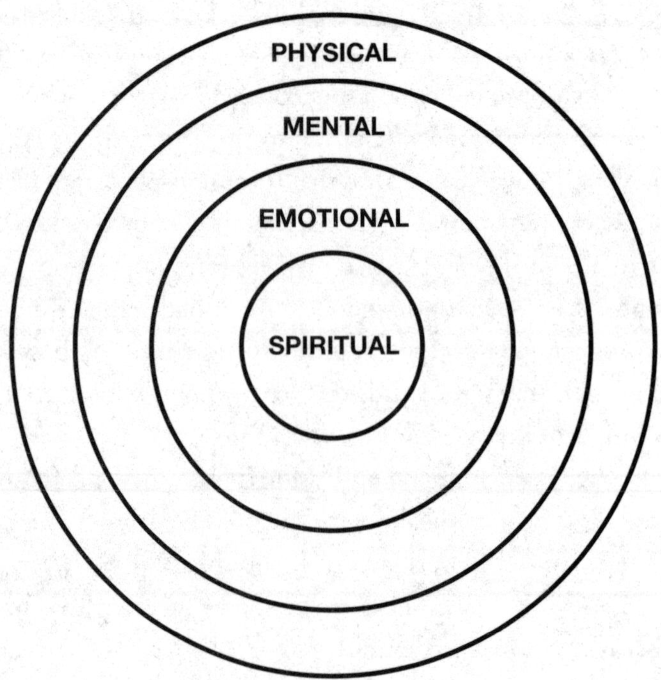

With the diagram complete, the instructor turned and said, "To develop into a whole human being, we need mental, physical, emotional, and spiritual education."

Listening to her explanation, it was clear to me that traditional schools were primarily about developing students mentally. That is why so many students who do well in school, do not do well in real life, especially in the world of money.

As the course progressed over the weekend, I discovered why I disliked school. I realized that I loved learning, but hated school.

Traditional education was a great environment for the "A" students, but it was not the environment for me. Traditional education was crushing my spirit, trying to motivate me with the emotion of fear: the fear of making mistakes, the fear of failing, and the fear of not getting a job. They were programming me to be an employee in the E or S quadrant. I realized that traditional education is not the place for a person who wants to be an entrepreneur in the B and I quadrants.

This may be why so many entrepreneurs never finish school — entrepreneurs like Thomas Edison, founder of General Electric; Henry Ford, founder of Ford Motor Company; Steve Jobs, founder of Apple; Bill Gates, founder of Microsoft; Walt Disney, founder of Disneyland; and Mark Zuckerberg, founder of Facebook.

As the day went on and the instructor went deeper and deeper into these four types of personal development, I realized I had spent most of my life in very harsh educational environments. After four years at an all-male military academy and five years as a Marine pilot, I was pretty strong mentally and physically. As a Marine pilot, I was strong emotionally and spiritually, but all on the macho-male development side. I had no gentle side, no female energy. After all, I was trained to be Marine Corps officer, emotionally calm under pressure, prepared to kill, and spiritually prepared to die for my country.

If you ever saw the movie *Top Gun* starring Tom Cruise, you get a glimpse into the masculine world and bravado of military pilots. I loved that world. I was good in that world. It was a modern-day world of knights and warriors. It was not a world for wimps.

In the seminar, I went into my emotions and briefly touched my spirit. I cried a lot because I had a lot to cry about. I had done and seen things no one should ever be asked to do. During the seminar, I hugged a man, something I had never done before, not even with my father.

On Sunday night, it was difficult leaving this self-development workshop. The seminar had been a gentle, loving, honest environment. Monday morning was a shock to once again be surrounded by young egotistical pilots, dedicated to flying, killing and dying for country.

After that weekend seminar, I knew it was time to change. I knew developing myself emotionally and spiritually to become a kinder, gentler, and more compassionate person would be the hardest thing I could do. It went against all my years at the military academy and flight school.

I never returned to traditional education again. I had no desire to study for grades, degrees, promotions, or credentials again. From then on, if I did attend a course or school, I went to learn, to become a better person. I was no longer in the paper chase of grades, degrees, and credentials.

Growing up in a family of teachers, your grades, the high school and college you graduated from, and your advanced degrees were everything. Like the medals and ribbons on a Marine pilot's chest, advanced degrees and brand-name schools were the status and the stripes that educators wore on their sleeves. In their minds, people who did not finish high school were the unwashed, the lost souls of life. Those with master's degrees looked down on those with only bachelor degrees. Those with a PhD were held in reverence. At the age of 26, I knew I would never return to that world.

Editor's Note: In 2009, Robert received an honorary PhD in entrepreneurship from prestigious San Ignacio de Loyola in Lima, Peru. The few other recipients of this award are political leaders, such as the former President of Spain.

Finding My Path

I know some of you are now asking: Why is he spending so much time talking about non-traditional education courses?

The reason is, that first personal-development seminar rekindled my love of learning, but not the type of learning that is taught in school. Once that seminar was over, I became a seminar junkie, going from seminar to seminar, finding out more about the connection between *my* body, *my* mind, *my* emotions, and *my* spirit.

The more I studied, the more curious about traditional education I became. I began to ask questions such as:

- Why do so many kids hate school?
- Why do so few kids like school?
- Why are many highly educated people not successful in the real world?
- Does school prepare you for the real world?
- Why did I hate school but love learning?
- Why are most schoolteachers poor?
- Why do schools teach us little about money?

Those questions led me to become a student of education outside the hallowed walls of the school system. The more I studied, the more I understood why I did not like school and why schools failed to serve most of its students, even the "A" students.

My curiosity touched my spirit, and I became an entrepreneur in education. If not for this curiosity, I might never have become an author and a developer of financial-education games. My spiritual education led me to my path in life.

It seems that our paths in life are not found in our minds. Our path in life is to find out what is in our hearts.

This does not mean a person cannot find their path in traditional education. I am sure many do. I am just saying that I doubt I would have found my path in traditional school.

Why Is a Path Important?

We all know people who make a lot of money, but hate their work. We also know people who do not make a lot of money and hate their work. And we all know people who just work for money.

A classmate of mine from the Merchant Marine Academy also realized he did not want to spend his life at sea. Rather than sail for the rest of his life, he went to law school after graduation, spending three more years becoming a lawyer and entering private practice in the S quadrant.

He died in his early fifties. He had become a very successful, unhappy lawyer. Like me, he had two professions by the time he was 26. Although he hated being a lawyer, he continued being a lawyer because he had a family, kids, a mortgage, and bills to pay.

A year before he died, I met him at a class reunion in New York. He was a bitter man. "All I do is sweep up behind rich guys like you. They pay me nothing. I hate what I do and who I work for."

"Why don't you do something else?" I asked.

"I can't afford to stop working. My first child is entering college."

He died of a heart attack before she graduated.

He made a lot of money via his professional training, but he was emotionally angry, spiritually dead, and soon his body followed.

I realize this is an extreme example. Most people do not hate what they do as much as my friend did. Yet it illustrates the problem when a person is trapped in a profession and unable to find their path.

To me, this is the shortcoming of traditional education. Millions of people leave school, only to be trapped in jobs they do not like. They know something is missing in life. Many people are also trapped financially, earning just enough to survive, wanting to earn more but not knowing what to do.

Without awareness of the other quadrants, many people go back to school and look for new professions or pay raises in the E or S quadrant, unaware of the world of the B and I quadrants.

My Reason for Becoming a Teacher

My primary reason for becoming a teacher in the B quadrant was a desire to provide financial education. I wanted to make this education available to anyone who wanted to learn, regardless of how much money they had or what their grade-point averages were. That is why The Rich Dad Company started with the *CASHFLOW* game. This game can teach in places I could never go. The beauty of the game is that it was designed to have people teach people. There is no need for an expensive teacher or classroom. The *CASHFLOW* game is now translated into over sixteen languages, reaching millions of people all over the world.

Today, The Rich Dad Company offers financial-education courses as well as the services of coaches and mentors to support a person's financial education. Our programs are especially important for anyone wanting to evolve out of the E and S quadrants into the B and I quadrants.

There is no guarantee that everyone will make it to the B and I quadrants, yet they will know how to access those quadrants if they want to.

Change Is Not Easy

For me, changing quadrants was not easy. It was hard work mentally, but more so emotionally and spiritually. Growing up in a family of highly educated employees in the E quadrant, I carried their values of education, job security, benefits, and a government pension. In many ways, my family values made my transition difficult. I had to shut out their warnings, concerns, and criticisms about becoming an entrepreneur and investor. Some of their values I had to discount were:

- "But you have to have a job."
- "You're taking too many risks."
- "What if you fail?"
- "Just go back to school and get your masters degree."
- "Become a doctor. They make a lot of money."
- "The rich are greedy."

- "Why is money so important to you?"
- "Money won't make you happy."
- "Just live below your means."
- "Play it safe. Don't go for your dreams."

Diet and Exercise

I mention emotional and spiritual development because that is what it takes to make a permanent change in life. For example, it rarely works to tell an overweight person, "Just eat less and exercise more." Diet and exercise may make sense mentally, but most people who are overweight do not eat because they are hungry. They eat to feed an emptiness in their emotions and their soul. When a person goes on a diet-and-exercise program, they are only working on their mind and their body. Without emotional development and spiritual strength, the overweight person may go on a diet for six months and lose a ton of weight, only to put even more weight back on later.

The same is true for changing quadrants. Saying to yourself, "I'm going to become an entrepreneur in the B quadrant," is as futile as a chain smoker saying, "Tomorrow I'm going to quit smoking." Smoking is a physical addiction caused by emotional and spiritual challenges. Without emotional and spiritual support, the smoker will always be a smoker. The same is true for an alcoholic, a sex addict, or a chronic shopper. Most addictions are attempts to find happiness in people's souls.

This is why my company offers courses for the mind and body, but also coaches and mentors to support the emotional and spiritual transitions.

A few people are able to make the journey alone, but I was not one of them. If not for a coach like my rich dad and the support of Kim, I would not have made it. There were so many times I wanted to quit and give up. If not for Kim and my rich dad, I would have quit.

Why "A" Students Fail

Looking at the diagram again, it is easy to see why so many "A" students fail in the world of money.

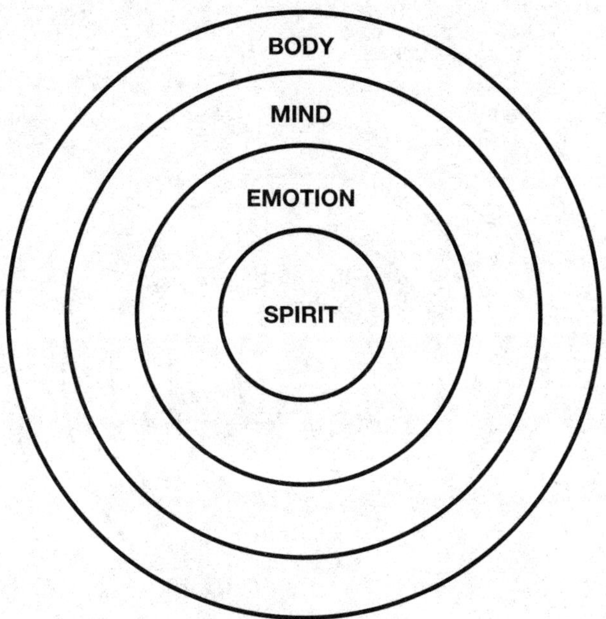

A person may be highly educated mentally, but if they are not educated emotionally, their fear will often stop their body from doing what it must do. That is why so many "A" students get stuck in "analysis paralysis," studying every little detail, but failing to do anything.

This "analysis paralysis" is caused by our educational system punishing students for making mistakes. If you think about it, "A" students are "A" students simply because they made the fewest mistakes. The problem with that emotional psychosis is that, in the real world, people who take action are the ones who make the most mistakes and learn from them to win in the game of life.

Just look at Presidents Clinton and Bush. Clinton could not admit he had sex and Bush could not recall any mistakes he made during his presidency. Making mistakes is human, but lying about your mistakes is criminal, a criminal act known as perjury.

When criticized for making 1,014 mistakes before creating the electric light bulb, Thomas Edison said, "I did not fail 1,014 times. I successfully found out what did not work 1,014 times."

In other words, the reason so many people fail to achieve success is because they fail to fail enough times.

Looking at the diagram again,

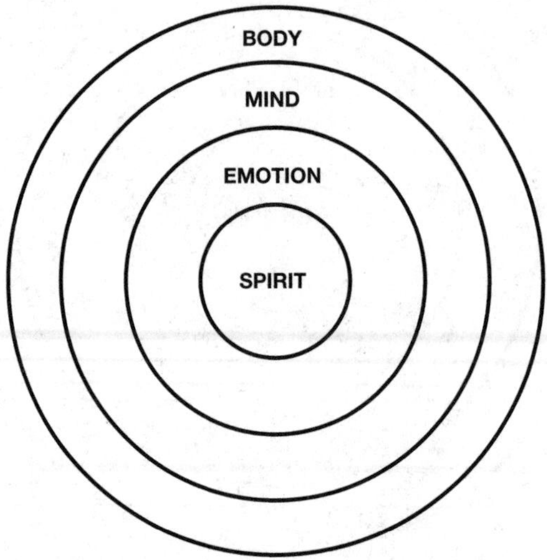

one of the reasons so many people cling to job security is because they lack emotional education. They let fear stop them.

One of the best things about military school and the Marine Corps is that these organizations spend a lot of time developing young men and women spiritually, emotionally, mentally, and physically. Although it was a tough education, it was a complete education, preparing us to do a nasty job.

The reason I created the *CASHFLOW* game is because the game educates the whole person. The game is a better teaching tool than reading or lecture, simply because the game involves the body, mind, emotions, and spirit of the player.

The game is designed for players to make as many mistakes as possible with play money, and then learn from those mistakes. To me, this is a more humane way to learn about money.

The Path Is the Goal

Today, there are thousands of CASHFLOW clubs all over the world. One reason why CASHFLOW clubs are important is because they are a shelter from the storm, a way station on the path of life. By joining a CASHFLOW club, you get to meet people like you, people who are committed to making changes, not just talking about change.

Unlike school, there is not a requirement of past academic success. All that is asked is a sincere desire to learn and make changes. In the game, you will make a lot of mistakes in different financial situations and will learn from your mistakes, using play money.

CASHFLOW clubs are not for those who want to get rich quick. CASHFLOW clubs are there to support the long-term mental, emotional, spiritual, physical, and financial changes a person needs to go through. We all change and evolve at different rates of speed so you are encouraged to go at your own speed.

After playing the game with others a few times, you will have a better idea of what your next step should be and which of the four asset classes (business, real estate, paper assets, or commodities) is best for you.

In Conclusion

Finding one's path is not necessarily easy. Even today, I do not really know if I am on my path or not. As you know, we all get lost at times, and it is not always easy to find our way back.

If you feel you are not in the right quadrant for you, or you are not on your life's path, I encourage you to search your heart and find your path in life. You may know it is time to change if you are saying things like the following statements:

- "I'm working with dead people."
- "I love what I do, but I wish I could make more money."
- "I can't wait for the weekend."
- "I want to do my own thing."
- "Is it quitting time yet?"

My sister is a Buddhist nun. Her path is to support the Dalai Lama, a path that pays nothing. Yet, although she earns little, it does not mean she has to be a poor nun. She has her own rental property and investments in gold and silver. Her strength of spirit and her financially educated mind allow her to follow her life's path without taking a vow of poverty.

In many ways, it was a good thing I was labeled stupid in school. Although emotionally painful, that pain allowed me to find my life's path as a teacher. And like my sister, the nun, just because I am a teacher does not mean I have to be a poor teacher.

Repeating what Thich Naht Hahn said: "The path is the goal."

Introduction

WHICH QUADRANT ARE YOU IN?

The CASHFLOW Quadrant®
is a way to categorize people
based on where their money comes from.

Are you financially free? If your life has come to a financial fork in the road, *Rich Dad's CASHFLOW Quadrant* was written for you. If you want to take control of what you do today in order to change your financial destiny, this book will help you chart your course.

This is the CASHFLOW Quadrant. The letters in each quadrant represent:

E for employee
S for small business or self-employed
B for big business
I for investor

Each of us resides in at least one of the four sections (quadrants) of the CASHFLOW Quadrant. Where we are is determined by where our cash comes from. Many of us are employees who rely on paychecks, while others are self-employed. Employees and self-employed individuals reside on the left side of the CASHFLOW Quadrant. The right side is for individuals who receive their cash from businesses they own or investments they own.

The CASHFLOW Quadrant is an easy way to categorize people based on where their money comes from. Each quadrant within the CASHFLOW Quadrant is unique, and the people within each one share common characteristics. The quadrants will show you where you are today and will help you chart a course for where you want to be in the future as you choose your own path to financial freedom. While financial freedom can be found in all four of the quadrants, the skills of a B or I will help you reach your financial goals more quickly. Successful E's need to become successful I's to ensure their financial security during retirement.

What Do You Want to Be When You Grow Up?

This book is, in many ways, Part II of my book, *Rich Dad Poor Dad.* For those of you who may not have read *Rich Dad Poor Dad,* it is about the different lessons my two dads taught me about money and life choices. One was my real dad, and the other was my best friend's dad. One was highly educated and the other was a high school dropout. One was poor, and the other was rich.

Poor Dad's Advice

Growing up, my highly educated, but poor, dad always said, "Go to school, get good grades, and find a safe secure job." He was recommending a life path that looked like this:

Poor dad recommended that I become either a well-paid E, employee, or a well-paid S, self-employed professional, such as a medical doctor, lawyer, or accountant. My poor dad was very concerned about a steady paycheck, benefits, and job security. That's why he was a well-paid government official, the head of education for the State of Hawaii.

Rich Dad's Advice

My uneducated, but rich, dad offered very different advice. He said, "Go to school, graduate, build businesses, and become a successful investor." He was recommending a life path that looked like this:

This book is about the mental, emotional, and educational process I went through in following my rich dad's advice.

Who Is This Book For?

This book is written for people who are ready to change quadrants, especially for individuals who are currently in the E and S categories and are contemplating moving to the B or I category. This book is for people who are ready to move beyond job security and begin to achieve financial security. It's not an easy life path, but the prize at the end of the road, financial freedom, is worth the journey.

When I was 12 years old, rich dad told me a simple story that guided me to great wealth and financial freedom. It was his way of explaining the difference between the left side of the CASHFLOW Quadrant, the E and S quadrants, and the right side, or the B and I quadrants. The story goes like this:

"Once upon a time there was this quaint little village. It was a great place to live except for one problem. The village had no water unless it rained. To solve this problem once and for all, the village elders asked contractors to submit bids to deliver water to the village on a daily basis. Two people volunteered to take on the task, and the elders awarded the contract to both of them. They felt that a little competition would keep prices low and ensure a backup supply of water.

"The first person who won the contract, Ed, immediately ran out, bought two galvanized steel buckets and began running back and forth to the lake which was a mile away. He immediately began making money as he labored morning to dusk, hauling water from the lake with his two buckets. He would empty them into the large concrete holding tank the village had built. Each morning he had to get up before the rest of the village awoke to make sure there was enough water for the people. It was hard work, but he was very happy to be making money and for having one of the two exclusive contracts for this business.

"The second winning contractor, Bill, disappeared for a while. He wasn't seen for months, which made Ed very happy, since he had no competition.

"Instead of buying two buckets to compete with Ed, Bill wrote a business plan, created a corporation, found four investors, employed a president to do the work, and returned six months later with a construction crew. Within a year, his team had built a large-volume stainless-steel pipeline which connected the village to the lake.

"At the grand-opening celebration, Bill announced that his water was cleaner than Ed's water. Bill knew that the villagers had complained about the water's lack of cleanliness. Bill also announced that he could supply the village with water 24 hours a day, 7 days a week. Ed could only deliver water on weekdays because he didn't want to work on weekends. Then Bill announced that he would charge 75 percent less than Ed did for this higher-quality, more-reliable water. The villagers cheered and immediately ran for the faucet at the end of Bill's pipeline.

"In order to compete, Ed immediately lowered his rates by 75 percent, bought two more buckets, added covers to his buckets and began hauling four buckets each trip. In order to provide better service, he hired his two sons to give him a hand on the night shift and on weekends. When his boys went off to college, he said to them, 'Hurry back because someday this business will belong to you.'

"For some reason, his two sons never returned. Eventually, Ed had employees and union problems. The union demanded higher wages and better benefits and wanted its members to only haul one bucket at a time.

"Meanwhile, Bill realized that if this village needed water, then other villages must need water too. He rewrote his business plan and went off to sell his high-speed, high-volume, low-cost, clean-water delivery system to villages throughout the world. He only makes a penny per bucket of water delivered, but he delivers billions of buckets of water every day. Whether he works or not, billions of people consume billions of buckets of water, and all that money pours into his bank account. Bill developed a pipeline to deliver money to himself, as well as water to the villages.

"Bill lived happily ever after. Ed worked hard for the rest of his life and had financial problems forever after. The end."

That story about Bill and Ed has guided me for years. It has assisted me in my life's decision-making process. I often ask myself:

"Am I building a pipeline or hauling buckets?"

"Am I working hard, or am I working smart?"

And the answers to those questions have made me financially free.

That is what this book is about. It's about what it takes to become a B and an I. It's for people who are tired of hauling buckets and are ready to build pipelines for cash to flow into their pockets.

This Book Is Divided into Three Parts

Part One The first part of this book focuses on the core differences between people in the four quadrants. It shows why certain people gravitate to certain quadrants and often get stuck there without realizing it. It will help you identify where you are today in the quadrant and where you want to be in five years.

Part Two The second part of this book is about personal change. It's more about who you have to be, instead of what you have to do.

Part Three The third part of this book explains how to find success on the right side of the CASHFLOW Quadrant. I will share more of my rich dad's secrets on the skills required to be a successful B and I. It will help you choose your own path to financial freedom.

Throughout *Rich Dad's CASHFLOW Quadrant,* I continue to stress the importance of financial intelligence. If you want to operate on the right side, the B- and I-quadrant side, you must be smarter than if you choose to stay on the left side, the E- and S-quadrant side. To be a B or I, you must be able to control the direction of your cash flow.

This book is written for people who are ready to make changes in their lives to move beyond job security and begin to build their own pipelines to achieve financial freedom.

We are in the Information Age which offers more opportunities for financial reward than ever before. Individuals with the skills of the B's and I's will be able to identify and seize those opportunities. To be successful in the Information Age, a person needs information from all four quadrants. Unfortunately, our schools are still in the Industrial Age and still prepare students for only the left side of the CASHFLOW Quadrant.

If you're looking for new answers to move forward in the Information Age, this book is for you. It doesn't have all the answers, but it will share the deep personal and guiding insights I gained as I traveled from the E and S side to the B and I side.

My Environment...

The six adults I spend the most time with are:

Name________________________________ Quadrant______

Name________________________________ Quadrant______

Name________________________________ Quadrant______

Name________________________________ Quadrant______

Name________________________________ Quadrant______

Name________________________________ Quadrant______

Get connected...
and stay connected
with our global
Rich Dad Community

Visit RichDad.com
for

News • Blogs
Tools and Resources
***CASHFLOW* games**
Podcasts
The Rich Dad Store

Follow Robert on...

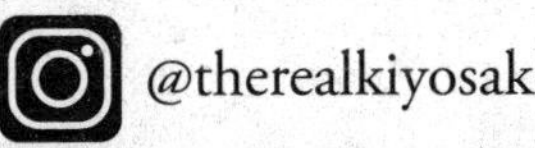

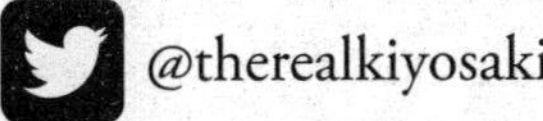

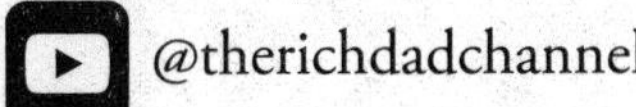

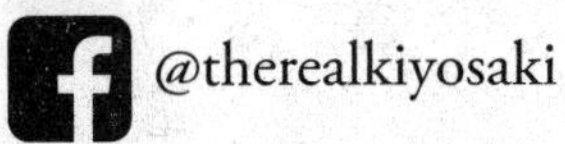